# The politics of old age in Europe

RETHINKING AGEING SERIES

Series editor: Brian Gearing
School of Health and Social Welfare
The Open University

The rapid growth in ageing populations in Britain and other countries has greatly increased academic and professional interest in gerontology. Since the mid-1970s there has been a marked increase in published research studies which have stimulated new ideas and approaches to understanding old age. However such knowledge has not been widely disseminated. There continues to be concern about the education and training in gerontology of professional workers and whether research findings about ageing reach professionals and the general public.

The *Rethinking Ageing* series aims to fill this need for accessible, up-to-date studies of important issues in gerontology. Each book is intended to review and enhance understanding of a major topic in ageing, and to have particular relevance for those involved in age care, whether as researchers, service providers or carers. All the books in this series address two fundamental questions. What is known about this topic? And what are the policy, service and practice implications of this knowledge? At the same time, authors are encouraged to *rethink* their subject area by developing their own ideas, drawing on case material and their research and experience. Most of the books are multi-disciplinary and all are written in clear, non-technical language which appeals to a broad range of students, academics and professionals with a common interest in ageing and age care. The very positive response from readers and reviewers to the books published so far has encouraged us to extend the series with new titles while retaining this approach.

*Current and forthcoming titles:*
Simon Biggs *et al.*: **Elder abuse in perspective**
Ken Blakemore and Margaret Boneham: **Age, race and ethnicity**
Joanna Bornat (ed.): **Reminiscence reviewed**
Bill Bytheway: **Ageism**
Maureen Crane: **Homeless people in later life**
Andrew Dunning: **Advocacy and older people**
Mike Hepworth: **Stories of ageing**
Frances Heywood *et al.*: **Housing and home in later life**
Beverley Hughes: **Older people and community care**
Tom Kitwood: **Dementia reconsidered**
Eric Midwinter: **Pensioned off**
Sheila Peace *et al.*: **Re-evaluating residential care**
Moyra Sidell: **Health in old age**
Robert Slater: **The psychology of growing old**
John Vincent: **Politics, power and old age**
Alan Walker and Tony Maltby: **Ageing Europe**
Alan Walker and Gerhard Naegele (eds): **The politics of old age in Europe**

# The politics of old age in Europe

Edited by
ALAN WALKER
and
GERHARD NAEGELE

OPEN UNIVERSITY PRESS
Buckingham · Philadelphia

Open University Press
Celtic Court
22 Ballmoor
Buckingham
MK18 1XW

*HQ
1064
.E8
P65
1999*

email: enquiries@openup.co.uk
world wide web: http://www.openup.co.uk

and
325 Chestnut Street
Philadelphia, PA 19106, USA

First Published 1999

A catalogue record of this book is available from the British Library

ISBN   0 335 20007 9 (pb)   0 335 20008 7 (hb)

*Library of Congress Cataloging-in-Publication Data*
The politics of old age in Europe / edited by Alan Walker and Gerhard Naegele.
        p.   cm. — (Rethinking ageing series)
     Includes bibliographical references (p.    ).
     ISBN 0-335-20008-7   ISBN 0-335-20007-9 (pbk.)
     1. Aged—Government policy—Europe. 2. Aged—Europe—Political activity. I
Walker, Alan. II. Naegele, Gerhard, 1948–  . III. Series.
HQ1064.E8P65 1999
305.26′094—dc21                                                             98-8177
                                                                               CIP

Copy-edited and typeset by The Running Head Limited, London and Cambridge
Printed in Great Britain by St Edmundsbury Press, Bury St Edmunds

# Contents

# Notes on contributors

SANG-HOON AHN, Doctoral Fellow, Department of Sociology, Uppsala University, Sweden.

SARA ARBER, Professor of Sociology, University of Surrey, UK.

DOMINIQUE ARGOUD, Researcher, Centre de Sociologie des Politiques Sociales, Université Paris 1 – Panthéon Sorbonne.

CHRISTIANE BAHR, Assistant General Manager, Social and Health Centre Gnigl, Salzburg, Austria.

ADALBERT EVERS, Professor of Comparative Health and Social Policy, Justus Liebig University, Giessen, Germany.

LUCIA LAMEIRO GARCÍA, Researcher, Department of Sociology and Social Gerontology, Free University, Amsterdam, the Netherlands.

JAY GINN, Research Fellow, Sociology Department, University of Surrey, UK.

ANNE-MARIE GUILLEMARD, Professor of Sociology, Université Paris V, France.

KEES KNIPSCHEER, Professor of Sociology and Social Gerontology, Department of Sociology and Social Gerontology, Free University, Amsterdam, the Netherlands.

KAI LEICHSENRING, Research Fellow, European Centre for Social Welfare Policy and Research, Vienna, Austria.

MARIA LUISA MIRABILE, Researcher, IRES (Social and Economic Research Institute), Rome, Italy.

GERHARD NAEGELE, Professor of Social Gerontology and Director of the Institute of Gerontology, University of Dortmund, Germany.

SVEN E. OLSSON HORT, Director, Welfare Research Centre, Mälardalen University College, Sweden.

SARA E. RIX, Senior Policy Advisor, American Association of Retired Persons Public Policy Unit, Washington DC, USA.

BERND SCHULTE, Senior Research Fellow, Max-Planck-Institute for Foreign and International Social Law, Munich, Germany.

THEO SCHUYT, Senior Lecturer, Department of Sociology and Social Gerontology, Free University, Amsterdam, the Netherlands.

CHARLOTTE STRÜMPEL, Researcher, European Centre for Social Welfare Policy and Research, Vienna, Austria.

ZSUZSA SZÉMAN, Scientific Research Worker, Institute for Social Conflict Research, Hungarian Academy of Sciences, Hungary.

ALAN WALKER, Professor of Social Policy, University of Sheffield, UK.

JÜRGEN WOLF, Professor of Social Gerontology, Fachhochschule Magdeburg, Germany.

# Preface

All editors rely on the knowledge, skill and time-keeping of their contributors, and we have been very fortunate to be able to collaborate with this group of outstanding social scientists. We are extremely grateful to them all and especially for the patience of those who excelled in the third contributors' virtue as well as the other two! We are very grateful also to Christine Marking for her help with the conclusion, and to David Williams and Sandra O'Neill for their creative copy-editing. Marg Walker deserves very special thanks for taking full responsibility for the preparation of the manuscript for publication and for carrying out that task so efficiently.

In researching and writing about the politics of old age we have been inspired by many academic researchers but, also, by the older people who have been actively engaged in the political struggles to secure the rights of all older people to a decent income and to overcome social exclusion, people such as the late, great Maggie Kuhn. We dedicate this book to those currently leading the pensioners' movements in Europe, too numerous to mention, in the hope that it might contribute, albeit in a very small way, to their campaigns for European citizenship and intergenerational solidarity.

*Alan Walker*                                   *Gerhard Naegele*
*Department of Sociological Studies*            *Institute of Gerontology*
*University of Sheffield*                       *University of Dortmund*

# 1

# Introduction

ALAN WALKER AND GERHARD NAEGELE

The politics of old age in Europe have entered a critical new phase. On the one hand policy makers in most countries are raising questions about the sustainability of national pension systems while, on the other, older people are becoming more active politically. These conjunctive developments are of profound importance for two reasons. First of all, pension systems are the foundations of the European welfare states; changing them therefore has broad implications for the provision of welfare in a particular country. Second, population ageing is raising questions about the democratic institutions which were constructed when European societies had very different age structures. Are those institutions still appropriate? Can they accommodate the rising aspirations of older people to speak for themselves? In other words, the assumptions that older people will 'retire' from participation in political life when they leave the labour force and that they are content to do so, are increasingly out of step with the active forms of citizenship being pursued by some older people and their calls for greater political involvement.

The main purpose of this book is to explore, for the first time, the extent and nature of the political participation and representation of older people in Europe. Our primary focus is the European Union – with general overviews of political participation and representation followed by case studies of seven Member States – but we have also included chapters on Hungary and the USA for comparative purposes. Leading experts from nine countries were asked to examine the politics of old age in their countries by providing an overview (main developments, introduction to the main organizations and actors, classification of types of organization and references to any class, gender or race dimensions); an account of recent developments, covering major policy changes and their impact on political mobilization and changes in the nature of the political participation and representation of older people at local, regional and national levels; a description of measures taken by national or local government to increase participation; the key barriers to the political participation of older people in each country; and comments on the future politics of old age (for example the impact of demography on the political system and policy-making process, attitudes of younger age groups, impact on traditional forms of representation of older people, likely direction of intergenerational relations and actions required by policy makers and older people). These national case studies form the core of the book.

In addition we have sought to provide a European perspective by analysing developments across the European Union (EU) as a whole. Thus Part 1 of the book takes a comparative perspective towards the political participation and representation of older people, both within the Member States of the EU and at European Commission level. Our concluding chapter synthesizes the main issues raised by the national case studies. Chapter 2 is intended to set the scene for the volume and, therefore, very few additional words are required here.

The backcloth to the analyses in this book is the changing demography of Europe and its implications. Since the facts of this demographic revolution are so widely known we will not repeat them at length here (see Walker and Maltby 1997). In 1993 people aged 60 and over represented one fifth of the total population of the 15 Member States of the EU. By the year 2020 they are expected to represent more than one quarter (Walker and Maltby 1997: 11). Women predominate in the higher reaches of the 'age pyramid' for all the countries of Europe, which means that, as the population of each Member State ages, it becomes increasingly 'feminized' (Chapter 2). The two main factors in European population ageing are declining fertility and mortality , the rates of which differ between Member States. As a result the pace of ageing differs: Ireland has the youngest population of all EU countries and Sweden the oldest, followed by Germany, France and then the UK.

As well as the ageing of its population, Europe is witnessing a profound transformation in the meaning and experience of old age. Retirement is no longer the dominant entry-point to old age that it was in the modern stage of development and, therefore, it is increasingly useless as a definition of old age. More and more people throughout the EU are leaving the labour force in different ways: early retirement, partial retirement, redundancy, unemployment, disability, and so on. The pension and welfare systems of most Northern EU countries successfully delivered relative affluence to large sections of the older population. At the same time, with increased longevity, older people are living healthier old ages and, as a result, the threshold of frailty is being pushed back. These changes in age structure, health, economic security and patterns of employment are transforming the nature of old age. They are, thereby, posing sharp questions about the traditional, passive roles expected of older people and the extent to which policy makers and major economic and political institutions have adjusted to socio-demographic change. In essence the question at issue is what role do the majority of older people occupy in the new millennium: passive consumers and welfare recipients or active citizens?

Population ageing is a mainstream political issue mainly because of the numerical importance of older people and the fact that they are the largest group of current welfare state beneficiaries. Current changes in the life course affect welfare states in two critical ways. On the expenditure side, pensions are the largest single item of social expenditure and older people are the main users of health and social services. On the funding side, the widespread European trend towards earlier exit from the labour force reduces the income from taxes and social contributions (and also adds to the expenditure side of the account). Population ageing means workforce ageing, and the early exit trend also deprives employers of skilled labour while fuelling age discrimination in the labour market (Walker 1997).

General readers may wonder why we chose to devote a whole book to the politics of old age. We have noted already that these have entered a new and critical phase in Europe and this development is analysed in Chapter 2. However, despite the political significance of population ageing there has been surprisingly little scientific commentary on the politics of old age in Europe. There are exceptions (Walker 1986, 1991; Ginn 1993; Carell *et al.* 1997) but this issue has not been explored on this side of the Atlantic to anything like the depth found in the United States (see for example Hudson 1981; Williams *et al.* 1982; Binstock 1983; Estes 1986; Quadagno 1988; Myles and Quadagno 1991; Torres-Gil 1992). The differences between the political systems of the US and Europe is probably the main reason for this academic lag. The pluralistic political system of the US facilitated the growth of age-interest politics and age awareness among both policy makers and social scientists more than two decades ago. In contrast Europe is only just witnessing the emergence of a fully fledged age-interest politics (even if this is not destined to achieve the same prominence as experienced in the US in the mid-1980s [Minkler 1986]). Therefore this volume is intended to fill a glaring gap in the European literature, and we are confident that this will only be the first of a series of social science analyses of the politics of ageing in Europe.

In the light of the changing meaning of old age and the more active citizenship being adopted by older people on a local, national and European level, the terminology used to describe this group and their associated metaphors – 'the elderly', 'old', 'retired' – seem to be out of step with reality. Throughout this text we have adopted the terms favoured by older people themselves in the different Member States – 'older people' and 'senior citizens' – though we do have to acknowledge both that there is no consensus among different nationalities on this issue and that language and translation get in the way of a universal resolution to this longstanding issue (Walker 1993).

**Plan of the book**

This book is divided into two parts. The first provides a European overview of the main issues. Chapter 2 sets the scene for the volume by outlining the changing reality of the political participation and representation of older people in Europe, the rise of the new politics of old age, the economic, social and personal barriers inhibiting older people from becoming more active politically; and the future politics of old age: that is, whether or not age will become more significant as a basis for political mobilization. In Chapter 3 Bernd Schulte describes the legal, institutional and infrastructural machinery which promotes the participation of older people at EU level and within the Member States. In Chapter 4 Adalbert Evers and Jürgen Wolf report the results of their empirical investigation of the organization, representation and political participation of older people in five EU countries – Austria, France, Denmark, the UK and Italy.

These three chapters create a European analytical and empirical framework for the national case studies contained in Part 2. Chapters 5 to 11 consist of case studies of EU countries, covering all four of the welfare regimes represented within the EU: Beveridge, Bismarck, Scandinavian and Southern (Leibfried 1992). Also, as the analyses in Part 2 show, the EU is composed of countries with different political as well as welfare traditions. Following the seven EU countries there are chapters on Hungary and the US. The former is included to provide a perspective from Central/Eastern Europe to compare with those from Western Europe. The USA is also included for comparative purposes because the politics of old age have achieved great prominence there.

In the final chapter we synthesize the main elements of the country case studies. This emphasizes the three main dimensions of the politics of old age which represent continuous analytical threads running throughout the book: the politics of social policies, political behaviour among older people and the issue of their political representation. Although our conclusion concerning the political representation of older people is optimistic, this is mainly a reflection of the new grassroots politics of old age – the changes in political behaviour and representation documented in this volume. However, in contrast at the macro level, we echo the concerns expressed by a majority of contributors that the new politics of social policy may not only be detrimental to older people's economic security but could also undermine solidarity between the generations.

# PART 1

# European overview

# 2

# Political participation and representation of older people in Europe

ALAN WALKER

The purpose of this chapter is to provide a general context for the subsequent detailed analyses of political participation among older people and the politics of old age in different countries. In doing so the chapter covers three main issues. First of all there is the changing reality of the political participation and representation of older people in Europe. In most countries the post-war period has seen the exclusion of this group from many of the institutions of political participation and representation, including trade unions and political parties. This process of social exclusion has not been conscious discrimination, for the most part, but a failure to adapt institutions to take on board the changing socio-demographic structure; it has, therefore, been part of a general policy failure that is age discriminatory (or ageist) in its impact. The result is the political paradox of old age: large numbers but small influence. It also suggests that age *per se* is not a sound basis for political mobilization – a point I return to later. It is important to recognize that the politics of old age are in flux in all sorts of respects, including the growth of more direct action on the part of older people themselves. It is necessary to consider the reasons for this transformation and its political ramifications.

However, although there is a trend towards greater political activity on the part of older people, we must not get it out of proportion. The majority of senior citizens in all EU countries are not part of this new social movement. Therefore, secondly, we should consider briefly the economic, social and personal barriers that are inhibiting older people from becoming more active politically.

The third part of this chapter directs attention to the future of the politics of old age: will older people become a more unified and outspoken political force – along the lines of their US counterparts? What impact will the changing demographic structure of the populations of the EU Member States have on the political participation and representation of older people? In other words, will age become more significant as a basis for political mobilization?

## Trends in political participation and representation

For much of the post-war period the politics of old age in Europe were characterized by acquiescence. Older people were largely excluded from the political and policy-making systems by a process of disengagement whereby, on retirement, they withdrew from participation in formal economic structures and institutions. Thus retirement operated as a process of both social and political exclusion which detached senior citizens from some of the main sources of political consciousness and channels of representation. In the northern EU states this exclusion contributed to a popular perception of older people as being politically passive whereas, in the southern states, the image of passivity was also a product of culture and the continuing strength of family solidarity. This popular perception fed into age-discriminatory stereotypes which portrayed older people as inactive, acquiescent, family-oriented and, therefore, not interested in political participation. The scientific community contributed social theories which purported to explain the social and political passivity of older people. For example the sociological theory of 'disengagement' was introduced from the US in the early 1960s. This argued that old age consisted of an inevitable and mutual process of disengagement between the ageing individual and other members of society (Cumming and Henry 1961). In other words, older people were not expected to be active participants in social and political life. Of course in every country there were living examples of active senior citizens which contradicted the stereotype, but this did not negate the general trend.

Other factors operated to limit the extent of political participation on the part of older people in the early post-war period. In a general sense age was less significant than it is today: there were fewer older people and they were less healthy, and retirement was still acting as the key regulator of entry into old age. In political terms, too, age was less salient because attention was directed chiefly at rebuilding the physical infrastructure of Europe and constructing the major institutions of the welfare state. Thus the politics of old age reflected the general politics of European societies at the time: dominated by traditional class and religious divisions, with corporatism containing policy conflicts within the political system.

During this phase of the European politics of old age, pressure groups representing the interests of older people were created in most northern countries either at local or national levels, or at both. Often the national pressure groups represented specific sections of the older population, such as retired civil servants. They appeared on the political scene at different times in different countries. In the UK such pressure groups date from the 1940s and 1950s, though some can trace their origins to the early part of the century. In Portugal they sprang up in the mid-1970s. In Germany the association of war victims, disabled people and pensioners (VdK) was formed in 1917 but re-established in the Federal Republic in 1950 and currently has about 1 million members. A similar association represents civil service pensioners (BRH) and has some 80,000 members (Alber 1995). In the Netherlands the three associations of older people reflect the three ideological pillars of Dutch society (Protestant, Catholic and Socialist). A dual pillar structure may be found in Austria but it is a purely political one: the social democrats and Catholic conservatives have sponsored particular organizations across a wide field. Pensioners' organizations have existed since the 1950s – the Pensioners' Organizations (Social Democratic) and the Seniors' Federation (Conservative) claim around 38 per cent of all senior citizens (60+) as members (Leichsenring 1996). In a few countries national trade unions established special sections for retired workers but only in Italy did these develop into major sources of direct representation (with more than 20 per cent of the older population belonging to the retired sections of the three main unions).

Despite the large membership of some of the pressure groups and other organizations formed in the 1950s, '60s and '70s, they were not primarily concerned with the political mobilization of the older population. Instead they were oriented towards the representation of older people in the policy arena. They formed the European equivalent of what Estes (1979) referred to in the US as the 'ageing enterprise'. In this sense, therefore, the politics of old age in this period may be described as consensual: pressure groups representing older people were bargaining for public policy advances within a context of shared understanding about the possibilities of politics, the assumption of both progressive welfare development and the deservingness of the case they espoused.

Looking back now, with all the confidence of hindsight, we can see that period in the evolution of the politics of old age in modern European society as a formative one which witnessed the birth or re-birth of many of the organizations that continue to represent the interests of older people today. Now, though, we are in a qualitatively different phase in the political fortunes of older people in Europe.

## The new politics of old age

What is meant by a 'new' politics of old age? There are two distinct but causally related macro and micro features. I will focus mainly on the micro level but, at the macro level policy makers first began to question, more openly and frequently than hitherto, the cost of population ageing. The first wave of this critical approach to welfare and particularly the public expenditure implications of pensions and health care occurred in the mid-1970s following the world oil price shock and the ensuing fiscal crisis (O'Connor 1977). This was followed by a second wave of criticism in the 1980s when the macroeconomic implications of pension system maturation and the financial costs of long term care were the subject of sometimes heated debate across Europe. Indeed, several reports from the OECD (1988a, 1988b), which were influential in these debates, emphasize the fact that this issue extended well beyond the borders of Europe. Thus, at a macro policy level, the new politics of old age poses a fundamentally different set of questions to those that led to the creation of welfare states in

Europe. The essence of these new questions may be gleaned from the following quotations:

> The key social policy concern arising out of current demographic trends is whether the ageing of populations is likely to lead to a major increase in the cost of public social programmes and whether society, and in particular the working population, will be able or willing to bear the additional financing burden.
>
> (OECD 1988b: 27)

> Under existing regulations the evolution of public pension schemes is likely to put a heavy and increasing burden on the working population in the coming decades. Such a financial strain may put inter-generational solidarity – a concept on which all public retirement pensions are based – at risk.
>
> (OECD 1988a: 102)

Again, it must not be assumed that this new agenda is accepted without question by all policy makers: that is patently not the case. There are very wide variations among the Member States in the extent to which they have pursued the policy prescriptions dictated by this macroeconomic perspective. However, there is no doubt that all EU governments and leading political actors now place this issue high on their list of priorities.

At the micro level the new politics of old age consists of a rapid increase in direct political involvement on the part of older people, a transformation that can be observed in different parts of the EU, north and south, though it occurred sooner in the former than the latter. For example, in Germany the Senior Protection Association or 'Grey Panthers' was formed in 1975. The Grey Panthers now have some 200 local groups with roughly 15,000 members (Alber 1995: 133). In the UK the National Pensioners Convention (NPC) was created in 1979 and reconstituted in 1992 by an amalgamation of different pre-existing grassroots and trade union groups. (This includes one of the oldest pensioner pressure groups in Europe, the National Federation of Retired Pensioners Associations, which was established in 1939 as a radical grassroots campaigning organization.) The NPC has up to 2 million affiliated members in the local pensioner action groups that have mushroomed under its aegis (Carter and Nash 1992). Also a Pensioners Protection Party was started in 1991 and a Pensioners Rights Campaign was formed in 1989 to press for a Pensioners Charter. In Denmark in the early 1990s a new grassroots movement of older people was established called the C Team. This group is independent of established organizations representing older people as well as political parties; it arranges mass demonstrations and other actions aimed at preventing cuts in health and social services and improving provision for frail older people (Platz and Petersen 1995: 63). In Portugal the Party of National Solidarity (PSN) was formed and secured the election of a deputy to the National Assembly in 1990 (out of 100,000 votes for the PSN, 90,000 were cast by older people) (Perista 1995). In 1992 the Italian pensioner party, the oldest such party in Europe, had its first representative elected to the regional government in Rome. A year later seven pensioner representatives were elected to the Netherlands parliament.

These examples are sufficient to show that, in a very short space of time, the EU has seen a mushrooming of pensioners' action groups at local and national levels and, with them, the emergence of what appears to be a newly radicalized politics of old age. Of course the new social movements among older people involve only relatively few pensioners – activism is a minority pursuit in all generations – but many more are involved than previously and more actively so. Furthermore the nature of political participation and representation is changing: there are more and more examples of direct action by senior citizens, and the new action groups are grassroots organizations composed of older people who want to represent themselves. It is too soon to say how permanent these new social movements will be, as we may still be in a transitional phase. Indeed insecurity is a familiar feature of grassroots organizations, and it is predictable that some will fail, as happened to the political party for older people in Belgium. I will come back to the question of future directions in the final part of this chapter, but for the moment, how do we explain this rapid transformation in the political participation and representation of older people?

First of all, the growth in political action by older people is merely a reflection of the global upsurge in social movements spanning almost every element of political life (Jenkins and Klandermans 1995). This may be seen as one facet of the transition from modernity to postmodernity which, on the one hand, means the breakdown of the traditional economic and social certainties of modernity and, on the other, the opening up of new concepts of citizenship and consumerism, and new channels of political action (Harvey 1989). The emergence of new social movements outside of the familiar political institutions – political parties and trade unions – is not surprising given the profound realignments under way in the social and economic orders of the advanced industrial societies of Europe.

Second, some of the socio-demographic developments have supported both a heightened political awareness of old age as a political issue and the likelihood that older people will participate actively. I mean that there are more older people and, therefore, they are more visible than 15–20 years ago in social terms and in policy/political terms. Also the combination of the massive growth of early exit from the labour market (Kohli *et al.* 1991; Walker *et al.* 1993) and the cohort effects of a healthier and better educated older population has produced a potentially active pool of older people in their third age (50–74).

Third, the negative changes in the macroeconomic policy context referred to earlier have had an impact on the radicalization of the grassroots politics of old age in some countries. In Denmark the C Team was set up to protest against cuts in public social services. The primary focus of the UK pensioners' campaigns is the government: both local and national campaigns have been concerned almost exclusively with the last government's cuts in pensions and social services provision and related issues, such as the introduction of VAT on electricity and gas bills. Obviously the precise impact of such policies on activism among older people depends on a variety of factors including the adequacy of welfare provision for this group in each country and the extent of the public expenditure reductions being proposed by particular governments. Thus the mobilization or activation effect of adverse public policy changes is uneven across the EU.

Fourth, the growth of political participation among older people has been openly encouraged in several countries by policy makers at both local and national levels.

### Participation in local decision making

Local authorities in Europe play an important part in encouraging and facilitating the participation of older people in decision making. Most of the participation of older people in daily life takes place at a local level; this unit of administration is responsible, directly or indirectly, for many of the services that they receive. It is useful, however, to distinguish two different sorts of participation in decision making at the local level. On the one hand there is the macro public policy-making process which determines the general direction of services and the distribution of resources between groups; while, on the other hand, there are policy decisions taken at a micro, interpersonal, level often by professionals employed by municipalities which concern the delivery of specific services to older people. The distinction corresponds to that in Denmark between senior citizens' councils and user councils.

As far as the local municipal policy-making process is concerned there has been a great deal of activity in recent years in different EU countries to try to improve the participation of older people. Local authorities in Austria, Denmark, France, Germany, Italy, the Netherlands and Sweden have all established advisory boards of senior citizens. In the case of Sweden, advisory councils must be established by law in all municipalities and, in 70 per cent of them, there are ombudsmen with special responsibilities towards older people. Denmark has advisory boards or similar bodies in the majority of its municipalities. Under a 1982 decree in France, regional and departmental consultative committees were established to ensure the participation of older people in policy making concerning health and social services programmes. At the same time a National Committee for Pensioners and Old People (CNRPA) was created to facilitate participation in national policy making. In Germany, local councils of senior citizens began to be formed in the early 1970s in an attempt to open new channels of access to the policy-making process. Initially the adoption of these senior councils spread very slowly, but during the 1980s their numbers more than trebled (Alber 1994: 135). Italy has recently established consultative committees at regional and communal levels – though their composition and function varies widely. The larger municipalities in the Netherlands have seniors' boards operating in an advisory capacity. Advisory boards for senior citizens have been established, during the last five years, in most Austrian provinces (Leichsenring 1996). Local consultative councils of older people have begun to appear in Belgium: 50 per cent of municipalities in the Flemish-speaking part of Belgium have an advisory committee, and their numbers are increasing. Councils of older people at local, regional and national levels have been set up under Spain's gerontological plan.

The example of Denmark gives some flavour of the rapid increase in activity at municipal level in the recent past. In 1980 only four local authorities had senior citizens' councils, but by 1995 this had increased to 200 (out of 275). Also, in Germany, there has been a very rapid growth recently in senior councils from 500 in 1995 to 730 in 1996.

The formation of advisory bodies provides both an important basis for participation by older people in municipal affairs and a potential network for local administrators to activate. However, we should not overstate the role of such councils. Their existence does not mean that the voices of older people will actually be heard within the policy-making process or that the councils will be able to stand up for their interests, especially those of the most vulnerable. Moreover, as Verté *et al.*'s (1996) study of advisory councils in the Dutch-speaking part of Belgium shows, such bodies may reinforce the exclusion of some groups of older people. He found that members of the advisory bodies were mainly drawn from organizations of retired people and were overwhelmingly men. When women did participate they were rarely members of the council's executive boards. The main participation was from ex-skilled and semi-skilled manual workers and farmers.

His survey also found that when an important issue was put on the agenda only just under half of the members consulted other members of the organization they represented. One third of advisory group members were judged to be passive participants. Most members of advisory councils of older people said that once they had advised the municipal council it depends on the goodwill of the mayor or the alderman if the advice is acted upon. The majority of those who participate in the advisory councils were of the opinion that their efforts are not taken seriously by the local authorities. To quote Verté and his colleagues:

> Our study showed that, although many local policy makers took the initiative of forming an advisory body for the elderly, only a few of them asked for the opinion of the members of the advisory body. The attitude of local policy makers towards their own advisory bodies is characterised by a low commitment to these projects of political participation.
>
> (Verté *et al.* 1996: 12)

The key elements in this negative picture seem to be the absence of a legal framework governing the establishment of advisory councils (as in Sweden) and the existence among some policy makers of age-discriminatory attitudes which lead them to minimize the potential contribution of older people to policy making.

On the positive side, there are examples of advisory councils successfully mobilizing older people and making an impact on policy making. Moreover, there is some good evidence that it is possible to overcome the problems in organizing the local participation of older people. It is clear, though, that we must be mindful about the limitations of local advisory councils, and older people must be aware of the danger of co-option; indeed, some pensioners' organizations may prefer to retain an independent voice. None the less municipalities may still want to subsidize such activities to encourage older people to be independent.

Thus, implicit in what has been said so far is that there are four different models of participation in the policy-making process at the municipal level:

- *independence*, where the organization lobbies the municipality from outside;
- *quasi-independence*, where the municipality provides some funding for the organization to help it to lobby;
- *partial co-option*, where an advisory body is established with representation from different organizations and which has limited access to the decision-making process;
- *full co-option*, where an advisory body is integrated within the municipality's decision-making structure, for example where the local authority has a statutory duty to consult the advisory body.

Each of these approaches entails advantages and disadvantages, and none of them guarantees impact on policy making.

Turning to the second dimension of participation in decision making at local level, we are faced with a very complex interplay of personal and professional relationships. The health and social services are key agencies in the construction of dependency in old age. Professional groups have been trained to regard themselves as autonomous experts, and this has had the effect of excluding older people and their family carers from decision making about the services required to meet their care needs. Thus one of the most important issues confronting local health and social care providers, including local authorities, is how to promote the participation of older people (and service users) and their informal carers in the processes of care.

There are pressures building up for increased participation in decisions previously regarded as the sole province of professionals. These are coming, first, from the rise of consumerism (the transition from modernity to post-modernity) and the reassertion of individualism. This social change is creating twin pressures for greater choice and for a participating voice. Second, there are grassroots pressures from service users – some of whom are demanding a greater say in what services are provided – and from informal carers, who are complaining about being, at best, taken for granted by service providers. In the Netherlands and the UK self-help groups of carers have been formed to represent their views. They are calling for a recognition of their right to be consulted on an equal basis with service users. Third, there are changes within professionals in their orientation and practice that are beginning to question professional autonomy and which are opening up professional practice to user involvement. Together these processes are beginning to set a new agenda favouring the participation of older people and older service users.

Signs of this culture shift can be seen in some countries, notably those Scandinavian ones which emphasize rights to services. Thus the Users' Councils in Denmark are representing the interests of older users with regard to home care, institutional care and other services. Even in the UK, which has a more paternalistic service tradition, user groups are being established by some local authorities.

But there are still formidable barriers in the way of effective participation and there is a very long way to go before older people are genuinely empowered in the face of professional service allocators and providers. Clearly the local authorities have a crucial role to play in promoting a *culture of empowerment* at all levels and encouraging professionals to operate in more open participative ways (Barnes and Walker 1996).

*Participation in national decision making*

Several countries have set up national advisory boards consisting of the representatives of older people. The French National Committee for Pensioners and Old People (CNRPA) and Spanish national council have been mentioned already. The Senior Citizens' Consulting Council was set up in Belgium more than 40 years ago. In the Netherlands the National Council for Elderly Policy was established in 1988 (but disbanded in 1996); in Ireland the National Council for the Elderly advises the Minister of Health, and a National Economic and Social Council has just been set up. In Luxembourg there is a Higher Council for Older People. In Austria a Federal Senior Council was established in 1995. It consists of 35 representatives of the three most important seniors' organizations, the ministries, the provinces and local authorities, meets 3–4 times a year and is chaired by the Chancellor (Leichsenring 1996). Although these national bodies reflect a consensual model of policy making and may be regarded by politically active seniors as part of a process of co-option, they, none the less, have probably assisted the development of the new politics of old age by both raising the profile of older people in the policy-making process and by helping to legitimize their political concerns. The Ombudsman role in Sweden is also a mechanism which raises the profile of older people's rights and, particularly with regard to frail older people, helps to include them in decision making.

*Participation at European level*

European institutions also have begun recently to encourage directly and indirectly, the political participation of older people and to act as an important source of legitimacy for their political action. The European Commission and Parliament have provided a focus for the formation of European-wide networks of older people or their representatives. The main European trade union and NGO umbrella groups are EURAG (European Federation for the Welfare of the Elderly), Eurolink Age, FERPA (European Federation of Retired and Older People) and FIAPA (International Federation of Older People's Associations). The Commission granted these groups a special place in its policy-making machinery by appointing them to an NGO Liaison Group for the 1991–3 Actions Programme. Moreover, in awarding them resources and allocating them a key role in the European Year of Older People and Solidarity Between the Generations the Commission has both enhanced their status and directly facilitated the participation of older people. The European Parliament similarly has been a stimulus to participation, particularly through the very active Intergroup on Ageing and the mounting of a Seniors' Parliament in 1992. The European Court of Justice has also had a radicalizing effect on older people in some countries by providing them with a focus for political action on pensions and equal opportunities issues and by increasing awareness of rights among pensioners.

Thus the recent mobilization of older people in Europe and the development of what appears to be a new politics of old age must be regarded as the consequence of two distinct impulses. From *below* there are undoubtedly pressures on the part of older people seeking a political voice; while from *above*, policy makers at local, national and EU levels have consciously encouraged the political mobilization of older people.

Before concluding this review of trends in political participation and representation among older people it is worth noting that the new forms of political action seem to be in tune with public opinion. For example opinion polls in Denmark have found that over half the population considers the C Team's demonstrations to be quite reasonable, and only 10 per cent regard them as unreasonable. Ironically, the lowest level of support for such forms of direct action was given by older people themselves (Platz and Petersen 1995: 65). In the 1992 Eurobarometer survey conducted in all of the then 12 Member States we asked the general public whether or not older people should stand up more actively for their rights. Very large proportions of the public in all countries said that they should: on average more than four out of five EC citizens agreed. The combined FDR and GDR proportions were 84 per cent – the same as in the UK – though more of the latter agreed strongly (Walker 1993: 32).

## Barriers to political participation

There can be no doubt about the importance of the transformation that is taking place in the politics of old age in Europe. Equally, however, we must not overstate what has happened. So far it has impinged on only a minority of senior citizens, and this suggests that the barriers to political participation may be more formidable than has been recognized generally. There are five main impediments to such participation by older people in specifically age-related politics, and these include both demand and supply factors.

In the first place, contrary to popular perceptions and some scientific analyses, older people do not necessarily share a common interest by virtue of their age alone which transcends all other interests. Thus it is mistaken to regard senior citizens as a homogeneous group which might coalesce around or be attracted by a one-dimensionsal politics of old age. In other words, there is not only one but several forms of socio-political consciousness which depend, not on age as such, but on factors such as socio-economic status, race, gender, religion and locality. This perspective is at odds with the long-standing tendency for social gerontologists to regard older people as a distinct and homogeneous social group, separate from the rest of the social structure and, in particular, as a group cut off from their *own* status and class position formed at earlier stages of the life-cycle. Although no longer prevalent in social gerontology this is still a view held by policy makers in many different countries and in international economic agencies such as the OECD (Walker 1990; OECD 1994). As Estes (1982, 1991) has argued, a largely classless view of old age has been incorporated into public policy.

In fact, older people are just as deeply divided along social class and other structural lines as younger adults. This contrasts with both commonsense notions and pluralistic analyses suggesting a common interest among older people, with age acting as a sort of leveller of class and status differentials (a view which may have some relevance in the US – see Pampel and Williamson [1989] – but not in Europe). There is no doubt that the process of retirement, not ageing, does superimpose reduced socio-economic status on a majority of older people – for example net replacement ratios for a married man with a full working life of contributions are 69 per cent in Germany, 83 per cent in France and 64 per cent in the UK (Walker *et al.* 1993: 15) – but, even so, retirement has a differential impact on older people depending on their prior socio-economic status. For example there is unequal access to second-tier pensions. Women and other groups with incomplete employment records are particularly disadvantaged in most EU countries. Moreover, the size of second-tier pensions differs considerably according to socio-economic grouping. There are also inequalities between generations of older people arising from their unequal access to improved private and occupational pension opportunities. Very elderly lone women are the most disadvantaged financially in all EU countries.

Second, the majority of older people in Europe remain powerless politically. Traditionally the main source of working class political power has been the economic base provided by the workplace and trade union organization. The social processes of exclusion created through retirement and, more recently, early exit, not only remove older people from their main source of income but also from collective activities and potential political influence. Indeed the process of exclusion itself is likely to encourage conservatism because it detaches older people from collective workplace activities and sources of socio-political consciousness as well as practical information, and replaces them with privatized and individualized home-based activities. Of course I am well aware that this is predicated on a 'Fordist' model of work organization which is increasingly inappropriate as a description of the post-modern world of work (Harvey 1989), but paid employment remains a collective activity for the majority of those in employment. Thus Simone de Beauvoir's (1977) observation retains some element of truth: having been removed from playing any economic role in society, older people lack both cohesion and a means of challenging their inferior economic and social position.

Retirement (including early retirement) appears to entail an element of depoliticization or political disengagement, though it is impossible to disentangle any cohort effects from the available data. The observation of a relationship between political efficacy and occupation dates back more than 30 years to the US research by Almond and Verba (1963). Using a similar approach, later British survey analysis has found that propensity for collective action is lowest among the retired and, in contrast to the employed and other groups in the labour market, retired people have a preference for personal over collective action (Young 1984). (These findings echo those Danish opinion poll data reported earlier.) The explanation for this acquiescence on the part of older people consisted of a sense of powerlessness or non-competence which, in turn, reflected a lack of real resources on which to gain political influence. There was, predictably, a close association between both socio-economic group and education and subjectively assessed power.

Third, pensioners often lack formal channels through which to exert political influence. Indeed, the political representation systems of some countries effectively exclude older people from key institutions. For example few of the established political parties in Europe provided an organizational context for pensioners or made special efforts to include them in their decision-making machinery. The main exception is Germany, whose political parties have tried to take such steps (Alber 1995: 131). The Christian Democrats were the first to establish a special party organization for older people, in 1988. It is called the Senioren-Union and is open to all people over 60, including non-members of the party. The Social Democrats rejected the creation of a special subgroup for older people and instead issued an appeal, in 1979, to mobilize senior citizens within the party. Subsequently a network of senior circles was built up at district and regional levels within the party. More recently the Social Democrats created senior representative posts at district, state and federal levels.

Similarly, some trade unions in Europe have been poor at involving ex-members and in providing continuing membership after labour force exit. Again there are important exceptions and also signs that the trade union movement generally is becoming more aware of the need to involve older people. In Italy, more than 20 per cent of pensioners belong to the special retirement sections of the three main unions. This relatively high participation rate appears to be the result of a combination of bottom–up and top–down impulses. On the one hand older people want to defend the rights they have acquired, particularly pension rights, and on the other Italian trade unions have taken specific steps to increase the social and political involvement of older people (Florea *et al.* 1995). Other national unions in the EU lag some way behind their Italian counterparts. Germany has a relatively high union participation rate among pensioners compared with other EU countries: 13.3 per cent of the 11.7 million union members are pensioners (with higher than average rates in the public sector and metal workers unions) (Alber 1995). Union membership after retirement is also significant in the Netherlands, at least among men (for example 14 per cent of men aged 70–74 are in unions) but is very low among women (1 per cent aged 70 and over). In Spain the two major unions each have a federation of the retired but their membership is low (less than 1 per cent of all pensioners). The two confederations of Portuguese unions have sub-organizations of older people (created in 1986 and 1989), and the FGTB in Belgium established a national coordinating commission of retired members in 1988.

Fourth, there are important physical and mental barriers to political participation in old age. Disability and socially disabling later life course events, such as widowhood, may further fragment political consciousness and discourage political activity. The experience of ageing itself creates barriers to collective action and political participation for a minority of older people. For those with intellectual or learning disabilities who are now reaching old age, the ageing process merely confirms their socio-political exclusion (Walker *et al.* 1996b). Other social structural factors that militate against political participation include poverty and low incomes, and age, gender and race discrimination. For instance, we know from the work of the EU Observatory that there is a significant minority of older people experiencing poverty in all Member States and, in some, the size of the minority is quite large (Walker *et al.* 1993: 16). Those suffering social exclusion as a result of poverty face substantial material and psychological barriers to participation and are among the least likely to be represented within the formal political system. In addition a large number of older people, particularly women, are actively engaged in caring for spouses and others in need and, therefore, may not have the physical energy and mental space to be active on the political scene as well.

Finally, there is conservatism. It is not necessarily the case that people become more conservative as they grow older – despite the commonplace nature of that assumption (see for example Hudson 1980). Although there is evidence that older people are more conservative in certain respects than younger ones – certainly voting patterns in different EU countries suggest this – the reasons are not related primarily to age. Several key factors have been mentioned already, including the removal of sources of potential influence and activity, but in addition there is a generational dimension. The present older generations have different reference points to younger people, and early economic life is of particular importance in the formation of political consciousness and party allegiance (Westergaard *et al.* 1989). Many of their formative years occurred between 1915 and 1950, a unique historical period in Europe. Older people are also likely to retain loyalty to a particular political party. All of this suggests that older people are *not* more conservative in voting terms but, rather, they have a tendency to vote for the party they have always voted for. Also it is likely that conservative voters, on average, live longer than social democratic ones – because of their different social class origins. This class/demographic effect will tend to reinforce pro-conservative voting patterns among very elderly people, the majority of whom are women.

These five demand and supply factors represent substantial barriers to political participation on the part of some older people, and cast serious doubt on the development of any major age-specific political groupings in the EU. They also help to explain why it was that the politics of old age in Europe was dominated for so long by consensus.

## The political challenges of an ageing Europe

The third and final section of this chapter concerns the future evolution of the politics of old age. Will older people in the EU develop a more unified and outspoken voice, like their US counterparts? What will be the impact of societal ageing on the political process? These are some of the crucial questions that Europe must confront in the next two or three decades.

More than 20 years ago Neugarten (1974) predicted the emergence in the US of a more activist population of older people (the 'young-old') challenging traditional stereotypes of ageing. One manifestation of that change is the powerful American Association of Retired Persons (AARP) with 30 million members – one quarter of all registered voters in the US (Torres-Gil 1992). The AARP has substantial resources and is able to exercise considerable influence on the US government. The potential for older people in Europe to develop such a mass movement is likely to be limited for four reasons. First, there are the major divisions among older people outlined earlier which, at a European level, also include nationality and cultural differences. Second, old age is a more marginalized status in Europe than it is in the US, where older people are more ready to identify themselves as such and to exhibit what is referred to there as 'age consciousness' (Torres-Gil 1993). Third, the superior welfare systems of Europe, in comparison with the US, have reduced some of the mobilization potential of social need (CEC 1993). Fourth, pluralistic political systems, such as the US, are particularly amenable to the influence of interest groups, including age-interest groups (Williamson *et al.* 1982; Pampel *et al.* 1990). In contrast, the corporatist traditions of most European politics have not been so conducive to the emergence of a mass movement of older people.

Although we have seen the development of a more militant tendency among older people in some EU countries – a trend that is likely to continue – these factors will inhibit the development of a unified age-interest politics in most countries and at EU level. There will be variations between Member States, and some political systems in Europe are more open than others, but, overall, current trends suggest that age-based movements and political parties are likely to remain relatively marginal features of national and European political life. At the present time there does not appear to be a great deal of enthusiasm on the part of European elders to join political parties devoted primarily to the issue of age – except in the cases of Greece, Italy and Portugal (Table 2.1).

In the 1992 Eurobarometer survey we asked older people if they would be prepared to join a political party formed mainly to further the interests of their age group. Across the EC as a whole only just under one quarter said that they would, a not insignificant but none the less small minority. Even in one of Europe's most pluralistic political systems, the Netherlands, the associations of older people take the view that the creation of an age-related political party is not desirable (Rijsselt 1995: 326). However, this does *not* mean that age will be unimportant in political terms: European politics are likely to be influenced increasingly by older people at all levels.

The main pressure will come from demography. As Table 2.2 shows, there will be an increase of nearly 10 per cent in the proportion of potential voters over the age of 55 between 1990 and 2020. Countries which now have almost one third of potential voters in the over 55 age group will see this proportion grow towards one half by 2020.

**Table 2.1** Percentage of older people saying they would or would not join a political party formed mainly to further the interests of older people in the European Community

|  | Yes | No | DK |
|---|---|---|---|
| Belgium | 16 | 75 | 9 |
| Denmark | 20 | 74 | 6 |
| France | 22 | 72 | 6 |
| Germany | 14 | 73 | 13 |
| Greece | 33 | 47 | 20 |
| Ireland | 16 | 79 | 5 |
| Italy | 34 | 51 | 15 |
| Luxembourg | 21 | 73 | 5 |
| Netherlands | 21 | 76 | 4 |
| Portugal | 42 | 36 | 22 |
| Spain | 18 | 70 | 12 |
| UK | 20 | 76 | 4 |
| Total | 22 | 68 | 10 |

*Source*: Unpublished data from 1992 Eurobarometer (Walker 1993)

**Table 2.2** Percentage of voters over 55 in the EU

|  | 1990 | 2000 | 2010 | 2020 |
|---|---|---|---|---|
| Austria | 32 | 34 | 37 | 43 |
| Belgium | 33 | 34 | 37 | 43 |
| Denmark | 32 | 34 | 39 | 44 |
| Finland | 30 | 32 | 40 | 44 |
| France | 32 | 32 | 36 | 40 |
| Germany | 32 | 37 | 39 | 45 |
| Greece | 35 | 36 | 38 | 40 |
| Ireland | 27 | 26 | 27 | 31 |
| Italy | 33 | 35 | 39 | 44 |
| Luxembourg | 32 | 35 | 40 | 45 |
| Netherlands | 29 | 31 | 37 | 42 |
| Portugal | 32 | 31 | 34 | 38 |
| Spain | 32 | 32 | 34 | 39 |
| Sweden | 35 | 36 | 39 | 42 |
| UK | 34 | 34 | 36 | 41 |

*Source*: Wilson (1993: 96)

If we lower the cut-off to the starting point of the third age (i.e. 50) it can be seen that most of the northern Member States will have half of all potential voters aged over 50 in 2020 (Table 2.3).

Having already criticized the simplistic view that growing numbers of older people will automatically mean more power for, (and expenditure on) this group, I am not suggesting that a majority of potential voters in the 50+ age group will mean that they will vote as a block. They will not, the majority is a heterogeneous one. But the sheer size of the electoral numbers imply

**Table 2.3**   EU countries in which more than half the voters are over 50 by 2020 (per cent)

|            | 1990 | 2000 | 2010 | 2020 |
|------------|------|------|------|------|
| Austria    | 40   | 43   | 46   | 53   |
| Belgium    | 41   | 42   | 47   | 52   |
| Denmark    | 39   | 43   | 48   | 53   |
| Finland    | 38   | 43   | 49   | 53   |
| Italy      | 41   | 44   | 47   | 54   |
| Luxembourg | 40   | 44   | 50   | 54   |
| Netherlands| 36   | 40   | 47   | 52   |
| Sweden     | 42   | 46   | 48   | 51   |
| UK         | 41   | 43   | 45   | 50   |

*Source*: Wilson (1993: 97)

that political systems and, in particular, political parties, will not be able to ignore them. Even if the majority of older voters split along class or other lines they will still be able to exercise influence.

This demographic pressure will reinforce the growth trend in political participation among older people. There are sure signs of a changing political mood on the part of European elders. One of these is the symbolic issue of what older people want themselves to be called collectively. In the 1992 Eurobarometer survey we found that in most of the then 12 countries the term 'elderly' was rejected in favour of 'older people' and 'senior citizens' (Walker 1993: 6). In Germany, Ireland and the UK the clear signal was that older people want to be regarded, in positive terms, as civic actors with the full rights and duties of citizenship. There are also signs in several EU countries of increased participation among older people in local political action. A pilot project organized by the Free University in Amsterdam and funded by the European Commission has found a great deal of support in municipalities for increased participation among older people. The project involved teams of action researchers in Belgium, the Netherlands, Spain and the UK, and aimed to create the conditions necessary for social and political participation at a local level. The trend towards greater local participation is likely to gain further impetus from the fact that future cohorts of older people will be healthier, more educated and more consumerist in orientation than previous ones (Dane Age 1990).

Although it is impossible to predict the future with any certainty, there can be little doubt that these pressures will present irresistible challenges to the existing systems of political representation in Europe. Local, national and European political systems will have to adjust quickly to this new sociodemographic reality; as has been shown, some important steps have been taken already in this direction. The age-interest groups that represent the views of older people within the policy systems of Europe will have to adapt to the growing demands from senior citizens for a greater voice in their own affairs – in the same way that disabled persons have moved to the forefront in advocating their own cause. At EU level the pan-European NGOs will have to face the challenge of creating a unified movement. The inclusion of

**Table 2.4**   Women over the age of 50 as a percentage of total voters

|            | 1990 | 2000 | 2010 | 2020 |
|------------|------|------|------|------|
| Austria    | 23   | 24   | 25   | 29   |
| Belgium    | 23   | 23   | 25   | 28   |
| Denmark    | 21   | 23   | 26   | 28   |
| Finland    | 21   | 23   | 26   | 28   |
| France     | 22   | 22   | 24   | 26   |
| Germany    | 24   | 24   | 26   | 29   |
| Greece     | 24   | 24   | 25   | 27   |
| Ireland    | 18   | 17   | 19   | 21   |
| Italy      | 23   | 24   | 26   | 29   |
| Luxembourg | 22   | 24   | 27   | 29   |
| Netherlands| 19   | 22   | 25   | 29   |
| Portugal   | 22   | 22   | 25   | 26   |
| Spain      | 21   | 22   | 23   | 26   |
| Sweden     | 23   | 25   | 26   | 28   |
| UK         | 22   | 23   | 24   | 27   |

*Source*: Wilson (1993: 102)

the concept of European citizenship in the Maastricht Treaty (Social Chapter) opens the way to the inclusion of older people in the previously employment-dominated citizenship criteria. Also the addition of health to the competence of the EU is of potentially great significance to older people (Spicker 1991), as is the reference to age in the Amsterdam Treaty. The European Commission is likely, therefore, to be the focus of even more lobbying by older people's groups.

But it is at the local level that we are likely to see the greatest impact of the new politics of old age. Social movements of older people are already present in many municipalities and, partly in response to the encouragement by policy makers and partly due to the mounting desire for empowerment, we are likely to see more and more pensioner action groups operating at local and regional levels. Many of the most immediate issues that impact on older people are determined locally, and community politics enable people to participate despite some of the personal barriers that may be in their way. Conflict over the local rationing of health and social care resources will reinforce the tendency towards local action. The European handbook for increasing the participation of older people being developed by the EU project mentioned earlier (based on the Dutch prototype *Seniors Help Decide*) will undoubtedly assist this process of local mobilization. Indeed, we may see the development of a new 'neighbourhood effect' in terms of a localized political consciousness on the part of older people. This will be especially strong in the traditional retirement areas of Europe.

Because women outnumber men in old age the new politics will be feminized increasingly (Table 2.4). Again policy makers will need to adjust, and the often male dominated pensioner unions will likewise have to respond to the pressure from women for positions of leadership and campaigns that reflect their needs. Of course women will also form an increasing proportion of voters as European societies age. This raises the prospect of issues that affect women in particular gaining a higher political profile – issues such as the long term care of older people and the rights of family carers. These are issues that have a local impact, and local authorities will have to adjust to older women playing a greater role in decision making.

## Conclusion

Over the last decade the politics of old age in Europe have begun a transition from consensus to a more conflictual approach. The origins of this change lie in twin top–down and bottom–up pressures. On the one hand there has been a shift in the orientation of policy makers concerning the relationship between old age and the welfare state; on the other, a growth in political participation among older people at grassroots level. We cannot say for certain that this will be permanent but it looks as though it will be. The demographics suggest the increasing prominence of older people as political actors. This is not just a matter of numbers but also the cohort effect of improved health and education. Also the transformation of societies as a whole to more consumerist and participative forms will reinforce this trend.

Europe is not likely to see the emergence of a full-blown US style age-interest politics: both the structural divisions among older people and the majority of political systems in the EU will militate against this. In any case such a development would not necessarily further the cause of older people because it could lead to age-specific opposition. The more likely course in Europe is the continued growth of older people's participation in local politics. Also the politics of old age will become increasingly feminized. All of which poses some major challenges to the existing political systems of Europe – local, national and European – and the organizations that are involved in the representation of older people.

Municipalities are likely to occupy the centre stage in the increasing participation of older people, and they will have a vital role in ensuring that older citizens are able to exert a reasonable influence on policy making without creating reactions from other age groups. This will be a difficult balancing act. Local (and national) politicians will have to be aware of the danger of age-based politics but, equally, it is essential to overcome exclusion, to bring older people in from the political wilderness. The future goal should be consultative groups of all generations but, for now, there is a need to redress the age imbalance in political participation.

# 3

# The legal structures
# of representation

BERND SCHULTE

Despite the real upsurge in research on older people in Europe there is still very little comparative work on the legal, institutional and infrastructural prerequisites for an adequate life for older people. There is a lack of comparative analyses which shed light upon the overall systems which form the wider context for an understanding of 'assistance for older people'; there are also few studies on the objectives, individual measures and legal basis of assistance for this group within the context of the relevant national systems of social security. This applies particularly to the *representation of the interests of older people and the forms of their political involvement*, both in respect of their institutional and legal frameworks as well as of the traditions, actual practice and innovations in this sector.

## The voicing of interests at European level

The Council of the European Union and the Council of Social Affairs Ministers issued a basic declaration on 6 December 1993 to mark the official end of the European Year for Older People and Solidarity between the Generations, a project which attempted to take account of the considerable increase in the numbers of senior citizens in all the Member States. There were five sectors in which the Member States were called on to take tangible measures:

1. level of income and standard of living;
2. housing and mobility;
3. care and aid services;
4. the employment of older workers and preparation for retirement;
5. the integration of older people.

The EU Member States were called on to promote the full integration of older people into social life in all social groupings, by making available t them in an appropriate manner the information necessary for active an appropriate participation in all areas affecting them (Council for Socia Affairs 1993).

Although there are a few areas of policy important for older people whic are expressly subject to EU law (for example the equal treatment of men an women in working life and in social security, as well as in systems of socia welfare at company level) and the personal freedoms of the Commor Market (namely the right to freedom of movement) the Council's statemen recognizes that the Community has no fundamental competence to mak policy for older persons. Rather, social policy has remained fundamentall within the remit of the Member States. In accordance with the Communit legal principle of specific allocation, the Community is only responsible ir those cases expressly laid down in the founding treaty of the Europea Community, namely in connection with the personal freedoms of the indi vidual in the Common Market: freedom of movement of workers (Article 48–51 of the EC Treaty), freedom of the self-employed to set up in busines where they want (Article 52), equality of treatment for men and wome (Article 119), and – most recently – in the field of occupational safety (Arti cle 118a). In addition, there is now a further responsibility on the Membe States based on an extension of the majority voting principle (in contrast t the principle of unanimity which otherwise prevails in the sphere of socia policy) and deriving from the minutes and agreements on social policy a Maastricht in connection with the signing of the Treaty on the Europea Union. At the intergovernmental conference in 1996 and 1997 on the revi sion of the Maastricht Treaty (in Amsterdam) in June 1997, an agreemen was reached to return to a uniform, common EC social policy by incorpo rating the content of the agreement on social policy in the EC Treaty. Apar from this, an extension of the majority voting principle (and then also t include social policy) is under discussion anyway in view of the planne increase in the number of EU members. In the field of policy for olde people, however, the European Community is currently restricted: it is no allowed to operate directly through legislation, but indirectly through th exchange of information, cross-border contacts and cooperation; it may als work through the propagation of models for 'good practice'. This approac and method shows promise, not least with regard to fields of action such a the political and legal representation of older people, where the Membe States are largely lacking in traditional, established systems and where mor or less all of them are in search of innovations.

At the invitation of the Socialist Group within the European Parliament the first European Parliament for Senior Citizens was convened in 1992. A group of 518 older people from all walks of life met together at a two-da conference and adopted *A Social Charter for Senior Citizens*. In their final decla ration the group called for the establishment of a permanent advisory senio citizens' forum in the European Community. The declaration showed tha the efforts to involve older people in the making of decisions concernin their own well-being had progressed from local, regional and national leve and had now reached European level.

## Forms of political participation in European countries

A 1993 study, *Senior Citizens in Europe*, (Europa Research Group 1993) investigated the position, status and opportunities for the development of senior citizens policy in the Member States of the European Community and European Free Trade Association. It also looked into the issue of the political participation of senior citizens (Europa Research Group 1993). The study observed that as a rule senior citizens only play a subsidiary role in politics and also that political activities of older people – at that time anyway – were still an exception (disregarding the admittedly generally very high level of electoral turn-out of older citizens compared to other age brackets of the population). On this basis, the study made a distinction between two forms of institutionalized participation of older people: on the one hand, in decision making and advisory bodies dealing directly with the living conditions of senior citizens; on the other, in the more traditional forms of political organization, particularly political parties and associations (see Chapter 2).

As far as the first type of institutionalized participation is concerned, older citizens lack representation and opportunities to voice their interests: state agencies and bodies, employers and employees, the providers of social benefits, the associations of those providing services (e.g. doctors' associations), welfare associations and lobby organizations mostly decide on the main issues of policy for older people, without representing their specific interests at all. However, an increase in the (indirect) influence of older people in this type of organization was found. Most of the opportunities for senior citizens to further their interests by participating in institutions, were found at a local and regional level, where participation was as a rule restricted merely to consultation; there was no provision for older people to be involved in actual decision making. At supra-regional level even the opportunities for consultation only tended to be rare.

Something of a pioneering role with regard to the legal and institutional establishment of special bodies such as senior citizens' advisory boards was found in the Scandinavian countries. Here, senior citizens' boards are already widespread at local and regional level and have some decision-making powers, including budget and personnel matters. This leading position of the Scandinavian countries evidently has much to do with their legal constitution, administrative organization and political culture: the central role of the public sector in the sphere of social security and health care is still characteristic in Scandinavia. Another specific feature – especially in Denmark – is the decentralization of the administration. While the political guidelines and budgetary framework are decided at national level, the responsibility for the social and health services relevant especially to older people lies at local level, whose institutions both determine policy and provide for the collective participation of older citizens through senior citizens' boards.

### Denmark

In Denmark there are senior citizens' boards at local level almost everywhere, locally elected by older people and having an increasingly democra-

tic constitution. The influence of these boards on the local administratio
varies from community to community. It is, however, normally not restricte
merely to consultation but extends right up to influence on the loc
community budget. The increasing electoral turn-out in the elections to th
senior citizens' boards is a reflection of the growing awareness by olde
people of the significance of these bodies; at the same time, though, it als
increases their standing within the local community. The degree of politic
influence achieved by older people in this way is manifestly greater than i
all other comparable countries. Moreover, particular attention should b
drawn to the high degree of organized representation in all sectors of life i
Denmark. In addition to organizations for children, youngsters and parent
the largest are those which represent the sick, the disabled and pensioners

Associations directly connected with older people include the Academy fc
the Third Age, which has set itself the objective of researching the livin
conditions of older people (and which at present funds 30 study group
committed to this subject), the Regional Association of Active Pensioner
various church, party-political and trade union affiliated associations, an
the Alliance for the Development of New Opportunities in Old Age (whic
is active above all in adult education and in radio at a local level). The large
influence is ascribed to the C-Holdets (or C Team) alliance, a grassroot
movement which consists of people of all age groups and aims to represer
the interests of all people who are dependent on others for physical o
psychological support. Another association deserving particular mention i
Home Sharing for the Old, which concentrates its efforts on establishin
shared housing opportunities for people in the third age. It accepts member
from 40 years of age and upwards and also represents the corresponding ag
groups. Aeldre Sagen (Dane Age), a national association, sees itself as a non
political organization aimed at contributing to improving the quality an
conditions of life for older people; at local level, it offers cultural events an
maintains a voluntary network of visiting services, telephone chains, sel
help groups, and so on. The Association of Public Pensioners is active in th
field of social work, runs clubs for the elderly and organizes educationa
programmes in order to keep older people active. At a local level, finall
there is a wide range of groups providing advice, leisure activities, holiday
and further education courses for older people and the disabled (*omsorg*
*gruppe* and *OK-klubberne*) (Köhler 1997). These social groups lobby the stat
and particularly local authorities to further the specific interests of olde
people in matters of social policy. Another key area of their activities is i
representing the specific consumer interests of older people with trade an
business.

A recently completed comparative study into the legal, institutional an
infrastructural conditions of assistance for older people in Europe conclude
that the representation of senior citizens' interests by senior citizens is mush
rooming throughout Europe: there is a rapid increase in the number of advi
sory boards, representative bodies and so on at local, regional and even a
national level – but at the same time a legal and institutional framework fo
these developments is in most cases still lacking (Schulte 1996). Legal regu
lation is most likely to exist with regard to involvement in decision makin

or people living in residential institutions, such as old people's homes. In other words, such rights are granted to groups of older people in very special settings where their interests do no compete directly with those of other groups. In this context, a further trend is emerging of establishing advisory bodies – and in some cases even co-determination boards – for other institutions which also provide care, apart from the purely residential ones.

## The Netherlands

Developments in the Netherlands are particularly worthy of attention; here older people are involved in the establishment and administration of practically all institutions catering for them. So-called clients' boards (such as residents' boards, residents' commissions, patients' boards, tenants' commissions and the like) are the bodies which collectively look after the interests of those concerned. The members of such boards are mostly elected by long term and potential service users. In the case of institutions with a rapidly fluctuating clientele, on the other hand, the members are mostly chosen and appointed by the users' organizations.

The powers of the clients' boards may vary from institution to institution, and extend from mere consultation and the right to express an opinion on specific issues – the provision of services, for example – to the right to make suggestions with regard to the nature and organization of services and assistance. Their powers may also consist of the right of approval, whereby certain measures are dependent on a positive vote by the clients' board. The remit of the clients' boards is usually laid down in writing. Up to now these agreements have been individually negotiated – except in a few cases.

The Dutch law on old people's homes (Wet op die Bejaardenoorden – WBO) requires the setting-up of so-called residents' commissions in such homes and obliges the provinces and cities to draft corresponding legal regulations with further details on the establishment, organization and powers of such commissions. The residents' commissions represent the interests of and are elected by the residents of the homes; they are independent of the homes' management. Some of the most important functions of the commissions are to exercise an influence on the way the home is run, to make a contribution to ensuring a good atmosphere in the home, to support the residents in word and deed, to keep the residents, the management and also the staff of the institution informed on the activities of the commission, to influence policy for the older people also outside the home, and where necessary to receive complaints by the residents of the home and to follow them up. Whereas older people who have been accepted into institutions providing medical care can also have their interests looked after by residents' boards, older people in psycho-geriatric institutions are not normally credited with the ability to assess and look after their own interests. In this case, therefore, their interests are entrusted to so-called family boards, consisting of legal representatives or members of the families of the residents. These family boards have similar functions to the residents' commissions. However, they so far have no statutory basis, so their organization and functions are ultimately determined by the management of the relevant institution.

In 1993 the Dutch government tabled a Bill which is intended to give the co-determination arrangements already in existence a statutory basis (Wet medezeggenschap clienten zorginstellingen). This law (which was originally supposed to come into force before the end of 1996, but according to the most recent information has been temporarily postponed) will oblige all institutions which are financed by the state and/or from national insurance to set up clients' boards. This will affect old people's homes, nursing homes, institutions providing home help and nursing care as well as health care which are financed under the Sickness Insurance Fund Law (Zieken fondswet – ZFB), the General Law on Special Sickness Costs (Algemene Wet op de Bijzondere Ziektekosten), the Law on the Financing of Public Insur ance (Wet financiering volksverzekeringen) and, at provincial level, under the Welfare Law (Welzijnswet). Should an institution fail to meet its obliga tions, not only the clients' board itself but also individual members of it will have the right to take court action for the statutory obligations to be fulfilled. In other disputes between an institution and the clients' board, a special arbi tration commission can be set up in agreement with the clients' board in order to bring about a settlement, the commission's decision being final. On the other hand, there has been a right of complaint in existence since 1 August 1995 at a special commission in the care sector under the so-called 'klachtrecht clienten zorgsector'. This right has considerably reinforced the legal position of the individuals concerned as against the service providers. A corresponding arrangement also exists for psychiatric institutions under the Bijzondere Opneming Psychiatrische Ziekenhuizen which came into force on 17 January 1994. This has also significantly improved the legal position of the individuals concerned (Meijer 1996).

The representation of the interests of older people also at the general polit ical level is similarly very strong in the Netherlands. Two parties for senior citizens have been represented since 1994 in the parliament at The Hague. At local level as well as provincial level, there are regulations contained in the Local Authority Law and in the Provincial Law which require local and regional authorities to introduce so-called co-determination by-laws. There are three different senior citizens' associations, each with its own specific ideological or political orientation, which admit members on reaching the age of 50 and which seek to influence policies affecting old people locally, regionally, nationally and recently also at European level. The same applies to the pensioners' associations and the national umbrella organization of clients' boards.

At local and provincial level there are the so-called senior citizens' boards whose function is to advise the relevant authority concerning policy making for older people. The composition and structure of these boards may differ but they can be divided into three basic types. First, there are purely private organizations in the legal form of a foundation or society. This means that the body has complete legal independence from the local authority. Specific agreements with the respective local authority are then normal. Second, boards may be set up under public law on the basis of the Local or Provin cial Law. In this case, the local authorities also largely determine the compo sition of the boards; the senior citizens' associations, however, usually have the right to make proposals. In the latter case, the senior citizens' boards have to be included in the political decision-taking process by law. They have to be consulted on issues of policy concerning older people, and the public authorities must give reasons for rejecting their proposals. There is no national umbrella organization for these senior citizens' boards. Also, their role is by no means uncontested since some people believe that older people should not be specially and prominently singled out for political attention (Wildboer and Noordam 1997). Third and finally, there are bodies which have developed informally but whose existence is *de facto* acknowledged by the local communities because they are integrated into the work of local authorities along the same lines as the boards formally established under private law.

An outstanding example of this are the senior citizens' board regulations (*Verordening Ouderenadviesraad*) that came into effect on 1 January 1995 in the town of Breda. According to these regulations, the senior citizens' board has the function of contributing to the preparation, drafting and implementation of local authority functions in general and those specific to the old in particular (Article 1). The board has 13 members who must, among other things, be local residents, be aged over 55, and be appointed by the local council from a list of nominees. As a rule, the senior citizens' board meets in public six times a year. Resolutions are passed by a majority vote. In certain cases the mayor and local council are obliged to hear the views of the senior citizens' board; it must respond on matters submitted to it to the local council within two months in writing. Should the responsible local bodies then act in a way different from that proposed by the senior citizens' board, reasons must be given for doing so. The local authority must provide the board with all the information needed for it to carry out its functions, as well as the necessary premises, staff, and so on. This arrangement requires a high degree of formalization and institutionalization but should guarantee an effective contribution of older citizens to the local policy-formation and decision-making processes.

An overview of the scope of the advisory work of such senior citizens' boards is provided by the reports which are regularly submitted by these bodies, for example the *Adviezen 1995* report of the Municipal Advisory Commission on Age-Related Issues (Stedilijke Adviescommissie Ouderen-beleid) in Rotterdam. The views range from issues concerning the future organization of social services for the disabled, tax reductions under income tax law or local planning for the old, to traffic planning, the establishment of older people's centres and cultural questions.

*Norway*

In Norway there has been, since 1991, an Act on the Senior Citizens' Boards in Local Municipalities and 'Fylken' (which are about the same size as the federal states in Germany, but with a different structure). The Act came into force on 1 January 1992. The senior citizens' boards are advisory bodies for the relevant local authority or Fylken. They have an *advisory* function in respect of all matters concerning older people. According to the statutory provisions, a senior citizens' board should be elected in all local authority districts and Fylken. In the event that senior citizens' policy making is dele gated in larger local authority districts to sub-districts, corresponding board should also be established at this level. The local or regional (Fylken) assem bly decides on the number of members on the respective senior citizens boards. Senior citizens' associations are entitled to propose people for membership. The majority of members should be pensioners. The senior citi zens' board, which is elected by the older citizens of the local district or Fylken, in turn votes a chairperson and deputy chairperson from among the pensioners. Generally speaking, the regulations governing the local author ity committees also apply to the senior citizens' board. The senior citizens' board produces an annual report on its work, which is then submitted to the local assembly.

*Austria*

In Austria there are institutionalized senior citizens' advisory boards at local and regional levels; whereas at national level, talks are currently being held on the establishment of a national senior citizens' advisory board as a non-party lobby to represent the interests of older people. At regional level, the federal state of Vorarlberg, where there has been a well-functioning senior citizens' advisory board since 1989 (and established as early as 1974), has played a pioneering role in certain respects. Rules of procedure regulate the board's functions, which consist of *advising* the regional government; in addi tion, the senior citizens' advisory board may submit recommendations and proposals to the regional government. In practice, it concerns itself with issues which particularly affect older people, like for example health and pensions insurance, which is governed by federal law, or social security and old age nursing care, which is governed by regional law (Bahr *et al.* 1996). Austria is typical in that the evolution of political participation and repre sentation as described above shows that the initiatives which currently exist have not yet reached the stage where they are embodied in statute.

*France*

In France there are also manifold opportunities for older people to represent their interests, whether directly themselves or through associations, founda tions, societies and, in particular, the typically French *mutualités*. Neverthe less, as in the Netherlands, there is a lack of a comparable legal framework for the establishment and powers of such bodies.

Most of the associations active in the sphere of policy concerning older people are members of the National Committee for Pensioners and Old People (Comité National des Retraités et des Personnes Âgées). This commit tee, on which the minister responsible sits as chairperson, consists of repre sentatives of the government, parliament, numerous pensioners' and old people's associations, as well as eight other people who are nominated by the junior minister responsible on account of their particular specialist knowl edge or the importance of the organizations which they represent. The committee only has an advisory function, but it can also initiate consideration of specific subjects. There is a committee for pensioners and older people at regional level in every *département* (Comité Départemental des Retraités et des Personnes âgées – CDERPA). The function of these committees at regional level is to provide information on the social situation of older people and also to ensure their participation in the policies affecting them. To this extent, the involvement of senior citizens is embodied in law; the representation of older people both at national and *département* level also has a statutory basis.

The National Association Council (Conseil National de la Vie Associative – CNVA), to which representatives of pensioners' and older people's organizations also belong, concerns itself in general with the activity of associations and in particular with making suggestions for improving the associations; to this extent, therefore, it is also of significance for senior citizens' associations.

Pensioners and older people are also represented on the administration boards of the social insurance agencies (including the supplementary pension insurance). The General Association Act of 1901 is the legal basis for the work of associations which are politically active on behalf of the old. This type of association plays a significant role in the social and medical-social sphere in France because up until now social legislation has specified any compulsory requirements for the shape of the organization and management structure of the bodies responsible for facilities and institutions; therefore there is no statutory provision for the representation of those concerned. Such associations act in an advisory capacity at a national level through their representation in the National Council for Social Work (Conseil Supérieur du Travail Social), whose viewpoint has to be heard on many matters (Kaufman 1996).

The co-determination of those concerned is different, being defined in greater legal detail. All socio-medical establishments within the meaning of the Social Act of 1975 must have an in-house council (conseil d'établissement). This body deliberates on questions of organization and function of the establishment and can submit its views. The in-house council consists of between nine and 17 members who represent the residents of the establishment (clients, their relatives, the management and the staff). The residents and their relatives always make up more than a half of the in-house council, members of which are elected by the various groups which are represented on the council.

Even if the law does not actually require it, the in-house council can in fact develop from being merely a consultative body to being a co-determination body. Whether this happens depends on the commitment of its members and a corresponding willingness of the management to accept such a far-reaching involvement of a third party.

## Spain

In Spain, the laws on social services and particularly the national plan for older people (Plan Gerontológico) provide for the participation of those concerned. So-called older people's councils (Consejo de Vejez) exist at local, regional and national level, and have an advisory capacity in all matters concerning the needs of older people.

In old people's homes which are under the auspices of the National Institute for Social Services (Instituto Nacional de Servicios Sociales – INSERSO) or, at regional level, the autonomous communities (Comunidades Autónomas), and likewise in private old people's homes which are supported out of public funds, there are home advisory boards which are intended to protect the interests of the residents. Day centres are as a rule managed by the users themselves; there are legal regulations for this at regional level.

At local, regional and national levels there are advisory boards in which elected representatives of the people concerned sit beside members appointed by law, for example managers of establishments and directors of local authority social services departments.

In 1995 a National Senior Citizens' Council (Consejo Estatal de las Personas Mayores) convened for the first time to represent the interests of older people, with the main task of supervising the implementation of the plan for older people. This body – which is presided over by the Minister for Social Affairs and (in the capacity of dual vice-presidents) the Director General of the National Institute for Social Services and a representative elected by the delegates from the old people's associations – consists of a further 50 delegates (one representative each) at least at the rank of a director general, for the Ministries of Finance, Cultural Affairs, Labour and Social Security as well as Consumer Affairs, four elected representatives of the autonomous communities, two elected representatives of the local authority associations, one representative for each regional senior citizens' board of the autonomous communities, as well as 23 representatives of the registered senior citizens' associations. A standing committee consisting of one chair and 18 delegates steers and coordinates the activities of the National Senior Citizens' Council as a kind of working party. The standing committee is presided over by the second vice-president of the National Senior Citizens' Council, who is elected by the delegates of the senior citizens' associations; other members of the committee are the four representatives of the government, two of the four representatives of the autonomous communities, one of the two local authority representatives as well as four representatives of the regional senior citizens' boards and seven of the senior citizens' associations.

The representatives of the senior citizens' associations are chosen by the Minister for Social Affairs on a predetermined points system (one point for each year of registration as an association, one for each 100 members registered on 31 December 1994, one for each autonomous community in which the association is active, one for each recognized programme of voluntary cooperation, one for each year of voluntary cooperation, and one for each member active on an honorary basis). In this way, the differing importance of the various older people's associations at local, regional and national levels is taken into account in the National Senior Citizens' Council. Representation of interests by a third party exists in the form of an Ombudsman (Defensor del Pueblo), who in 1989, for example produced a report on grievances in public and private old people's homes based on unannounced inspection visits (Reinhard 1996).

*United Kingdom*

In the United Kingdom, charitable organizations and unpaid activity, especially for the support of older people, have a long tradition. Accordingly, organizations such as Age Concern and Help the Aged can look back on many years of work. On the other hand, official representation of interests of older people is not in the hands of particular services or organizations, but is one task among many. There is no authority or other body established by the government which is specifically devoted to the problems of older people. The widespread work of ombudsmen and similar independent third parties – for example the Pensions Ombudsman, the Health Service Commissioner, the Local Authority Commissioner or the Parliamentary Commissioner for Administration, to whom general complaints about government bodies can be addressed – naturally also helps older people. The privatization of public utilities in the past few years has led to the creation of special arbitration panels, who concern themselves with complaints about water, electricity or telephone services. Last but not least, there is a long tradition of parliamentary committees to look into public grievances, and these also play a role in the specific British system for safeguarding interests, including those of older people and their problems (Walker *et al.* 1996a).

I will now turn to the question of how the problems arising nationally and the approaches to solving them can be systematized. In doing so, I will raise more questions than I will provide answers – though this, as the examples quoted above show, corresponds to the current level of development of the subject.

## The representation of older people – problems and solutions

The examples from the selected countries, international legal instruments of (for example) the United Nations, the Council of Europe and the European Community, the recent World Summit for Social Development in 1994, and programmatical declarations of older people's associations in the wider sense which are active on an international scale; all show that policy for older people in the European countries is at a *formative stage* (see Chapter 4). Against this background, policy for older people, for which even in the European Union the Member States bear and will in future continue to bear responsibility, can also be shaped by the exchange of information and experience, by conceptual work and by the activities of the Community institutions. In this sense, therefore, 'Europeanization' means above all an exchange of information and voluntary harmonization of individual policies, exchange of experience, coordination and cooperation at all levels of state and non-state activity. This ensures the compatibility of policy for older people in the Member States in view of the continually increasing importance of the common framework conditions and coordination needs; it also helps Member States to learn from, and with, one another.

Regarding the objectives of policy for older people (and in particular state assistance policy) a large measure of agreement exists in the European countries about the main aims, which are to do with preserving or regaining the greatest possible independence/autonomy in leading their lives, and participation in the life of the community. There is also agreement about the sub-goals: normalization, de-hospitalization/de-institutionalization, having outpatients rather than in-patients, integration/inclusion instead of marginalization/exclusion, and last (though not least), financial efficiency. However, individual national emphases can be found.

The common features of European policy objectives for older people may ultimately be seen as the result of general historical development. For European societies themselves have many things in common in the twentieth century which distinguish them markedly from other societies, such as the USA or Japan. For example, small households predominate to a greater extent in Europe than in Japan; the structure of employment in the European countries is more strongly characterized by industrial work than elsewhere; geographical, professional and social mobility is much less strong than in the USA; and the contrasts between rich and poor are less stark in Europe. Also the development of the welfare state is a distinguishing feature of Europe, where, generally speaking, state social security systems developed earlier and have up until recently been expanded more than elsewhere. Likewise, European countries have in the past tended to spend a significantly higher proportion of their annual national income on social purposes (Kaelble 1987; Schulte 1993).

The basis of the organization of state and society peculiar to Europe, and the broadly shared European policy objectives for older people, map out a broad framework in which the problems of political representation of the interests of older people in the respective state can be located:

- a *state system* which is based on *democracy*;
- an *economic system* which is predominantly based on *private property* and is determined by *free market principles*, with corrective intervention by the state;
- state objectives, which are directed towards the welfare of the citizens;
- a broad area of socio-political activity, the purpose of which is to eliminate discrimination and inequality of opportunity, to create opportunities for individual development and generally to integrate the members of society into society and its individual functional spheres ('inclusion');
- an advanced *system of social security*, the aim of which is to prevent the occurrence of social risks, and in the event of such risks occurring to take compensatory action;
- and also a *legal system* which guarantees the right of citizens to participate in social support – assistance and other benefits – usually in the form of individual legal entitlements (Schulte 1995).

Within this shared framework there are, however, also significant differences between the countries under review in their constitutional and legal systems and their societies, for which the federal element, regionalization, and the independent powers of the local authorities may serve as examples of decentralization in the broadest sense.

Thus in Germany, for example, with its *federal* structure, there is a fundamental constitutional and value orientation that favours the holding of powers and responsibilities by the federal states; the actual administrative structures are largely aligned to this, and hence also the efforts towards political participation, with the result that just as there is a multi-level structure of government responsibilities and duties, so there is also a multi-level structure of political participation. Similar effects are also produced by *regionalization* of the kind that can be observed – to different extents and in differing degrees of approximation to a federalist structure – in Belgium, Italy and Spain. Here, too, there is on the one hand, a centralist and, on the other, a part-state or regional decision-making level, on which, in the Member States of the European Community, a European level is further superimposed (though only to the – as yet – modest extent described above). Then there is also usually a *local* level. So when seeking for appropriate political forms for the representation of interests, the parallel nature of these different levels of decision making and action must also be taken into account.

In a national, legal and social structure of this kind, the task of giving appropriate consideration to older people also implies a commitment to giving them the opportunity to articulate and to represent their needs, interests, ideas and wishes. This task is particularly acute because old age is a stage of life frequently attended by restrictions which directly affect this process of articulation and representation.

At the same time it must be remembered that social services are not provided by the state alone, but also by charitable organizations in the broader sense of the word – independent welfare organizations or certain forms of social service associations – who also play a greater or lesser role. Whereas in Scandinavia and the United Kingdom the modern welfare state has in the past only allocated a comparatively modest role to independent welfare organizations, while specific lobby organizations have been of great importance, such associations have a broad sphere of activity for example in Germany and also the Netherlands (not least for historical reasons associated with the denominational heterogeneity in these countries) (Kersbergen 1995; Schmidt 1995). Where there are such associations, they represent on the one hand a vehicle for the political participation of older people; on the other hand, as both financiers and providers of services, they are themselves the object of political co-determination (for example by the residents of a residential establishment run by an independent welfare association).

It is therefore characteristic of the majority of countries under review that while institutions have developed which in many cases have a legally ordered internal structure and which represent specific age-related interests in public, at the various levels of political representation or within the framework of administrative and institutional establishments, there are nevertheless marked differences in their extent, form and institutional and legal structure. At the same time, the character of these institutions does not just depend on the general requirements of a welfare state, but also on structures which exist *beyond the state level*, such as the existence of independent welfare organizations, which so strongly set their stamp on social policies in the Netherlands and Germany, for example.

In the United Kingdom and in particular in Italy, on the other hand, the representation of senior citizens has developed out of the trade union movement in the form of associations representing the interests of older citizens, without any statutory requirement. To this extent, therefore, the trade union movement constitutes an independent source of age-related social commitment.

There is, therefore, at least in a number of countries, a certain institutional framework for the political participation of older people, which takes different forms and is at differing stages of development. However, these developments do not usually take place against the background of well defined and clear legal specifications and frameworks for activity, as there is generally an absence, both at constitutional and normal statutory level, not only of legal statements about the status of older people and about old age as a stage of life, but also – and in particular – about the question of political activity and participation of older people. In this regard (and this also applies to Germany), the lack of a statutory (and in particular constitutional) formulation of the specific rights of older people is a barrier to their political participation.

What has yet to be done everywhere is to create the legal framework for the political participation of older people in Europe. Trends – though again of differing intensity – towards the institutionalization and the legal embodiment of existing approaches and forms of participation are in fact discernible. There is, for example, a discussion in progress about legislation banning discrimination against older people similar to that which has been enacted most recently in Germany for disabled people.

Clearly the most advanced development has been in the participation *of those concerned*, notably in residential institutions (old people's homes, nursing homes, hospitals, semi-residential institutions). Their participation has been made possible through specific bodies (such as home advisory boards), the establishment of which is in some cases obligatory. These rights of participation are also matched by specific duties of the bodies running the institutions to provide information, submit accounts and so on. However, these duties are usually owed to the co-determination boards – the home advisory board or clients' board – but not to the individuals concerned (the residents of a home). To this extent, therefore, a clear distinction must always be made between the legal position of the individual and the legal status of the collective participation body – and the powers it may have. The powers of participation of such bodies are mostly restricted to the right to information and consultation; only in exceptional cases do they constitute rights of co-determination, which even then are usually only rudimentary. Nevertheless, such arrangements – even if there is little possibility of exercising influence – are manifestly capable of reinforcing the independence and self-responsibility of the people concerned. This should give occasion to pursue the question of creating appropriate forms of collective representation for the interests of the people concerned, especially in the social services sector as a whole.

Besides such internal participation of those concerned in the form of advisory boards as instruments for clarifying, collectively articulating and asserting their interests, also external participation by outside third parties is possible in cases where the people concerned are no longer in a position to participate by themselves as a result of age, illness or (in particular, mental) handicap. In this way, a user advocate may take the place of a user board. Moreover, these types of internal boards may also be given the functions of dealing with complaints and acting in a supervisory role. To avoid excessive demands being placed on them it is important to consider the involvement of outsiders (such as ombudsmen), particularly with regard to poor performance. Thus it should be possible to combine the strengths of both internal and external participation.

In connection with the representation of interests by third parties, mention should be made of the functional equivalents of the German system of guardianship (*Betreuung*) for older people, which for example in Austria takes the form of a *Sachwalterschaft*, including so-called 'patient *Sachwalterschaft*' for residential institutions, or under the English legal system are governed by the 'guardianship laws' (Hoggett 1989).

The participation of citizens in their role as insured people or benefit recipients, which exists in many cases within the administrative framework for social security systems, and particularly as part of the social self-administration of the social insurance organizations, is another starting point for the participation of older people in the issues concerning them in the field of social security, i.e. pensions, health care, geriatric nursing care and assistance for the old.

As regards political participation in the narrower sense of the word, a distinction must be made between the local, regional, national and now also the supra-national levels, whereby it is currently the case that the most intensive legal regulation and the most tightly-knit institutional provisions are to be found at local level. This is of course especially true in countries in which this level also has wide responsibilities in connection with the fulfilment of extensive functions.

A starting point for the participation of older people is the fact that they are the people affected and that they therefore have specialist knowledge of age-related problems. The more the local level is responsible for age-related problems, the more those affected by the consequences of this phase of life address their demands for participation and involvement to this level. Against this background, the establishment of older people's advisory boards is a suitable instrument for dealing with the specific interests of the older citizens (and will then stand side by side with the corresponding bodies for other specific interest groups, such as for example children, youngsters and foreigners).

In this context, it is possible (and Denmark appears to provide an example of this) for the participation of older people to go beyond mere political consultation and participation and extend to the actual performance of functions, though of course the democratic legitimation of this extended participation of a specific group of the population requires due justification, which will find its limits where such participation would not only supplement the 'normal' democratic participation of all citizens but may partially supplant it.

The greater reserve shown towards senior citizens' representation at regional and national levels is because representation based on the mere fact of people being directly affected by a particular situation is more difficult to justify here than at local level. In view of this, the representation of senior citizens at regional and national level is mainly restricted to promoting, co-ordinating and focusing the activities of representation at the lowest level. Moreover, at this level, older people bring in their specific interests and specialist knowledge on an advisory basis (particularly in France and Spain, for example).

The participation of those with special needs, such as users of social services, is thus supplemented by participation within the framework of general social self-government – that is, in the institutions providing social security – and also of local political self-government. Here, too, there are starting points for putting the political participation of older people on a firm institutional and legal base, as the use of social services naturally presupposes the involvement of the persons availing themselves of them; therefore not only the bodies providing social services but also the local authorities are places – the former in functional terms, the latter in functional and local terms – for higher participation levels of older people. Incidentally, it seems the opportunities for the participation of older people in the governing bodies of social services organizations are not taken advantage of as much as could be possible. Thus pensioner participation has so far generally only played a rather minor role in the governing bodies of the organizations responsible for pension provision.

A particular problem that is apparently perceived and addressed in greatly differing degrees (but which plays a major role for instance in Germany), is that of the democratic legitimation of the specific forms of participation of older people and, in particular, of the institutional arrangements intended for this purpose in the form of special boards and bodies. Naturally, the significance of this issue depends on the nature and degree of the participation accorded to the older people: information, consultation, discussion, involvement in decision making (if necessary with the right of veto) and in the implementation of action. The greater the extent to which participation becomes co-determination, the more pressing the question becomes of the democratic legitimation of those involved. This applies in particular where the level concerned is that of the state – as in the federal states of Germany – and for this reason requires democratic legitimation. In this respect, therefore, there is everywhere a fundamental necessity to ensure that the aimed-for participation and representation is compatible with the overall constitutional and legal system. Above and beyond this there is also the problem of the appropriate representation of women, all the more so since they represent a clear majority among the older generation.

## Conclusion

If one looks for a justification for the striving towards an institutional and legal embodiment of the political representation of the interests of older people, a common starting point can be found in all the countries under review in the ideal of 'independence' and 'participation' for older people, on which policy for this group is everywhere claimed to be based. 'Independence' in this context means the ability for people to lead their lives and to act according to their own ideas.

Opportunities for influence are restricted by given social structures as well as by legal and institutional factors, and the possibility of participation in the form of involvement and influence on decisions and actions is also affected by one's life stage. Accordingly there exists an obligation by the state bodies, within the context of preserving or creating the opportunity for everyone to develop their own personality, to ensure that older people also have the opportunity for involvement and participation, right up to the level of political interests.

While there is to a large extent agreement about this objective in all European countries, and action can be seen everywhere, in view of the differing traditions and differing political and legal backgrounds and frameworks, different paths are being pursued in the individual countries in order to reach this objective. But in this process, the individual countries can learn a great deal from one another.

However, a uniform – or as it were, 'European' – model of political participation is not to be expected. The background situations in the individual countries are too disparate and the steps towards increased participation of older citizens are going in far too diverse directions for this to happen.

# 4

# Political organization and participation of older people: traditions and changes in five European countries

ADALBERT EVERS AND JÜRGEN WOLF

In 'ageing' societies the representation and participation of older people is likely to become a crucial question not only for the politics of pensions and living standards in old age but also for society in general. This becomes obvious when we look at the present political context. Apparently there is a widespread breakdown of the former broad consensus about what has been achieved and what should be done regarding older people. In the area of economic and social welfare policies the living conditions and the attitudes and perspectives of older people (Walker *et al.* 1993) are affected by new and different conflicts and by a common policy orientation towards reducing the costs of public pensions and the health care sector.

This apparently broad political consensus for austerity is not built on stable and future-oriented cultural concepts of ageing and old age. There has been a shift from the older concept of a passive 'third age' – so well encapsulated in the French word *retraité* – to the concept of 'active ageing'. But what does it mean to be 'active'? Staying active in terms of continuing employment has become less realistic than ever for the majority of older people. Thus 'active ageing' emphasizes the older person as a consumer. Old age is recognized as a stage of life with intensified leisure activities (Parsons 1963). Only a minority of policy makers understand active old age in terms of intensified social and political participation. Older people are regarded in terms of their contributions to family life and potentially as active members of communities – as citizens rather than merely as consumers.

Thus this limited political consensus and a dual cultural concept are both important parts of a process which reflects the fact that the 'third age' is linked today with increasing uncertainty, both concerning the degree to which old age will remain socially and financially secure, and whether people have a chance to succeed in living an old age which is meaningful. On the other hand there has been an increase in the level of resources (pensions, health and education) which can be mobilized by today's older people.

The participation of older people at large and, more specifically, the ways they are organized, represented and involved in formal mechanisms of political participation has an impact on their social position, on intergenerational relations, and on the legitimation of the decision-making process – even though this impact is difficult to measure. In a pilot study[1] we compared the different forms of these three issues of organization, representation and political participation in five EU countries – Austria, France, Denmark, the UK and Italy. Our comparison aimed at indicating structural similarities rather than emphasizing national differences and peculiarities. Taking a number of countries into account can help eliminate nation-specific features when looking at structural trends, and it provides a broader range of reference when looking at innovations. The selection of the five countries was the outcome of different criteria. Some countries were well known to us from our prior research on political participation of older people and participative concepts in the area of care services (Evers *et al.* 1993; Wolf *et al.* 1994); the others have been added to represent a mix of larger and smaller countries as well as different welfare cultures such as the Nordic and southern ones. Germany was not included, even though we look on the forms of participation in different EU countries from the perspective of our German experiences.

In general we can say that older people are underrepresented in parliaments and in important positions in political parties and associations throughout Europe, despite the fact that there is a growing number of national and European umbrella organizations. So far it is unclear whether this mirrors first of all the rigidity of the respective organizations or the reluctance of older people in political participation (Olk 1997). But there is an ongoing process of change which takes different paths in the different European countries depending on the political context and traditions. We will reflect these specific conditions by an overview of the main forms of organized representation and participation for each country. Traditions, changes and innovations are the key words of our chapter. They reflect our thesis that the present state of thinking about political representation and participation does not suggest unitary coherence but, rather, the juxtaposition of different elements. Some of them are representing the historical past, others attempt modernization and changes towards alternative futures, and some are innovative in so far as they really challenge the restrictions of traditions.

## Approach: participation and political culture

The political participation of older people is related to basic questions of political theory and practice. In the following we want to list some of these questions, particularly those which influenced the way we looked at processes in the respective countries.

A first important question concerns the relationship between grassroots participation and the structures of representative democracy (for a more detailed debate in relation to the area of ageing and care policies see Evers *et al.* 1993). To what degree do group-specific demands for participation derive from the processes of dissociation in pluralist societies into different groups of social, cultural, ethnic, gender and situational identities? To what degree may it therefore be necessary to counteract the centrifugal tendencies linked with group-specific participation by strengthening representative governing bodies, legitimated by a majority and emphasizing the overall shared goals and values in society?

A second question concerns the real effects of organization and the articulation of group interests. They are preconditions of participatory politics which aim at the empowerment of the different groups in question by transforming them into active political minorities (Rödel *et al.* 1989: 190). But there are two interrelated problems which arise particularly in the case of participation in old age. First, it can be asked, to what degree age-specific interests, roles and identities can be distinguished from general social structural and cultural interests? Second, there is the risk that the self-organization of minorities within the broader group of older people may renew processes of exclusion, for example by neglecting the concerns of the weak section among the older age group: the poor, the frail, and those who are in need of care. This leads us to the theoretical and ideological backgrounds of the concepts of self-organization and participation as they have been raised in the debates between liberals and communitarians (Barber 1984).

There is a tradition of participation among older people which mirrors the dominant concepts of what has often been called 'interest group liberalism' – a practice where each group is just bargaining for the expansion of its own power and where the redistributive process which derives from this only reflects procedural rules rather than shared goals and values. Effective participation of this kind can be found in the US with the biggest and most powerful interest groups of older people. The membership of the American Association of Retired People exceeds 30 million. This association practises professional lobbying but only has limited direct participation by the members themselves (Day 1990 and Chapter 13). Mere interest group democracy can be very costly for weaker groups inside and outside of the respective lobbies (Mills 1956), and since it leads to confrontation rather than cooperation, it may thus restrict the chances of certain groups to participate – as with the intergenerational equity campaigns. A different perspective derives from communitarian discourses. Here it is not just the specific social and economic interests which characterize the behaviour of a participating group, but a plurality of identities and perspectives (Evers 1997). These include people's roles as citizens, implying awareness of some shared values and perspectives with other communities and therefore an ability to be more 'other regarding' (Cohen and Rogers 1995) and take into account the legitimate interests of other groups. The difference this could make can be illustrated with reference to the way social and health services would figure in such a discourse in the sphere of old age politics. A citizenship approach would not only ask questions concerning the improvement of professional assistance, it would also raise issues concerning the mutual responsibilities of professionals and public service systems, on the one hand, and of patients and dependent people and their family carers on the other. The improvement of services according to a citizens' perspective would mean not only a larger share in the national expenditure but would also contribute to a reorganization of services which, by making the system as a whole more effective, could be in the general interest of all citizens in a welfare state.

Finally, to the degree the communitarian discourse is politically and morally more rewarding, it might also be more beneficial with regard to the side effects of participation on political culture and social capital. Social and political engagement in groups and associations in general can contribute to the enhancement of the role of older people and their citizenship rights. Several studies have shown the positive influence of participation on the attitudes and images of old age (Ward 1977). The readiness to engage in the collective interests of older people is positively correlated to the membership of associations (Day 1990: 32). Membership and cooperation in associations is, beyond that, a means to produce and maintain the 'social capital' which enables people to engage in public affairs. A recently finished international study (Stolle and Rochon 1996) found that associations which represent a wider range of orientations and activities, such as social or cultural, are associated with a higher level of social capital than interest groups with a narrower scope of issues like pensioners, veterans and animal rights associations.

This, finally, leads to a question concerning the organizational forms of participation which crosscut political and ideological boundaries and which can be illustrated with the following alternative: if existing cross-generational organizations are able to expand their structures towards the direct participation of their older members – for example by abrogating age limits, forming age-specific sub-organizations, and providing formal rights for older members in the decision-making process – to what degree can this be a substitute for a separate organization of older people? Keeping this question in mind may open up different interpretations and conclusions about the following information on developments in a number of countries of the EU.

## Country reports

### Austria

Austria is a country with about 7 million inhabitants and more than 1.6 million people aged 60 and older who represent more than a quarter of the voters. It is characterized by a strong paternalistic state administration as well as by a high level of social and political organization and membership. The two big parties, the Social Democratic and the Conservative, have functioned for decades in a model of extensive institutionalized cooperation at all levels of civic and political life. As a result until recently many aspects of Austrian life were shaped by the dividing line between the Socialists and Conservatives. Due to their close cooperation a political culture was created where unofficial and informal consent-finding procedures usually precede formal decision making in official institutions, thus favouring compromise and consent over conflict. The Austrian welfare state, a result of this model of political cooperation, was until recently built on a high level of consensus (Gerlich 1991).

For about ten years this harmonious model has been breaking up, and Austrian political life increasingly shows similarities to other Western democracies, with less stable and institutionalized forms of membership and participation, a wider political spectrum and increasing conflicts which have already led to a questioning of a number of institutionalized social rights and status guarantees for older people. These include the stability and dynamics of the pension system, the conditions of early retirement and the financing of health care. In many aspects the Austrian system of representation and participation in the field of old age politics represents the political past in a changing present.

### Organizations of older people and their development

As with other countries, the origins of the organization of older people have been in the unifying aspects of pension problems. These issues continue to dominate the two big organizations which were founded after World War II and which are still by far the most influential interest organizations of seniors in Austria:

- the Austrian Pensioners Association (Österreichischer Pensionistenverband) which is closely linked to the Austrian Social Democratic Party; nearly 20 per cent of all Austrian people 60 and over belong to this association;
- the Austrian Seniors' Alliance (Österreichischer Seniorenbund), which is closely linked to the Austrian People's Party; more than 15 per cent of the Austrian population aged 60 and over are members.

The large membership reflects the overall high degree of party and organizational affiliation which has been characteristic of Austria. Even though individualization and fragmentation within the large group of older people has been as marked in Austria as in other countries, they have resulted only in a few quite small independent organizations, mostly in locations in major cities such as Vienna or Salzburg.

Until today, the policies of the two big organizations mentioned above have had neither much visibility nor clarity, but this does not mean that they have not been influential. The leaders and activists of both organizations are usually former politicians. Thus there are close informal channels connecting with party politics which can guarantee influence without any formal structures of political participation. Traditionally these organizations have combined three different roles:

- on the local level they have provided older people with a cultural and ideological framework – through clubs which were centred mainly around leisure activities, travelling and social events;
- both organizations have provided effective services concerned with the often complicated questions of social and insurance based rights, particularly eligibility for and levels of pensions;
- at federal and central state level they have acted as intermediaries, both lobbying for their members and, vice versa, reporting back the government's decisions.

So far this quite traditional paternalistic model of representation has not really been affected by the challenges and hardships of the welfare state crisis in Austria. In a way it fits with a traditional image of old age as a phase of dependency and need for protection, which is still strong in Austria (Majce 1992). In recent conflicts over legislation concerning older people, as in the case of a care reform plan, the small organization for disabled people had far more visibility and effect; and while potential pension cuts were an important issue in the recent election campaign, the pensioners' organizations did not make any significant contribution.

*Forms of political participation*

As far as the formal political participation of older people is concerned, nothing is prescribed by law but something has developed in practice (Leichsenring *et al.* 1997; see also Chapter 5). The two important elements are special representatives in charge of seniors' concerns and the institutionalized participation of seniors in the form of advisory councils. Such a council exists on a national level, but only in a small number of Austrian cities. It is at the level of the federal states, which play an important role concerning health and social services as well as social assistance, where the most institutionalized form of political participation by advisory councils can be found. In some states they are composed of representatives of the seniors' organizations only – sometimes according to their numerical size in the respective state. In other states there is a round-table approach, with representatives from social services and welfare organizations engaged in elderly help and care. This approach reflects the link between the development of welfare agencies and a type of participation which is about staying in tune with the clients. Most of these forms of participation were installed because of the interest of politicians or administrators; with a few exceptions, they are merely about the exchange of information and opinions. Conflicts are rare. As a research report has shown, these forms of participation meet scepticism from two different sides (Bahr *et al.* 1996). On the one hand, the professionals engaged in informal lobbying and consultation (that is, the former politicians of the big political parties) are sceptical. From their point of view it is hard to see what such forms of participation can really add to their business of informal lobbying and mediation between state/party politics and organized older people. On the other, senior citizens who are active in their own name in local initiatives and clubs independent from party-political life are sceptical as well. They think that the really controversial issues are mostly not articulated and touched upon by this type of participation by consultation.

*France*

In order to understand better the development of political participation among senior citizens, three peculiarities of the French socio-political system should be kept in mind. First, the French 'republican' political tradition and culture highlights the role of the state in society, giving special emphasis to the central state's authority and the role of universal regulations as well as to the rights and duties of its people as citizens. Second, prior to the ambitious and still unfinished project for a general decentralization by the Socialist government in the early 1980s, France has had an extremely centralized political system which set narrow limits to the self-governance of municipalities and to the autonomy of the *départements*. Third, in such a system with a statist bias there has been less room than in other countries for the flourishing and consolidating of civic self-organization, neither trade unionist nor in voluntary organizations.

*Organizations of older people and their development*
The organizations which form the basis for the most influential forms of political participation of older people in France have two major branches. The first branch can be described as a labour- and profession-based type of representation (for a detailed overview see Ministère de la Solidarité 1994). It is constituted by: organizations which represent seniors who have retired from working life, linked to the respective trade unions (260,000 are linked to the CGT; 85,000 to the CFDT; 200,000 to the FO; 60,000 to the CFTC); organizations which represent mainly or exclusively former employees from the public sector (CNR 500,000; FGR 100,000) and organizations which represent professions in fields like agriculture, craftmanship or commerce.

Older people have usually been considered in terms of problems with their pensions. At the local level the respective organizations provide for their members a certain level of continuity with their former work-based environment and its culture. However, with recent problems such as pre-retirement or plans for pension reform, only the trade unions themselves faced these challenges, while their sub-organizations for older members apparently took no action.

The second basis of self-organization of senior citizens is a part of the third, voluntary non-profit sector: the social movement of associations. Today there are between 600,000 and 700,000 associations in France; about 20,000 of them are made up by or intended especially for senior citizens. Associations consist of local clubs and initiatives in the fields of culture, leisure, sports and social affairs (including issues of help and care). This wide spectrum gets even more diverse if one takes into account that there are very small groups, restricted to voluntary membership but which include the maintenance of social and medical services, which are contracted in by the municipalities. The growth in numbers of the associations dates back to the cultural changes which surfaced at the end of the 1960s (Archambault 1993). A national policy which supported these changes as part of the third sector (or the social economy) was developed by the Socialists as part of their decentralization policy. The associational sector has national umbrella organizations like the National Federation of Associations of Retired People (FNAR) which represents about 3,500 associations with about 50,000 members, and the National Federation of Clubs for Older People in the Rural Parts of the Country (FNCRA). They represent local clubs which go beyond mere cultural aspects by providing important services in the thousands of very small villages in France (more than 13,000 clubs with 1.2 million members). The generalization of themes which concern older people has favoured the growth of associations with a rather looser, cultural approach.

Here older people are considered first of all as local citizens rather than as former workers or professionals. Instead of conflict there seems to be a kind of complementarity between the trade unions (which defend the social welfare rights of older people) and the associations (which represent primarily cultural aspirations linked with the growing demand for an active and participative third age, whether concerned with work, volunteering or political participation) (Théry 1993; Gaullier 1995).

*Forms of formal political participation*

Formal political participation of older people in France is the product of an initiative by the Socialist government. In the beginning of the 1980s a Secretary of State for the Ageing and a National Committee for Pensioners and Old People (CNRPA) were created by law, as well as similar committees in the 90 departments. This was followed up by the attempt to build up such boards at the newly created regional level (about 20 regions) and at the local level. Since then political participation has been ever-present at the central and departmental level, where the boards can be described as a unique mixture of state-official and social institution. The Departmental Councils of Retired and Older Persons (CDERPA) are presided over by the *préfet* (governor). They consist of three main groups (16 representatives of older people's organizations from the trade unions and associational sector, ten persons dealing with health and social services, and another ten persons representing local and financing institutions).

The legal framework in its 1988 renewed version is very ambitious, stating that these councils should be a forum for dialogue, information and reflection, allowing the representatives of older people to take part in working out and applying measures of all kinds which concern older people. In reality, however, the role of the CDERPA's is much more limited and sectoral. Many of them meet only a few times a year and depend heavily on the initiative of the *préfet* as their president. Furthermore, in practice they concentrate on health and social care issues, with the elaboration of 'gerontological plans' (surveys of the social care infrastructure) as an issue of priority. While the majority is concerned rather with the rituals and symbolism of what in France is called *concertation*, this does not exclude occasional innovative measures, like setting up associations or cultural events linked to the problems of the third age.

Innovative forms of action and participation are therefore still ubiquitous and of a local character. They are backed up by the fact that the major switch from a passive to an active approach towards ageing is questioning all sociopolitical sectors which have a bearing on old age – not just pension plans or care services. The city of Rennes (Ville de Rennes 1995) has set up a model project called 'Senior Citizens in the Municipality'. A mixed group of experts and senior citizens worked out a concept for ten strategic areas such as family, neighbourhood, health, transportation, volunteering and citizenship. This concept has been publicly discussed in local districts and the major local organizations. These discussions were complemented by a survey among nearly 1,000 local senior citizens over the age of 50 concerning their opinions about the questions raised in the proposal.

Another approach, initiated by a mayor of African origin in a small city, has been duplicated in about 100 municipalities. It foresees the installation of what is called a 'Board of Wise Men' (Argoud 1997 and Chapter 6). Usually the mayor nominates a number of well-respected and experienced local senior citizens who form a board which can comment on any local political action. This approach differs from the usual discourses of political participation. It does not consider older people as just another social interest group but as a reservoir of citizens who perhaps are more free and experienced than others to comment on current issues and trends from a point of view of the public interest and the common good.

### Denmark

Even though Denmark with its 5 million citizens is the smallest country of our survey, it has become well known for its reform policy in the field of elderly housing and care. There are some peculiarities of the political and social welfare system which Denmark partly shares with other Nordic countries. First, political participation is shaped by the fact that most citizens see the state and its institutions as what the Swedish have called a *volkshuset*: a protective environment for society and its groups to live in. Given this background, civic participation, a participative planning culture and a kind of cooperative spirit have had a better chance to develop than in countries where state institutions are mistrusted or where their representatives claim to have a special authority over their social partners. Second, the Danish welfare state, like other Nordic countries, is a very much decentralized institution. The 277 municipalities have many tasks and far-reaching autonomy in their decision making. A lesser degree of uniform state-wide regulation by the central national policy is accepted in order to safeguard that political decisions are appropriate for specific local problems and priorities. Third, a complex reform programme concerning older people's housing and care services which started nine years ago is about to be finished. It is based on a consensual concept of ageing with the guidelines of ensuring biographical continuity, providing roles for older people as active participants and of creating decentralized and largely home-based networks of services.

### Organizations of older people and their development

The basis for participation is formed by a lively infrastructure of about 1,000 associations, clubs and committees, with about 600,000 members. Most of them come under the umbrella of one of the two big organizations that represent senior citizens nationally.

The first is Dane Age (Landesforingen Aeldresagen), which is a part of the Dane Age Foundation (Evers *et al.* 1993). It developed out of a church-based charity founded at the turn of the century. With the enormous steps towards reconstruction and modernization which have taken place since the late 1960s, it is nowadays often viewed as an innovative model with international relevance for a specific type of consumer-oriented interest representation. The organization as a whole is a kind of multifaceted enterprise. There are seven sub-organizations, some of them commercial (a consultancy firm for municipalities planning older people's services, a travel agency, a publishing branch and a research centre). Dane Age is the membership organization; enrolment is open to all ages (with about 15 per cent of its members under the age of 55), and there are about 150 local groups. Dane Age aims (among other things) to influence old age politics. Especially at the local level it can help its activists by offering professional advice. The organization considers older people primarily as individuals rather than as members of groups or clubs. Older people are viewed at least as much as consumers in a variety of different markets than as clients of different public welfare services or as citizens. Since the majority of facilities which consider older people as active and healthy persons are market based, while state-based services are usually more linked with need and needy persons, there is an affinity between such a consumer approach and an emphasis on 'active' and 'successful' ageing.

The second national organization of older persons is Aeldre Mobiliseringen (Mobilizing the Elderly) which organizes a number of trade union and party affiliated sub-organizations, many of them dating back to the beginning of the Danish welfare system. Local clubs can be based on one of the sub-organizations. The national umbrella organization is subsidized by the trade unions and the Ministry for Social Affairs. Aeldre Mobiliseringen was founded as a joint force in 1991, partly in reaction to the growing impact of Dane Age, and like the latter it tries to have a democratic structure and to cover more than merely pensions questions. Like Dane Age, Aeldre Mobiliseringen tries to act as a multifacet-organization which provides services, helps in articulating issues, and backs local networking and measures of community-building among older people. The main difference is, however, that this organization can be characterized as state/citizen-oriented, with former politicians playing a key role. The emphasis is on social policy rather than consumerist issues; organizationally, older persons are considered more as group members than as individuals.

*Forms of political participation*

Formalized political participation takes place at two levels. First, at national level, there are the ministries. The Social Ministry has installed a contact board where different groups are represented, among them Aeldre Mobiliseringen (Dane Age has not yet [1997] been invited as a member). Participation is not restricted to spreading information but also includes cooperation in preparing laws and carrying out action programmes. One example is the joint project of the Social Ministry and Aeldre Mobiliseringen which is called 'Elderly Help Elderly'. It started in 1996 and aims to support the initiatives of those who are able and willing to give voluntary help to weaker people and groups from the older population. The national law enforcing the setting up of senior citizens' councils in every municipality since January 1997 has been prepared with the participation of Aeldre Mobiliseringen; it is concerned with the main tasks and structures of the senior citizens' councils and the ways of establishing them by elections among the citizens aged 60 and over.

Second, the main centre of participative action is the municipalities.

Participation at local level (Mathiesen 1997) is a firmly established part of the political and welfare culture in sectors like urban planning, housing, health and social services, leisure and cultural affairs. Most municipalities had already installed boards of senior citizens (with varying structures and procedures) before the national legislation came into effect. Usually the boards of seniors are not restricted to a single field of action and can claim to represent strongly the viewpoint of older persons in all aspects of local life. The Board of Senior Citizens of Odense, for example, has worked out a detailed paper on local politics in the field of cultural affairs. Because many of the local old age organizations have reached a considerable degree of professionalism, some municipalities are currently discussing the contracting out of some of their activities and services to them (Dochweiler 1993).

Unlike most of the other countries we observed, these Danish innovations seem not so much special and marginal phenomena; they are parts of a broad reform movement which is part of the mainstream and able, therefore, to shape the course of the key issues of old age politics in Denmark. Two lessons from Denmark deserve special attention. First of all there is the development of two different though overlapping directions of change and modernization in the long-established organizations for older people: Aeldre Mobiliseringen as predominantly welfare- and citizen-oriented, and Dane Age as much more market- and consumer-oriented. Second, attention should be given to a type of local political participation which seems to guarantee representatives of older people a real influence on the development of local politics (for a critical discussion see Holm-Christensen 1997; Lundsgaard and Raahauge 1997). This achievement depends both on the nature of the broad political culture and on the characteristics of older people and their organizations, which have to qualify and sometimes to professionalize in order to engage in this kind of participation.

## United Kingdom

As with Denmark, France and Italy, one of the historical roots of the UK's current organizations representing older people is the trade union and cooperative movement. Just as in Austria, Denmark and France, they are also based on charity/voluntary organizations traditionally caring about the concerns of older people, who have mostly belonged to the weakest parts of the population. In the UK some of these organizations have developed into effective representatives of and service providers for and with older people. The way both historical traditions have developed – and the way their offshoots operate and participate today – is shaped by some of the peculiarities of the UK political and welfare system. First, the once-strong trade union movement and the work-based identity of older people have seen a decrease for both socio-cultural and political reasons. Second, in contrast to countries like Germany, voluntary bodies have not developed along ideological principles but in order to solve specific problems and for particular purposes. Thus there are organizations for children and older people rather than, for example, an Austrian or German Catholic organization adopting all kinds of social issues and competing with similar (e.g. Protestant), organizations. Furthermore, with a strong civil society distinct from the state, UK voluntary associations were until recently able to define their own business and priorities independent from public authorities, depending less on public money (compared to Germany) and being less obliged to provide mainstream services. Until some years ago, this was indeed the case for the two charities working on a nationwide basis for and with older people: Age Concern and Help the Aged. Third, during the last decade the Conservative government tried to restrict those parts of the pension system which are public. It modernized and streamlined the social service sector, and in particular health and care services. The comparably modest level of pensions and of rights for services in the care sector produces basic problems of social provision and social inequalities among older people (Laczko and Phillipson 1991).

*Organizations of older people and their development*
UK pensioners' organizations date back to the 1930s (Age Concern 1994). One of the central claims of the National Federation of Old Age Pension Associations illustrates well the overall situation at that time: the National Federation requested the Prime Minister to double the pension, up to £1 per day. Other pensioners' groups have been fostered through trade union membership links, and some unions now support national organizations for their retired members. Since 1972 the UK Pensioners and Trade Union Action Association was formed with groups often known as Pensioners Action Groups. Most campaigning, however, has been fostered by the National Pensioners Convention, founded in 1979 under the aegis of the Trades Union Congress (TUC) with representatives from 17 pensioners' organizations. With a prominent former trade union leader (Jack Jones) as its president, it has a dynamic protagonist. It works on the basis of a charter calling for, among other things, an increased obligatory minimum pension level. Since 1988 there has also been a TUC Pensioners Committee. Its only task is to report and advise to the General Council on all issues of concern to pensioners.

The programmes and the activities of such bodies as the National Pensioners Convention are extending very slowly from the single issue of pensions to a broader range of questions of social welfare, especially the reliability and quality of health and care services. But it is not 'older people' in general who are represented by these organizations but only those who rely to a considerable extent on the public sector. Despite some interesting catalogues of demands and charters, the centrist UK trade-union based pensioners' organizations (like the French but unlike the Italian) often lack visibility and dynamics, partly because their issues and requests are finally handled directly by the TUC and the trade unions and not by the old age organizations themselves.

There is a lot of change and development in the sector of voluntary organizations taking up the concerns of older people. Help the Aged is a small organization, while Age Concern is big and widespread. Help the Aged is a service provider rather than a membership organization. It supports local groups and projects of other associations by technical and social support (for example 'community alarms' and telephone information lines, 'Seniorline', as well as volunteers to help older people in need). Their new programme is guided by the key words of 'enabling' and 'empowerment' of older people. This orientation is shared with a second big organization, Age Concern (Age Concern 1995), which was founded as a registered charity in 1940. Today it has nearly 1,000 local Age Concern groups in England and more than 100,000 volunteers. The main fields of action include social campaigning and public information through reports, conferences, etc. A typical example has been the 'Cold Crisis' campaign, which looked at combining practical help for poor older people in need with publicizing their heating problems. It also provides advice and information, through handbooks like *Your Rights for Pensioners* or a *Survival Guide for Widows*, but it also offers personal assistance too: more than 100,000 people each year call local groups directly for advice. Age Concern also provides services, both traditional but also innovative, like practical help by repair and improvement schemes for housing, visiting and transport services, day care schemes and so on; Age Concern funds model experiments as well as research; it also organizes leisure and social activities.

Age Concern, however, as in many other voluntary organizations during the last few years, has been becoming increasingly reliant on government money. Its absolute share is growing even though it was not more than one fifth at the end of the 1980s and 30 per cent in 1994/5. Furthermore, it is the government's policy to substitute the former open grants to the organizations by special contracts which allow payments only for services rendered. This makes some Age Concern services part of a policy which is designed by public authorities. It is a delicate question as to how much the service-providing and the independent advocacy role of Age Concern will come into conflict.

Until the general election in spring 1997, organizations like Age Concern as well as Help the Aged had to survive in a political climate where the government denied support for social concerns and favoured an individualist 'self help' mentality. This climate was more convenient for a new generation of organizations, which responded to an overall individualistic and consumerist orientation. The Association of Retired Persons over 50 years of age (ARP), with its 100 local friendship centres, is directly modelled after the concept of the American AARP; its appeal of lobbying, service and leisure/consumer orientation is far less concerned with questions of inequality among older people than pensioners' organizations or charities.

While organizations like Age Concern try hard to do effective work by social campaigning and public opinion-building, like the trade unions and pensioners' organizations they face enormous difficulties in making an impact which is strong enough to influence public politics effectively (Ginsburg 1992; Scharf 1993).

### Forms of political participation

It is debatable whether the complete lack of formalized law-based participation schemes is an additional reason for the pattern of UK development. While there are boards and commissions where some of the organizations mentioned above are invited, there is nowhere a formal agreement on the duties of central or local governments regarding the participation of senior citizens' organizations. Some interesting participation structures have been built up at the local level, however, for example the Senior Citizens Forums which started in the late 1980s in the Greater London region; 30 out of 32 boroughs have such a forum today (1997). This concept has spread to a number of municipalities in England and Scotland. The forums are often run by activists from the trade union-based organizations, but they are open to all senior citizens and take up all kinds of local policy issues (education, leisure, environmental, housing and urban issues). Quite often priority is given to questions concerning the development of care services, because (following a series of reforms in the 1980s and early 1990s) more services have been contracted with commercial providers, and there has been an increasing problem of public financing due to limited government grants, difficulties in raising additional local money or raising the charges on services. Since there is no legal framework for the forums, they are very different in structure and the way they work – only a minority receive local support from the municipality or can establish a continuous exchange with the local authorities; others have yet formally to constitute themselves, to win reputation and acknowledgement and to network with other organizations in the field of local old age politics. At the level of central government there are no formalized participation platforms like the forums. It will have to be seen to what degree the general election of 1997 did in fact mark the beginning of a new and different chapter in the relationship between government and old age organizations.

*Italy*

(Major parts of the information in this section are based on an earlier study by Rosanelli and Wolf 1994.) The situation in Italy is peculiar because the trade union-based pillar of representation of older people is more important than in any other country of our survey. The Italian trade unions have managed to modernize their structures and politics and to overcome the limits of a traditional pensionist trade unionism. This development has taken place in a specific political context. First, there is a considerable difference between different regions of the North and the South – even more than in other countries. Second, the Catholic church is strongly influential in charities, voluntary bodies and other similar organizations in the third sector which have a direct link with the interests of older people. Typically relationships with older persons in general remain paternalistic in many respects. This situation has produced a kind of intertwining with the political institutions which could be labelled 'clientism' rather than regulated political participation. Third, in a number of fields of welfare – especially those which are relevant for older people like pensions, health and social care – Italy can be seen as a latecomer. Its pension system, which is less robust than in other countries but rather expensive due to incremental decision making in the past, has been a constant political theme and source of conflicts over several decades.

*Organizations of older people and their development*

Each of the three most important trade unions in Italy – the CGIL (Commu nist), the CISL (Socialist) and the UIL (Christian Democratic) – has estab lished its own pensioners' trade union. These pensioner unions are special in so far as they form a kind of additional branch alongside the other branche representing the different occupational sectors. This close integration of pensioners into trade unionist structures – instead of their separation – is distinctive of the Italian situation, and makes it different from France and the UK. This equal position within the trade unions has made the pensioners unions quite powerful. The increase in trade union membership in the 1980 is mainly a result of the disproportionate increase of membership in the pensioners' trade unions: in 1991 they held 46 per cent of the CGIL, 38 per cent of the CISL and more than 20 per cent of the UIL members. In the CGIL the pensioners are the biggest branch. In contrast to the other countries of our survey, in Italy any organized form of representation of older people is tantamount to talking about the pensioners' unions. Other forms of self organization are insignificant.

This central position would have been hard to achieve without the changes of attitude, concept and identity which took place in modern Italian trade unionism, especially among pensioners' unions. Since the late 1960s when trade union struggles intensified in Italy, up to the early 1980s, the action and attitudes of the trade unions and their pensioners' organizations were of a traditional character and similar to those in other countries. The main (if not the exclusive) issue was the struggle for basic pension rights. It has to be taken into account that the trade unions had the majority on the supervisory board for private sector pensions insurance, while at the same time a pension system under constant reform had developed into a maze of paragraphs. Thus the help of the *patronati* – local bureaux for advice and consultancy – became indispensable. The trade unions run such *patronat* themselves, and more than 60 per cent of all applications are done by them This service always had the important side effect of attracting new members At the same time the trade unions were effective pressure groups in the ongoing reform of the pensions system.

A number of factors of this approach – combining central pressure group functions with local services in a clearcut but restricted field – changed, however. The trade unions learned to put more emphasis on the differences in orientation between different groups of workers and members – including their retired members. Also, with the recent extension of welfare state insti tutions they had to get prepared for new themes and issues like health and care, social services, housing and urban planning; today their overall goal is to give a new shape to the welfare state. Furthermore, through their effec tive role as brokers of rights and services the pensioners' unions attracted a considerable number of new members who had not been unionized before, people with different experiences and from other social strata; this had a clear impact on the character of the respective organizations.

Unions have traditionally fought for a wider participation by their older members in society through national actions like demonstrations and campaigning. But dealing with issues like general living conditions, health nd social services has made other types of action increasingly important. From the end of the 1980s this has encouraged local action supported by self-organized groups, clubs and initiatives. It has led towards the adoption of additional themes like the lack of social integration and loneliness among older people. The biggest of the pensioners' unions, which is organized in the CGIL, founded a special national organization in 1989 called the Association for the Self-Organization of Services and Solidarity in Old Age. Only one year later it had grown to more than 160 local associations and over 25,000 member-volunteers in areas like social tourism and culture ('silver tourism' and 'university of the third age'), initiatives for solidarity (helping hotlines like the 'silver telephone'), social circles and centres (own housing projects) and environmental projects ('silver-green'). With this strategy the strength of local action and central organization and support could be combined. This way of extending and diversifying membership, themes for action and forms of organization helped to create a more positive image of old age: from old age burden and old age in need towards old age as a resource for society.

### Forms of political participation

Given this background it seems at first surprising that there are no regulations for political participation by older people in Italy. But it was the mobilization and the increase of the *social* participation of older people that was a priority in the trade unions' original concept. The mobilization of massive membership in central campaigns and demonstrations had always helped in confronting the political system with their power. It helped to make the trade union leaders – but increasingly also the leaders of the pensioners' unions – partners and opponents in conflict situations, where their participation became unavoidable. It must be noticed, however, that the recent pension reforms could not be very much influenced by this strategy of confrontation, manifestation and negotiation. At local level, where almost no formalized participation structure exists, it is important to take into account what the trade unions call the transition from a quantitative to a qualitative membership. This means a membership defined by the active involvement of each individual – such as the areas of services and living conditions. In many cities it is therefore routine to have *ad hoc* and informal consultations with the local representatives of the pensioners' unions. A special contract between the three unions settles their cooperation in order to prevent them being played off against each other.

In this context it is understandable why there is a new orientation taking place which calls for the development of the former pensioners' trade unionism into a citizens' trade unionism, and why the Italian trade unions at present are having difficulties with political participation in terms of finding the right status for their powerful organizations of older members within their own organizations.

## Four summarizing theses

The findings of our pilot study have led us to some observations about shared trends, typical changes and basic alternative paths for the future, which we

summarize in this section. They have also further stimulated the initi
debate on the different and controversial meanings to be given to forms (
participation among older people.

First of all, the present forms of representation build on a structur
pattern of change which is similar in all of the countries of the survey, eve
though it has taken place in the various countries to different degrees. Th
trend is from single-issue organizing, one-dimensional identities and stron
cultural and political loyalties towards organizations which raise a broade
range of questions and which do so more independently of specific ideolog
ical camps.

Some examples in the study show the continuing legacy of the past: o
the one hand, strong state authorities and, on the other, old age organiza
tions tied to special ideological and social camps such as pensioners' organi
zations, where membership and milieu is dominated by relationships forme
at the workplace and where the scope of action is limited to a single issue c
social policy: their rights as pensioners. The process of modernization i
partly the result of the changing role of the state, where the state establishe
dialogues as part of its planning role. Partly it has been pushed by the orga
nizations themselves, which strive for an up-to-date representation of th
interests of older people. Issues which traditionally have been viewed a
private and which were often raised at the community rather than at th
national level have become a matter of a more public and global concern
The issue of 'care' is a typical example of this trend. The organizations ar
widening their scope of themes towards living conditions and the socia
welfare of older people in general. Party politics and trade unionist bond
remain important, but not in the sense of stabilized ideological camps. Th
members are identified more as senior citizens or as an age group witl
specific concerns, less as retired workers. These are the hallmarks of what w
call the modernization process. It can be observed in both organizations witl
a workplace and trade union background and those which build on th
legacy of voluntary organizations or charities, working with and for olde
people as clients or volunteers.

Second, the present modernization of organizations repesenting olde
people can take different courses regarding the balance of issues of social citi
zenship and consumerism.

The first alternative emphasizes older people as citizens rather than forme
workers; this view stresses questions of social policy, social rights and soli
darity in collective action. The second alternative identifies the older persor
as a participant in the consumer market with the same rights as othe
consumers. This emphasizes their role as individuals; a participatory politic
for older people would enable them to get the best deal available a
consumers of leisure, health and care services. Both approaches – active citi
zenship and consumer democracy – have consequences for attitudes toward
participation. These can range from an ethical claiming of social and demo
cratic entitlements as values in their own right, up to the pragmatic fight fo
those rights and opportunities which can help make older people equa
consumers in a consumer society.

Third, there is the important issue of self-organization. One can hav considerable influence with little formal participation. But does this also work the other way: can strong legal participation substitute for a low level of active self-organization? Organizations of older people have developed a broad repertoire of ways to make their voices heard, from the traditions of informal lobbying to new forms of campaigning and media work. Organized representation and participation which enables the members to develop perspectives and action may be important for the broad participation of older people, their role in society, their self-image and self-esteem. This kind of participation is, however, a multifaceted issue, expressed by supporting local community-building, associations and every kind of social, cultural and economic activities on the local and everyday level. It can be achieved by offering information, professional advice, expertise and all kinds of services. Formal political participation is just one item among others – perhaps even not the most important one when it comes to enhancing the wider participation of older people.

Fourth, there are different types of formalized political participation with differing roles and aims. Some of them are even harder to transfer between countries than others. The survey revealed at least three approaches. First, 'Information/consultation': a formalized, often regular dialogue and exchange of opinions on a representative level, which helps the leaders and administrators on both sides to stay in tune which each other; the initiative usually comes from the state administration. Second, 'Negotiation': a formalized, *ad hoc* or regular cooperation in legislation, plans, or programmes. Third, 'Brainstorming': a casual, *ad hoc* or temporary exchange, often motivated by the search for new cultural orientations or a shared new understanding of problems.

These different types of political participation are often related to different organizational forms. In some of the senior citizens' councils or forums (such as the UK senior citizens' forums) these different tasks and types merge together. Each of them raises specific problems when it comes to the question whether they should or can be transferred to other countries. The first type of formalized exchange of *information* and *consultation* (such as the advisory councils in Austria or the CDERPAs in France) can be found frequently in different countries. Taking our empirical observations into account, however, it can be asked whether this type of representation has any real impact – or is it as important as the frequency of its appearance in the political rhetoric of all sides would lead us to believe. The main reason for this scepticism is the fact that older people themselves, even members of the respective organizations, usually cannot participate in this process.

The second type of *negotiation* varies on a range between 'almost no influence' to 'real impact on decision making'. The latter was found in only two countries, with either a high level of integrated reform policies (like Denmark) or a form of mass representation of older people (like Italy). It should be noted, however, that this type of participation (as measured by its effectiveness in facilitating genuine involvement in decision making) cannot be simply installed or exported, because it seems to be inextricably linked with unique socio-political preconditions. For example, transporting the Danish 'model' to a different socio-political context where, as in Germany,

the respective organizations of older people are less independent and hav
developed less political and social competences and professionalism, coul
result in a different outcome, possibly something better called co-option tha
co-determination (see Chapter 2).

The third type of joint *'brainstorming'* is less institutionalized and depend
very much on current concerns. It is very flexible and it can meet both side:
current needs and interests. Furthermore, it may be relatively easy to trans
fer. But it should be kept in mind that creating future scenarios and negoti
ating the distribution and redistribution of real resources are two ver
different forms of participation. While the 'brainstorming' model looks suit
able for the former it seems to be inappropriate for the latter. So it could b
argued that the political task is to find complex up-to-date forms of consult
ing and representing older people that help them be 'present' in and be par
of the broad spectrum of social participation. Regular and legally bindin,
political participation is only one aspect of this basic process.

## Conclusion

The political participation of older people in Europe is developing fast. From
our point of view, informed by our pilot study, there are two main chal
lenges.

First, how can we blend and balance notions of citizenship and 'th
common good' with a consumerist and lobbying perspective? Toda
consumer-based politics endorses individual consumers' rights to mak
rational economic choices; the opposite viewpoint wants to draw limits t
this implicit simple 'more of everything' philosophy and tries to frame it
demands in terms of social mutuality and what it thinks should be share
values. But is it really totally impossible to agree that both perspectives coul
be linked to a certain degree in real politics?

The second challenge concerns a general question which is of specia
importance for older people as a group, which has gone a long way from
being a typical 'weak' group to a strong and powerful one in a short space o
time. To what degree must politics for older people still protect the needs o
people who are vulnerable and weak, and who often lack the degree o
competence and alertness showed by other groups in society? Or do th
changes among older people, towards 'active ageing', allow for much mor
impact of 'enabling' policies (Gilbert 1993), which not only aim at more indi
vidual and collective self-determination but which also presuppose a certai
level of competence already achieved? To give a concrete example: shoul
the provision of care continue to be based on publicly financed services, o
is it better to switch to cash payments or vouchers? To what degree shoul
there be specific protective measures for older citizens?

With an eye on such debates we should be aware that older people wil
remain a group which is particularly vulnerable. Their status derives les
from their market power as producers than from their social rights based or
the welfare system (Wolf 1990). The position of today's older people depend:
in many respects on a culture of respect and on the legitimacy of old ag
security as we have understood it up till now (Walker 1996). Older peopl

are ascribed weak status according to the ethos of the productive 'work society' (Kohli *et al.* 1997), and are left in a vulnerable position; the future course of development of the moral and normative boundaries is under threat by a mere instrumentalist perspective wherein older people appear to be 'useless' in many aspects. The more these moral prerequisites become fluid, and the more productivist orientations gain a dominant role, the more difficult the integration and participation of older people will be, because they will be viewed as a burden rather than a resource.

This leads us finally towards questioning a concept of participation which builds exclusively on 'one's own strength' as a separate group. We should not forget that what is undeniable at the level of care problems and family responsibility – the good will and advocacy role of other strong persons – can also be important at a broader community and societal level. The weaker and more dependent older people get, the more they will need this acceptance by society as a whole; they will also need advocacy to make their voices heard (Evers *et al.* 1994). This is important given the discourse on political participation which usually has an activist bias.

From such critical reflections three demands on concepts of the political participation of older people can be formulated. First, we should preserve and renew the moral and normative resources which contribute to the definition and recognition of the status of older people; second, we should give an incentive to acknowledge older people's manifold productive contributions to social welfare and development rather than just consider them in terms of their utilizable functions; and third, we should encourage the establishment of ties to groups of fellow citizens, as a way of intergenerational integration. From this perspective a look at the problems of participation among older people may teach us something about the participation of groups and minorities in general. This is important because somewhere and somehow we all belong to a minority.

## Note

1   The study was funded by grants of the German Federal Ministry of the Family, Senior Citizens Women and Youth from October 1995 to March 1996. The empirical data consist of expert interviews which were carried out by the authors. We are grateful to the representatives of old age organizations and experts in the respective countries for their readiness to provide a wealth of information.

# PART 2

# National case studies

# 5

# The politics of old age in Austria[1]

KAI LEICHSENRING, CHRISTIANE BAHR
AND CHARLOTTE STRÜMPEL

Today, more than 1.6 million Austrians (almost 20 per cent of the population) are above the age of 60. This group of the population currently represents about one quarter of the electorate, and demographic projections for the next 20 years show that the proportion of older voters will increase consistently. Given the fact that, at least in quantitative terms, the older generation seems to be well organized – about 38 per cent of older citizens are members of one of several seniors' organizations – the case of Austria is particularly interesting concerning intergenerational equity and the political influence of older persons.

A closer look at the situation however, shows, that the older generation is hardly visible in Austrian politics. Older persons and their organizations are represented rather marginally in parliaments and governments. In everyday politics they appear (at best) as clients of the welfare state, as beneficiaries of pension systems, and as care-dependent persons who consume the largest share of national health expenditure. Older voters have been addressed by political parties during election campaigns but their involvement in legal and political decision making has been rather negligible. The public opinion about ageing is characterized by typical stereotypes ('frail, sick, poor') and potential conflicts between the generations are still hidden by traditional family ethics (Majce 1992).

However, during the past few years a number of structural changes have taken place in the political system, which also affect the political participation of older persons. For instance, senior citizens' councils have been implemented at several levels. In the policy process issues concerning older citizens have become more visible, albeit not always in favour of this population group. In addition, some research projects about issues concerning the political participation of older persons have been carried out and documentation about them has been intensified (BMAS 1994). Hence in our chapter we shall, first, describe recent features of old age politics in Austria. This part will deal with the analysis of political participation in its strictest sense. It is therefore based on indicators such as voting behaviour, the organizational structure of seniors' organizations, and the representation of older citizens in party politics. Second, we shall focus on recent improvements concerning the political representation of older persons, including the implementation of senior citizens' councils at the provincial and the federal level. Third policy areas concerning older persons and generational equity will be highlighted, particularly the role of senior citizens' organizations in developing social policies in old age and in case of dependency. Fourth, the views on the political participation of older people in Austria and their perceived barriers will be introduced. In our final section we shall discuss recent reforms, innovations, challenges and future perspectives of the politics of old age in Austria.

## The politics of old age in the context of the Austrian political system

Since the post-war period, politics and policies for and by older persons have been closely related to the three main developments in Austrian political culture: first, the two major parties (the Socialist Party and the Christian Democratic Party) have dominated both the governments and most other spheres of society. Between 1945 and 1995, Austria was governed for about 30 years by 'big coalitions' and only for 17 years by single-party governments. Given the fact that both parties also have a wide range of affiliated organizations, e.g. sports associations, welfare organizations and older citizens' organizations, in international comparisons Austria has been characterized as a society demarcated into separate 'pillars' (Church, Socialists, Christian Democrats) with, however, an increased consensus orientation.

Second, the wish for political consensus – which is strongly related to the historical experience of civil war and fascism during the 1930s and '40s as well as to the occupation between 1945 and 1955 – is apparent, for instance, in the particular structure of labour relations in Austria. This has become paradigmatic as a model for an institutionalized 'social partnership', the influence of which has gone far beyond collective bargaining on wages and labour law. This unique way of reconciling the interests of workers and employers has been based on strong trade unions, an institutionalized system of interest organizations and steady economic growth. The constitutions of the nine provinces are another example of institutionalized cooperation between the main political streams. In the provincial governments all political parties are represented according to their seats in the respective provincial parliaments. Austria's particular way of moderating political divisions and structuring 'checks and balances' – together with a constant expansion of the welfare state – has protected the Second Republic from major social conflicts. However the reduced role of parliaments, the lack of democratic control and the far-reaching influence of the political parties on social and economic reality has given rise to increasing criticism of Austria's 'democratic quality', particularly since the beginning of the 1980s.

Third, another specific feature concerning the political framework of old age politics in Austria is the division of competences concerning older persons' issues. Many responsibilities (such as social assistance schemes, community care, old age and nursing homes, education and training of professionals, leisure and cultural activities) lie with the provinces. The result is that different policies and regulations do exist in the different provinces, whereas the federal government is only responsible for some remaining issues that are mainly divided between the Ministry for Labour, Health and Social Affairs (guiding and control of social insurance matters are administered by an autonomous body) and the Ministry for Environment, Youth and Family Affairs.

During the past decade, these features of the Austrian political system have been challenged not only by the economic restructuring process but also by the emergence of new political parties (Green Party, Liberal Forum), the redirection of the Freedom Party (FPÖ) towards a right-wing populism, and also an increasingly volatile electorate. As a consequence of the internationalization and privatization of nationalized industries, the social and economic influence of the hitherto leading political parties – the Socialists (now Social Democrats) and the Christian Democrats – has been reduced, although they still control a 'big coalition' government (since 1986). The historical legacy and the current political context is important in any evaluation of old age politics in Austria.

## The voting behaviour of older people in Austria

A number of studies have shown that older persons between 50 and 70 participate in political elections more than younger generations (Bürklin 1987; Brunner 1996). According to the assumption that the voting behaviour of each 'political generation' is formed at a younger age and rarely changes during later life (Fogt 1992), older voters ought to be less willing to change their voting behaviours. This assumption is underlined by Austrian reality. For generations, workers, inhabitants of larger cities and non-worshipping Catholics have traditionally voted for the Social Democrats (SPÖ), whereas farmers, the self-employed, active Catholics and persons living in the countryside made up the stable electorate of the Christian Democrats (ÖVP). Since the 1980s, however, voters' distinguishing characteristics have had to be analysed much more in terms of other than class dichotomies: such as education, gender and the differences between the young and the old.

During the 1970s the proportion of older voters who preferred the two big parties reflected the proportion of older people in the entire population. In the 1980s the proportion of older voters for these two parties increased while younger voters tended to vote for the newly founded Green Party or the reformed FPÖ. In the 1990s the 'ageing' of the big parties' electorate has continued to the degree that the share of votes for the 'big coalition' has been reduced to 48 per cent for the age group below 30, whereas the SPÖ and the ÖVP together are still supported by 78 per cent of the older generation above 60 (see Table 5.1; also Plasser *et al.* 1996; Haller and König 1997). In 1995, for instance, 30 per cent of the voters, but only 15 per cent of all those who had

**Table 5.1**   Changing party preferences in Austria by age group, 1986–95

|  | Parliamentary elections | Percentage of votes by age groups | | | |
|---|---|---|---|---|---|
|  |  | *20–29* | *30–44* | *45–59* | *60 and above* |
| SPÖ | 1986 | 39 | 43 | 42 | 44 |
|  | 1995 | 30 | 36 | 39 | 44 |
| ÖVP | 1986 | 33 | 37 | 48 | 45 |
|  | 1995 | 18 | 25 | 33 | 34 |
| FPÖ | 1986 | 12 | 11 | 6 | 8 |
|  | 1995 | 29 | 24 | 10 | 15 |
| Green Party | 1986 | 11 | 5 | 1 | 1 |
|  | 1995 | 10 | 5 | 2 | 0 |
| others | 1986 | 1 | 1 | 1 | 1 |
|  | 1995 | 9 | 5 | 6 | 2 |

*Sources*: Fessel and GfK, exit poll (Plasser and Ulram 1987: 67; Plasser *et al.* 1996: 174)

voted for a different party at previous elections, were above the age of 60. At the same time, 16 per cent of the voters were younger than 30, but they made up 23 per cent of those who had previously voted for a different party.

*Senior citizens' organizations*

The main political actors concerned with older persons' issues have been the senior citizens' organizations. In accordance with the traditional political culture of the country, the two main organizations are both affiliated to the two major parties. On the one side, the Austrian Pensioners' Association (Pensionistenverband Österreichs) is closely associated to the Austrian Social Democratic Party; on the other, the Austrian Senior Citizens' Federation (Österreichischer Seniorenbund) is a sub-division of the Christian Democratic Party. With around 300,000 members in the Austrian Pensioners' Association and about 250,000 in the Senior Citizens' Federation, the total number of members of these two bodies is quite impressive. In some regions, the number of members of the senior citizens' organization even exceeds the respective party's number. Including some smaller associations, senior citizens' organizations have altogether reached a level of organization averaging around 38 per cent of all Austrians above 60 (see Table 5.2).

Austrian senior citizens' organizations have quite a long tradition. For instance, the Austrian Pensioners' Association was founded in 1949. The Austrian Senior Citizens' Federation has also existed since the 1950s but was reformed during the 1970s when it eventually became a formal sub-division of the Christian Democratic Party. Both organizations have a hierarchical structure which results in a rather clear division of political and social functions. In general, the federal and the provincial organizations are responsible for political strategy (in particular concerning pensions and other social secu-

**Table 5.2** Membership of senior citizens' organizations and the share of organized older persons in Austria

|  | Membership* | Share |
|---|---|---|
| Austrian Pensioners' Association | 305,000 | 19.5% |
| Austrian Senior Citizens' Federation | 245,000 | 15.6% |
| Austrian Seniors' Ring | 40,000 | 2.5% |
| Central Federation of Austrian Pensioners | 10,000 | 0.6% |
| Others§ | 5,000 | 0.3% |
| Total | 605,000 |  |
| Population above 60 | 1,564,728 | 38.5% |

*Sources*: Pensionistenverband (1996); Own research on Seniorenbund and Seniorenring; ÖSTAT (Census 1991)
* Based on information given by the organizations
† Share of organized persons, for all citizens above the age of 60
§ Die Grauen, Verband der Sozialversicherten and Die Grauen Panther [The Greys, The Association of the Socially Insured and The Grey Panthers]

rity matters) whereas the widespread local organizations are occupied with the organization of leisure activities (for example weekly club meetings, excursions). For the individual member, these leisure activities are much more important than political debates or strategies. For instance, in Lower Austria there are about 800,000 participants in the about 28,000 activities that are organized by the Austrian Pensioners' Association in this province (Pensionistenverband Österreichs 1996). In addition, the Austrian Pensioners' Association runs its own travel agency, which is one of the largest travel agencies in Austria.

As a consequence of the close relations with each respective party, the chairmen and other officials are usually politicians who have retired from being Members of Parliament, ministers or party officials. For instance, the current president of the Austrian Pensioners' Association was the parliamentary chairman at one time. The chairman of the Austrian Senior Citizens' Federation was the vice-president of a provincial government earlier. The leading positions of the senior citizens' organizations are predominantly held by men, although most of the members are women.

On the federal level there are two more senior citizens' organizations. The Senior Citizens' Ring (with approximately 40,000 members) is affiliated to the Freedom Party, whereas the Central Federation of Pensioners (with about 10,000 members) has its origins with the Austrian Communist Party (KPÖ). During the past few years, we have also witnessed the emergence of a number of smaller initiatives at the local level, as well as attempts to create senior citizens' parties (e.g. The Greys, The Grey Panthers or The Association of the Socially Insured). Some of the latter have even fielded candidates for parliamentary elections. They are, however, more or less marginal and ephemeral phenomena in the political sphere (Endl and Leichsenring 1994).

To summarize, Austrian senior citizens' organizations are characterized,

**Table 5.3**   Age structure of members and functionaries of the SPÖ and the ÖVP

|     |               | 20–29 | 30–39 | 40–49 | 50–59 | 60–69 | 70+ |
|-----|---------------|-------|-------|-------|-------|-------|------|
| SPÖ | members       | 11.2  | 16.5  | 19.4  | 17.6  | 20.3  | 15.0 |
|     | functionaries | 6.1   | 17.9  | 32.7  | 18.9  | 20.9  | 3.6  |
| ÖVP | members       | 14.0  | 16.1  | 21.3  | 20.0  | 17.0  | 12.0 |
|     | functionaries | 15.0  | 25.8  | 27.2  | 16.0  | 12.2  | 3.8  |

*Source*: Gehmacher (1990: 524)

on the one hand, by a few officials/politicians in the provinces and at the federal level, who deal with political issues concerning older people; on the other, the majority of members are at the local level, and are mainly engaged in leisure activities. Functionaries usually exert their political influence informally: since most of them used to be politicians, they have well-developed political contacts (a kind of 'old boys' network'). Apart from general interest representation, the most important activities of the senior citizens' organizations are the provision of service functions, the main emphasis being on the organization of leisure activities and travel, counselling and information on pension matters, and public relations activities.

### Political participation of senior citizens in party politics

The close relationship between the senior citizens' organizations and the respective parties does not necessarily imply that older persons' interests are represented adequately within the political parties.

The Austrian Pensioners' Association, for instance, is a formally independent association, but it has the right to nominate delegates to party committees and general assemblies of the SPÖ. However, in the lists of candidates for elections, representatives of pensioners are rather rare. For a long period this was due to a party-internal 'age clause' which prevented canditates above the age of 65 from taking on any political function in provincial or federal parliaments. Although this 'age clause' was abolished in 1995 there still are, for instance, only two MPs (both below pensionable age) who represent the Austrian Pensioners' Association in parliament.

The same is true for the Austrian Senior Citizens' Federation, even though it is an integral part of the ÖVP.[2] Although the 'age clause' that had existed since 1969 was officially abandoned in 1986, a 'hidden age clause' still prevents older candidates from becoming MPs or party functionaries. As a consequence, political matters in parliament concerning older persons are still tackled mainly by the party's Spokesman for Social Affairs. Table 5.3 illustrates that the ageing process of the two largest political parties in terms of membership is barely reflected in the age structure of the party officials. This is especially true for older women, since women are generally underrepresented in the official political functions.

As a corollary, pensioners' and senior citizens' interests remain dependent on informal lobbying within each party by those functionaries of the respective senior citizens' organizations who have shaped their contacts during their previous political life as MPs, ministers or party officials.

## Improving the representation of older people by senior citizens' councils

According to opinion polls, the majority of older persons (87 per cent) in Austria approves of the Austrian political system and the extent of Austrian democracy. About 78 per cent of them do not think they have any influence on governmental activities (Fessel and GfK/IFES 1989). This perceived lack of influence is higher than in all other age groups and is underlined in most items concerning opportunities for political participation. Nevertheless, the older population still favours traditional democratic elections to demonstrations, a referendum or any other activities of 'direct democracy' (Haller and König 1997). However, one instrument with the potential to increase the influence of older citizens in political decision making has never been evaluated in opinion polls but has gained in importance during the past few years: the founding of senior citizens' councils and other institutions concerned with older persons both at the provincial and federal level.

### Initiatives at the provincial level

As stated above, the provincial level is most important when it comes to implementing political issues concerning older persons. This is especially true for community care, old-age and nursing homes, as well as financial support in the framework of the different social assistance Acts. The fact that older persons are one of the main target groups of the provincial social assistance departments has increased the impression that old age politics is mainly a concern of the provinces and/or the voluntary non-profit organizations that are contracted-in to provide community care services. Given this structure, the negative stereotype of old age ('poor, sick, disabled') has been perpetuated or even increased. During the past ten years, however, the social assistance committees at the provincial level have increasingly dealt with other age-relevant issues.

Altogether, the drive for more participation and an enlargement of competences is not to be neglected. In our research (Bahr *et al.* 1996) we have distinguished different types of approaches that increase both the visibility of older persons' concerns and the participation of senior citizens at the provincial level.

*Institutionalizing senior citizens' councils*

One way of increasing the political influence of a specific population group consists of opening formal channels within the political system. In Austria, the instrument of senior citizens' councils has been chosen for this purpose, first of all at the provincial level.

An interesting prototype of a 'demanding' senior citizens' council can be reported from Vorarlberg. In this most western province of Austria, the senior citizens' council has existed since 1977 but was completely reformed in 1989. The most important change was that the chairman of the council was elected by its members, whereas before it used to be the respective head of the provincial government. Since that time, the meetings of the council have become more regular, more lively, and much more targeted towards the needs of older citizens. The council consists of 12 members who represent the seniors' organizations, the municipalities, and relevant providers of community care services. Representatives of the provinical government and/or administration may participate in an advisory capacity. During the past few years, the council has produced comments on provincial and federal Bills, and recommendations to combat age discrimination. Furthermore, the council has suggested several research studies and the foundation of local senior citizens' councils in the municipalities. Finally, a major success has been to install a senior citizens' office within the provincial administration, the aim of which is to increase social integration and activities among older citizens.

Between 1992 and 1996, in most other provinces, different senior citizens' councils have been set up. These are more or less based on a model from Styria, in which only representatives (delegates) of the larger seniors' organizations and of the provincial government (administration) are admitted. The chair changes every six months to one of the different organizations ('rotation principle'). The councils meet at least twice a year. The persons involved consider these councils as 'the first step' towards the increased political participation of older citizens; up till now, however, no major influence has been reported. Most functionaries of the seniors' organizations still tend to trust much more in their 'informal contacts' with politicians than in the institution of senior citizens' councils.

*Senior citizens' offices and round-table discussions*

Another way of promoting old age as a political issue and older persons as a politically important population group is to generate politically adequate administrative structures. Some first steps in this direction have been implemented not only in Vorarlberg but in all Austrian provinces during the past few years.

In the province of Salzburg, for instance, the support of older citizens was enlisted in a top–down process, when a Senior Citizens' Office of the provincial government was installed in 1992 (Seniorenbüro des Landes Salzburg 1993). As one aim of the office has been to develop an 'experimental old age policy' with the involvement of the older persons themselves, an informal 'round table for senior citizens' issues' was organized with representatives of all relevant groups. The discussions resulted in different action programmes, mainly concerning care for older persons in the community and in nursing homes. Because the providers of community care services had dominated these round-table debates, older persons themselves started to gather occasionally in a so-called Seniors' Forum. In addition, in most communities, councillors responsible for old age issues have been nominated. All these activities have contributed to increase the visibility of age-related issues not only in the area of care but also, for instance, in housing, traffic and the development of villages. In 1993, also in The Tyrol a Seniors' Office was installed (Amt der Tiroler Landesregierung 1993). The aim of this institution is to increase public consciousness about the situation of older persons and to represent their interests at the provincial government and other public bodies. An informal discussion forum serves to enhance cooperation and coordination with the relevant people.

These models triggered developments in all Austrian provinces so that each provincial administration has at least nominated officials as responsible for old age policies (see Figure 5.4). In some provinces, e.g. in Vienna, they are conceived as autonomous offices with direct links to the government so that the different policy areas concerning old age can be tackled without being limited by departmental boundaries.

## Advisory councils at federal level

The fragmentation of forces as a result of the affiliation to the respective political parties has triggered repeated efforts to establish at least a national umbrella organization for the senior citizens' associations. Despite several attempts, this level of official cooperation has not been achieved. This was partly due to personal conflicts between the previous chairmen of the two largest organizations. However, during the last few years the level of cooperation increased considerably and resulted in a common strategy towards the foundation of a Federal Senior Citizens' Council that was eventually installed at the Federal Chancellory in 1994. In addition, advisory councils of the social security bodies were installed, in which representatives of the senior citizens' organizations were admitted.

### The Federal Senior Citizens' Council

This council is presided over by the Federal Chancellor and meets three or four times a year. It has a purely advisory role and consists of 35 members representing the largest senior citizens' organizations, the provincial governments, the municipalities and the relevant ministries. The Curia of the 19 members representing senior citizens' organizations is responsible for the agenda and may invite experts to provide clarification on specific issues. Besides topical matters of senior citizens' policy, the focus of the first meetings has been on social policy issues of special relevance for pensioners (such as pension increases, provision for care in old age, exemption from radio and television licence fees).

The structure of this body has been criticized from different sides: one critical point is that only representatives of the large party-affiliated senior citizens' organizations are admitted; another is that the provinces are not sufficiently represented and that it is not democratically legitimated. In addition, the absence of experts in gerontology and the fact that the meetings exclude the public were criticized. It is still too early to evaluate the institution of this council but it must be said that it is the first attempt to

**Table 5.4**   Formal channels for the political participation of older citizens in Austrian provinces

| Province | Name of advisory body | Year of foundation | Chairperson | Members | Frequency of meetings |
|---|---|---|---|---|---|
| Vorarl-berg | Seniorenbeirat | 1988 | Elected by members | Senior citizens' organizations, social service providers, provincial administration | At least four times a year |
| Tyrol | Senioren-plattform | 1993 | Official of the Seniors' Office | Senior citizens' organizations, social service providers | Sometimes |
| Salzburg | Seniorenbeirat | 1997 | Official of the Seniors' Office | Senior citizens' organizations, social service providers, provincial administration | Irregular |
| | | | Official of the Seniors' Office | Senior citizens' organizations, and initiatives | Irregular |
| Steier-mark | Seniorenbeirat | 1992 | Representative of a senior citizens' organization ('rotation' every six months) | Senior citizens' organizations affiliated to parties represented in the provincial parliament, provincial government and administration | Depends on the respective chairperson |
| Burgen-land | Seniorenbeirat | 1993 | Representative of a senior citizens' organization | Senior citizens' organizations affiliated to parties represented in the provincial parliament, provincial government and administration | At least twice a year |
| Kärnten land | Seniorenbeirat | 1995 | Representative of a senior citizens' organization ('rotation' every six months) | Senior citizens' organizations affiliated to parties represented in the provincial parliament, provincial government and administration | At least twice a year |
| Nieder-österreich | Unterausschuß Senioren | 1988 | Provincial minister responsible for social affairs | Senior citizens' organizations, social service providers, provincial administration | At least twice a year |
| Wien | Seniorenbeirat | 1996 | City counsellor, responsible for social affairs | Senior citizens' organizations, municipal administration | At least twice a year |
| Ober-österreich | No advisory body | | | | |

*Source*: Bahr *et al.* (1996)

coordinate the politics of old age and to recognize older persons at a federal level.

*Participation in social security advisory bodies*

Another example that shows how old age politics in Austria is still at a rather symbolic stage can be seen in the way in which the participation of older persons in social insurance matters has been regulated. With the 52nd Amendment of the General Social Insurance Act (1993), the number of members in the general assemblies of the self-governing Social Insurance Agency was reduced, while at the same time, separate advisory bodies were created in order to allow pensioners and persons with disabilities to advocate their interests in the field of social insurance matters. However, these bodies only have an advisory role, while the main decisions are still made in the general assemblies and the management boards, in which only employers and trade unions are represented.

## Old age policies in Austria: pension reforms and the Care Allowance Act

As in most other European countries, there is no specific old age policy in Austria. This is not only due to the existing division of competences between different ministries and between the federal state and the provinces. It has often been said that old age encompasses such a wide range of issues that hardly any single institution, e.g. a ministry, could come to grips with them. However, the same might be said about environmental policies, and yet both ministries for environmental affairs and respective policy agendas have been developed all over Europe. Thus it seems that the argument is often used as an excuse for failing to make a decision. In the Austrian reality, old age policies are usually seen as policies concerning older people's social security.

*Pension policies*

For a long time, the implementation of a comprehensive pension system, based on preceding models,[3] was one of the main concerns of Austrian governments. In 1954, the General Social Insurance Act (ASVG) came into force. It provided social security for workers and employees but not for self-employed persons and farmers; they have been fully included into the system only since the 1970s. Given the historical experiences of Austrians during this century, the statutory guarantee for social security in old age was one of the major concerns of the Social Democrats. The following statement of Chancellor Bruno Kreisky (Gottschlich *et al.* 1989, translation by the authors) gives an impression of the discourse in social policy during the 1970s:

> An Austrian at the age of 65 years had to survive two world wars, heavy inflation after the wars, long-term unemployment and global economic crises. He has experienced the incredible devastations of

World War II and was repeatedly confronted with annihilation. Therefore, the problem of social policy in Austria cannot be solved by means of formulas that might be valid for economies that have experienced a more or less continuous development with short interruptions.

During the 1980s the problem of financing the welfare state in times of recession became evident. Since then, a number of pension reforms have been passed. They were characterized by rather conservative features such as, for instance, the strengthening of the 'insurance principle' (the individual pension entitlement is now much more dependent on the number of contribution years), the reduction or delay of pension indexation, the step wise equalization (until 2030) of the pensionable age to 65 for men and women and the reduction of public subsidies to pensions insurance (General Social Security Act). These measures have had a rather marginal impact on the income of current pensioners; some of them, however, will have considerable future importance. In addition, claims for 'more private provision' and/or increased contributions to pensions insurance have been gaining ground during the 1990s – up till now, however, without any signs of protest by younger generations. On the contrary, the organizations of older citizens have expressed their clear opposition towards any reductions of pension rights, for example by means of demonstrations. The fact that pension policies are still a politically highly sensitive issue, for older voters particularly, was illustrated on the occasion of the parliamentary elections in 1995. During the election campaign, the then Chancellor Franz Vranitzky (SPÖ) communicated in a letter to each pensioner that, in case of his re-election, pensions would be secured at the current level, whereas this would not be guaranteed by other parties. The result was that the Social Democrats regained the relative majority; commentators as well as opinion polls after the ballot showed that the 'pension argument' had had a particular impact on voters' decisions (SWS-Bildstatistiken 1996).

Currently, debates about pension reforms focus around the standardization of pension systems (civil servants enjoy disproportionately higher pension levels than employed and self-employed pensioners) and the possibility of introducing independent pensions for women in old age – in the existing system, women heavily depend on widow's pensions and means-tested supplements (Prinz *et al.* 1996).

## Care policies

Apart from pensions, social and health care has always been a traditional component of old age policies. In Austria, care was neglected as a public policy issue for a long time. The provinces, which are responsible for this matter by constitutional law, generally used their budget for care to finance institutions for older persons and, increasingly since the 1970s, to contract-in (reimburse) home care services that are provided by voluntary organizations. With the rising sums of money required for these activities, the provincial governments started to claim more support from the federal state, particularly since the mid-1980s. The political discussions about care reforms oscillated between two objectives. On the one hand, the continually poor services in community care needed further development with additional subsidies from the federal state. On the other, first and foremost, a comprehensive federal attendance allowance scheme should be installed. Apart from claims by the provinces, the main impetus for reforms – especially with respect to the cash-based solution – came from groups of well-organized younger people with disabilities, whereas senior citizens' organizations were not particularly involved (Evers *et al.* 1994).

After several years of political negotiations – which nevertheless had mainly focused on the difficulties of financing a reform costing between 7 and 10 billion ATS – the Comprehensive Attendance Allowance Act was passed by the Austrian parliament. Since 1 July 1993 it has provided for seven levels of attendance allowances which are not means-tested and which range from ATS 2,000 to ATS 21,000. In addition, the provinces pledged themselves to expand the networks of community care services over the next ten years (Leichsenring 1996).

Concerning 'modern' old age policies, such as innovations in care, voluntary work, 'productive ageing' and discrimination against older workers, it has to be underlined that these – with some exceptions (Evers and Pruckner 1995; Artner *et al.* 1996) – have not yet been adopted by public forums in general nor by senior citizens and their organizations. Also, the senior citizens' councils that have been established during the past few years are only slowly taking on these emerging concerns. It still remains to be seen if the new structural framework of old age politics will have an impact on future old age policies.

## Views on and barriers to political participation of older persons in Austria

The preceding description of politics and policies for older people in Austria allows us to identify several structural barriers to the political participation of senior citizens. First, on the societal level, there are still stereotypes of older people as 'frail, sick and poor' and a focus on issues dealing with the frail elderly in politics, public opinion and the media.

Second, in the political sphere, topics concerning senior citizens – as well as older politicians – are still largely marginalized in party politics. Also, the structure of the existing senior citizens' organizations (and their domination of the political landscape for older people), presents barriers for the mobilization of seniors: within each organization, political influence is chiefly exerted by a few functionaries whereas the great majority of the members mainly participate in leisure activities. In addition, the political division between senior citizens' organizations makes it more difficult for them to cooperate in advocating their interests, especially at the lower levels of the organizational hierarchy.

Third, the federal system in Austria leads to the diffusion of responsibility for issues concerning older people. This is because many powers are delegated to the provincial governments and there is no single body (such as a government department) responsible at federal level.

Fourth, this diffusion of responsibility and the lack of formal channels to exert political influence has slowly been improving since the senior citizens' councils as well as senior citizens' offices were founded. However, there are still some problems with the seniors citizens' councils at federal and provincial level as well as in the social insurance agencies: since their members are appointed and not elected there is the question of their democratic legitimacy. Also, some of them still function more as window dressing rather than having any real political power.

In summary, there is the tendency in the senior citizens' councils as well as in the senior citizens' organizations for the majority of seniors to be left out of the real decision making processes.

Despite the above barriers, as a result of our study ('Political Participation of Older Persons in Austria', Bahr *et al.* 1996) we assumed that many senior citizens were willing to participate in democratic processes; we were interested in the opinions of different groups of senior citizens concerning political participation. Thus, in the second phase of the European Centre's research project we organized nine workshops with different groups of seniors citizens (including older people who were unemployed or in early retirement, older women, volunteers, residents of a small town, members of senior citizens' organizations, inhabitants of old people's homes) in different parts of Austria. In these workshops, participants spoke about their concerns and expressed their views on existing forms of and barriers to participation.

The main finding of the workshops is that participants were very eager to give their opinions and participate in political processes, provided the issues concerned were close to their personal situation or geographically nearby (local level). The importance of personal affinity in political mobilization is true for persons of all ages but seems to be especially relevant for older people. Due to the different groups of older participants a variety of issues arose in the course of the workshops: older persons who were unemployed or in early retirement talked, for instance, about how they were treated in the job centres. Volunteers for the social services of the Austrian Red Cross discussed ways of improving the social services in their area. The inhabitants of a small town exchanged ideas on how to encourage their community to cater for the needs of older citizens. And persons living in old-age and nursing homes (average age 84) discussed how to succeed with installing a lift and to get a bus stop in front of their home.

The workshops showed, once again, that older people are a very heterogeneous group whose members focus on different needs and issues, making political mobilization difficult (see Chapter 2). There were a variety of issues in the workshops, however, that were of interest for almost all participants (for instance, the image of older people in society and in the media); most participants had some sort of an identity as a 'senior citizen'. All in all, the topics, barriers and possible solutions that were discussed were influenced by present living conditions, biographical factors as well as personal experiences in old age.

Participants in the workshops talked about the structural barriers mentioned above as well as more detailed and personal aspects of barriers which hampered their participation. Institutional structures, for example, in old peoples' homes or job centres were seen as discouraging participants from articulating their needs. Not being able to keep up with societal changes, problems with younger generations, as well as social exclusion resulting from changes in the labour market were mentioned by many participants. Deteriorating health was one of the most relevant personal barriers that were identified. Also, several participants mentioned the biographical aspect that their authoritarian upbringing meant they were not used to articulating their needs. Apart from that some older women are faced with caring for their relatives, which leaves no time or energy for political participation. Lastly, many senior citizens are so active travelling and participating in other activities that they do not have time for political involvement. Another very relevant set of barriers that were identified were matters of communication between different agencies and seniors: seniors reported that many political processes lacked transparency. In many cases seniors were not informed adequately about issues concerning them, or the information was presented in such a way that it was hard to understand. Apart from that, participants did not know who or which agencies to contact to gain more information or to articulate their opinion. Seniors also had the impression that many politicians were not interested in the needs of older people.

Based on these results, five group discussions were organized which gave some of the participants in the workshops the opportunity to share their ideas with decision makers (experts, civil servants, politicians). Some of the topics that were identified as important for older people in the second stage of the project, as well as possible ways of including older people in decision-making processes, were discussed. This allowed senior citizens and experts to view the same issues from different perspectives. It also helped seniors gain insight into how political processes function and which of their ideas for political participation are realistic.

While the workshops and the group discussions helped list barriers to seniors' political participation they were also a first step in overcoming some of these barriers and empowering the participants. The design of these workshops and group discussions allowed participants to talk about those topics concerning them and their personal situation and to articulate their opinion. For some people this was a new experience in the field of political participation. The senior citizens in the workshops became enthusiastic about the discussions and showed great interest in continuing work in similar forums.

## Conclusion

Austria is only just starting to create a politics of old age that goes further than questions of pensions and health care. As in matters concerning women or young people, the question is, of course, to what extent a certain external characteristic – in this case, age – makes it necessary or meaningful for a certain group of the population to be given special consideration within the structure of democratic institutions and respective policy processes. The heterogeneous nature of the interests and needs of this age group reduces opportunities for mobilizing older persons 'towards a common goal'. On the other hand, however, this diversity fosters a range of different activities and initiatives that can mushroom in the area of social and cultural integration.

The political representation of Austrian senior citizens is sharply defined by the two major senior citizens' organizations' close connections to the SPÖ and the ÖVP. Between these two organizations there is far-reaching consensus in social security matters concerning older persons. However, their political visions are barely influenced by new perspectives for the third age or ideas for the future of old age. Given the large membership of organizations for older persons in Austria, the explanation must be that the higher hierarchical levels take care of 'political matters', and local groups usually concentrate on the organization of leisure activities.

The increase in opportunities for older people's representation through the framework of senior citizens' councils and the setting up of offices for older persons in the administration are to be welcomed as an important step. However, optimal forms of organization have not yet been found. On the one hand, the impression is that the representation of older persons in the currently existing senior citizens' councils is being monopolized by the senior citizens' organizations that are affiliated to the political parties. On the other, it is argued that some of the new structures have been implemented in a top–down manner as one politician or another has 'discovered' and instrumentalized old age. Anyhow, whatever the reasons behind the new structures or institutions may be, they are perhaps the proverbial 'first step' towards improved interest representation; they are a framework which now has to be brought to life by older persons themselves.

In order to overcome existing barriers towards political participation within the group of older people as a whole, local and regional initiatives are needed. Our own research on some of these initiatives which have been developing in Austria during the past few years (Bahr *et al.* 1996) suggests that these activities might remain 'single-issue initiatives'. This means that the scope of both their contents and the respective target group may be limited to specific needs or projects: like, for instance, a housing project in the community, a family carers' initiative, an association of pensioners concerned about public security or a self-help group of pensioners with specific health problems.

A mere increase in numbers will not directly influence the status of old age policy in Austria. Nevertheless, the ageing process of traditional associations, unions, parties and institutions might have an impact on their activities and their political orientation. At the same time, the existing senior citizens' organizations might have to rethink their role and orientation when they perceive that membership is shrinking because 'younger pensioners' are scarcely interested in their activities.

The question remains, however, as to whether future older generations will be inclined to be more active in their political involvement. Unlike the current older generation, which has experienced war, fascism and famine, the coming generations of pensioners will look back at a steady democratic development linked to the expansion of social security systems, to which they have contributed during their working life.

Thus the potential for generational conflicts in the future have so far only been detected in relation to financing pensions. Currently, about 50 per cent of Austrians above 60 would not accept any pension cuts, and propose the imposition of higher contributions on the working generation; whereas 40 per cent of those below 40 years of age are not prepared at all to accept any increase in social security contributions – rather, pensions should be reduced. In reality, however, generational conflicts are not a decisive factor, nor do they play a major role in political discussions. Still, only 4 per cent of all Austrians think that the needs and interests of older persons are considered too much in politics and society while 50 per cent believe that they are not taken into account enough (Majce 1992).

In order to face up to potential conflicts and to support the concept of generational balance, not only in social security but especially in social integration, old age politics in Austria, like in most other 'ageing societies', has to consider the following features. Information about ageing and matters concerning older persons should be disseminated in a clear and transparent way. If political decisions about necessary reforms in the area of pensions are taken, they should consider the interests of all generations and should be announced as soon as possible so that adequate group-related or individual measures can be prepared. Second, the potential of older persons should be made more visible; the negative images of ageing and older people should be countered by the prevailing positive experiences of pensioners. Third, the experiences, needs and ideas of older persons should be activated when it comes to the planning of social services or other infrastructure in the communities. Fourth, supporting the initiatives of older persons does not necessarily mean only financial subsidies. Empowering older persons has to include ways and mechanisms that help to develop ideas and visions for later life. Fifth, intergenerational exchange has not yet been developed actively in Austria. Opportunities for getting acquainted with the perspectives and living circumstances of the other generation are of outstanding importance in order to help people learn to cope with new realities. Sixth, public support programmes have to take into account that older persons as a group are very heterogeneous. Therefore such programmes should focus on specific target groups and thematic features. Finally, even if older persons are not a homogeneous group, there are also common features and interests that can be identified. Thus instead of looking for the lowest common denominator by organizing afternoon teas and bridge circles, we should strive to find the areas of widest political concern in ageing societies.

## Notes

1 This chapter is based on a study by the authors on 'The Political Participation of Older Persons in Austria' (Endl and Leichsenring 1994; Bahr *et al.* 1996). The research project was funded by the Ministry for Labour and Social Affairs, and thus shows in itself an increasing interest in old age politics in Austria.

2 The Austrian Christian Democrats (or People's Party) is combined with different, independent sub-organizations: the Workers' and Employees' Federation, the Farmers' Federation, the Industry and Trade Federation, and the Austrian Senior

Citizens' Federation. In order to become a member of the party it is necessary to belong to one of these federations.

3  By the end of the last century, Austria was one of the first European countries to introduce a social insurance system. The health insurance scheme which was introduced in 1888 laid the basis for a continuous expansion in relation to other social risks, coverage and level of benefits. Also after 1945, the General Social Insurance Law (1954) perpetuated the principles of the traditional regulations, e.g. the classification of blue-collar workers, white-collar employees and self-employed persons in commerce, trade and industry, farming and the civil service.

# 6

# The politics of old age in France

DOMINIQUE ARGOUD AND
ANNE-MARIE GUILLEMARD

For a long time France's population has been ageing in comparison with those of neighbouring countries. The drop in the fertility rate, which demographers have called the 'demographic transition', took place earlier in France than elsewhere. Even though the 'baby boom' turned this trend around from 1942 until the early 1970s, this reversal ended earlier in France than in nearby countries, as the fertility rate once again lowered. A second demographic trend has also had an impact: the longer life expectancies attained thanks to progress in public health and hygiene. Along with Japan, Sweden and a few other countries, France has one of the longest life expectancies (over 81 years at birth) for women, that of men being nearly 74.

The consequence of these two trends comes as no surprise: by 1950 France was one of the countries with the most older people in its population structure. Nowadays it is not alone, but the state became preoccupied with older people's living conditions soon after World War II. It has allowed the setting up and promulgation of an Old Age Fund scheme. In the same way it has supported an increase in the standard of living of retired and older people, through different measures such as the setting in 1956 of the minimum benefits and the continuous reassessment of retirement funds. So, since the mid-1970s, retirees' standards of living have increased continuously. Retirement pensions have gone up faster than wages. Despite this overall improvement, disparities still exist. The least privileged are the oldest, especially women.

## The fragmentation of pensioners' organizations

Policy has been mainly negotiated between the state, trade unions and employers' associations (Guillemard 1986).The structures of retiree organizations bear two characteristics that considerably limit their leverage in old age policy, however.

First of all, older people's organizations have vertical structures. Their grassroots activities are at the local (often the communal) level, but these local units are usually fitted into a departmental and then a national hierarchy. The purpose of this grouping of local units is to increase the organization's visibility by reinforcing its means of support and by endowing it with a relatively homogeneous ideology. This structure also encourages political participation by grouping units at the level where decisions are made (Bloch-Lainé and Garrigou-Lagrange 1988). In a country like France where the centralized state is an ideal (despite laws about decentralization), federal structures representing 'civil society' tend to be modelled on the hierarchy characteristic of public administration. But the proliferation of such vertically built organizations reduces their scope and makes it hard for them to coordinate strategy. Whenever umbrella organizations do exist (such as the Bureau de Liaison des Organisations de Retraités – BLOR), they run up against the quite different institutional positions of their member organizations.

Second, the state has always played a central role in organizing French society. As a consequence, 'civil society' lacks cohesion. Big organizations – whether independent or affiliated to labour unions – that represent senior citizens tend to splinter. Their representatives come from various unions and federations of associations. Furthermore, there is no room at the national level for global discussions between state and society (Guillemard *et al.* 1994). Older people do not seem able to influence social policy. Their organizations have little impact whenever major old age policy reforms are drawn up.

None the less, we can draw up a typology of the interest groups representing older people at the departmental and national levels. These ideal types are based on the groups' major objectives and an interpretation of the world of retiree associations (Gallard and Argoud 1995). In our analysis we will present only the organizations that are turned inward, exclusively towards their members. Given the overlaps between ideal types, this typology is somewhat arbitrary. In fact, most retiree organizations swing back and forth between two poles of activity: pressing demands and the provision of leisure activities.

The first ideal type encompasses the organizations affiliated to labour unions. Defending the interests of older people has always been deemed a union assignment, since the retired used to be workers – one becomes a retiree because one has, during his participation in the labour force, obtained the right to rest. As Guillemard (1986) has shown, labour unions have participated in debates about the 'social rights' related to withdrawal from the labour force: they played an active role in the origins of the right to retirement and have, more recently, had a part in setting up early retirement arrangements. Hence labour federations have set up their own specific 'sections' for their retiree members in line with their own ideological persuasions. These sections help the unions keep their members active after the end of their working lives. But little is known about the size of these sections, or about their actual impact on the unions. According to INSEE's statistics (Héran 1988), the rate of membership of unions and occupational organizations drops after the age of 60, with the noteworthy exception of the self-employed.

In addition to union-affiliated organizations, this first ideal type also comprises major associations that, though not affiliated with any union, have clearly formulated their objectives as demands – for instance: the Union Nationale des Retraités et Personnes Agées, the Union Française des Retraités and the Confédération Nationale des Retraités.

In parallel, organizations (mostly associations) have sprung up for 'pre-retirees'. Since the late 1970s, public officials have fostered early withdrawal from the labour force in an effort to keep joblessness from rising. Owing to this policy, some pre-retirees have formed groups to defend their purchasing power and rights. Union-related organizations, which pre-retirees consider to be too 'generalist', have not always taken the defence of these interests into account. An example is the Association de Défense des Intérêts des Préretraités, Retraités et Assimilés.

The second ideal type refers to a motley group of generation-based interest groups. Such organizations are less forceful in pushing demands. The claimant role of these organizations is based on the defence of interests more specific than the first type. These organizations may have a particular socio-economic composition: for example, some of them bring together veterans, veterans' widows, or widows who are heads of household (the Fédération des Associations de Veuves Chefs de Familles). Associations formed on the basis of religious affiliations also belong to this second type (for example, the Mouvement Chrétien des Retraités); they have strongly influenced several generations of older people.

The third ideal type covers the groups whose members used to be employed in the same firm. Some associations try to keep alive the bonds between employees and their firm. These groups or clubs usually focus on leisure activities for retirees. According to INSEE's statistics (Héran 1988), the membership rate in such associations stays rather high till the age of 80, especially among men in the public sector.

The last ideal type concerns the movement formed around 'senior citizen policy'. These associations are important; they work less at pressing demands and lobbying. Since the late 1970s, when public authorities adopted a policy based on the way of life of older people, several initiatives have been undertaken on behalf of the 'third age' of life corresponding to senior citizenship (Lenoir 1979). This new policy was based on and, in turn, helped develop senior citizen groups in most communes throughout France. These groups are assembled in two big federations. The mostly rural Fédération des Clubs des Aînés Ruraux has close links with the Mutualité Sociale Agricole, a provident fund for farmers. It has nearly a million members. The mainly urban Fédération Nationale des Associations de Retraités sprung up among persons active in the magazine *Notre Temps*, and has more than 300,000 members. Other associations are also part of this senior citizenship movement, including the Fédération Française de la Retraite Sportive and the Union Française des Universités du Troisième Age.

## Recent developments in the politics of old age

*Provision for long-term care and the cost of dependence*

Although national and local authorities have constantly pursued the policy of helping older people remain living at home, implementation has been difficult. The resulting piecemeal variety of measures has not always lived up to expectations (Guillemard 1986).

Ideally the implementation of such a policy would be coordinated in such a way that older people, despite their social and physical handicaps, might continue living at home as long as possible. But coordination has turned out to be hard to achieve, given the diversity of actors, the variety of institutional rationales and the multiplicity of budgets (and budget headings) necessary for the implementation of all these measures. A major obstacle to coordination has been the clearcut division of the health and social service sectors in France. Each of these sectors is administered under a different body of legislation. The 1970 and 1991 Hospital Acts have laid down the rules for organizing and financing the health sector, whereas social services are administered under a 1975 law.

The increasing number of persons who have reached an advanced age has highlighted the limits and shortcomings of old age policies. In 1991, no less than two official reports were made on the topic of 'dependence' (Boulard 1991; Schopflin 1991). It stands to reason that we have to work out new policies for providing care to people who suffer from the disabilities and loss of function that so often come along with advancing old age. More and more families are facing the intractable problem of providing care, whether at home or in an institution, to elderly parents whose autonomy has been impaired. But successive governments have put off adopting a law that would fund a programme for dependent older people.

In fact, a 24 January 1997 Act instituted a 'specific dependency service' (*prestation spécifique dépendance*). This law is intended merely to precede the introduction of a genuine 'dependency allocation'. But given the unfavourable economic and budgetary situation, public officials have set up a temporary arrangement funded with a fixed lump sum. At present, the specific dependency service, which the *départements* manage and provide, is intended for persons 60 years old or older who have a certain degree of dependence as assessed by a team of health professionals and social workers, and whose income falls below a certain limit. Given the relatively restrictive eligibility conditions, only 250,000 to 300,000 persons are covered.

In 1991, a White Paper on retirement pensions was published. The idea was to prepare some reforms to overcome the financial crisis of the French retirement fund. Since 1993 the rules for calculating pensions under Social Security's general Old Age Fund have been modified. In particular, the number of years of employee contributions required for a full pension has been raised from 37.5 to 40. In 1993 and 1994, agreements were worked out that tightened the rules for calculating the benefits paid out by the complementary old age funds. In 1997, retirement savings accounts were created, but the enabling decrees have not yet been published. Other measures – such as the extension of the 'generalized social contribution' (CSG) tax to old age pensions, or the increase of the percentage of retiree contribution that is paid into Social Security's Health Fund – have motivated older people to vent their discontent. Changes in taxes, especially withholding taxes, have spurred reactions that reach beyond the problem of pensions and purchasing power.

These measures that have come out of discussions about financing old age pensions have led older people to defend their purchasing power. In the same way, for several years now, retiree organizations have demanded that dependence be recognized as a social risk covered by social security. These two topics have become major issues on the public policy agenda in recent years, and have politically mobilized older people: in 1996, for example, there were three demonstrations. A joint union demonstration was organized on 30 May 1996. Then on 6 June 1996, three big non-union-affiliated organizations belonging to BLOR called for their members to take to the streets. Finally, a joint demonstration by nearly all the major associations and labour unions took place on 22 October 1996 in Paris and a few other cities. Though not very big, these demonstrations were a new phenomenon in French politics and society. For the first time in French history older people used demonstrations as a collective means of protesting against public policy.

### The changing nature of political participation

France is often represented as the ideal type of the centralized state. The structure of the French state was indeed created by the abolition of provincial individuality and the introduction of a powerful administrative organization. A turn away from this began to emerge, however, with the adoption of the decentralization laws in the early 1980s, which transferred responsibility for social affairs to the *départements*. So how are the interests of older people structured within this context? Can it be assumed that at a time when they constitute 20 per cent of the population and a third of the electorate, they also have an influence on the decision-making processes?

In fact, the state has always played a central role in the organization of social life. This is reflected in the fragmentation of the major representative organizations, whether trade unions or associations of one form or another, and in the absence of a forum for understanding between the state and society at national level. That is why the influence of older people in the development of the major gerontological reforms is therefore relatively limited. This shortcoming proved problematic in the early 1980s when the new Socialist government sought to revamp its policy concerning pensioners and the elderly and to involve them substantially in the negotiations. The National Assembly of Pensioners and the Elderly held in 1983 was an indication of these efforts.

Primarily, the state promoted the creation of new places of representation. The circular of 7 April 1982 illustrates the state strategy: it introduced a representative structure in order to involve pensioners in the renewal of social policy for older people. Thus, by the decree of 4 August 1982, the Comités Départementaux des Retraités et Personnes Âgées [*Département* Committees for Pensioners and the Elderly] (CDERPA) and a Comité

National des Retraités et Personnes Âgées [National Committee for Pensioners and the Elderly] (CNRPA) were set up. In this way, the state has provided a remedy against fragmentation and the typically unrepresentative nature of traditional pensioners' organizations by creating a body consisting of an administrative structure[1] chaired by the minister responsible for affairs relating to older people.

The intention to extend the representation of the interests of retired persons nevertheless has remained only very limited and has had hardly any impact. The vitality of the CDERPAs varies widely throughout France; and political authorities at the departmental level are sometimes sceptical about, or wary of, a structure under central government authority. Owing to the quite diverse composition of all these committees, it has been difficult to adopt a very clear course of action. True, the CDERPAs and CNRPA are broadly representative: delegates from the 16 organizations that are the most representative of retirees and older people sit on them, along with experts and elected officials. But for this very reason, these committees reproduce the splintering of retirees' organizations and highlight the cultural differences between various associations. Consequently they have a hard time adopting a common set of policies.

Early retirement and the increasing distinction between age and retirement are resulting in the responsible bodies increasingly identifying with the interests of the 'retired and senior citizens' and not just with 'senior citizens' alone. But more widely, early retirement has given rise to new social practices for older people. So in France, since the 1980s, some so-called 'socially useful activities' have emerged (Théry 1993). Those new practices show that some retired people want to remain wholly or partly socially active citizens and are not only just consumers or recipients of services. They become involved in different fields (cultural, social, economic) and voluntarily offer their free time and experience (Guillemard 1991; CLEIRPPA 1993).

## Measures to increase participation in local or national decision making

At the national level, CNRPA is still the only advisory organization where the government, administration and older people can meet. A 4 May 1995 decree has made a change: CNRPA's vice-president is to be elected by older people's representatives instead of being appointed by the minister. None the less, this reform does not seem to have increased the low level of participation of older people in policy making. The issue of retiree representation in decision making is still important. In a survey conducted during the 6 June 1996 demonstration in Paris, 46 per cent of respondents cited this issue as their principal motivation (Viriot-Durandal 1996). In line with this demand, CNRPA has formed a work group for identifying the various bodies where retirees are not sufficiently represented (CNRPA 1995).

Unlike some other European countries, no law forces authorities at the local level in France to involve older people in decision making (see Chapter 3). In the past few years, however, 'councils of sages' and 'councils of elders' have formed at the communal or intercommunal level. Through them, some etirees can play an advisory role in civic affairs. Councils from several cities such as La Roche-sur-Yon, Mulhouse, Pressagny l'Orgueilleux) formed a ederation (Actes du Colloque de la Roche-sur-Yon 1992) and organized a irst national meeting.

Each council has been created in a specific local context. Significantly, one of the first such councils was set up in 1989 in the village of Saint-Coulitz, Brittany, whose mayor (Kofi Yamgnane) was of Togolese origins and, at the ime, Minister of Social Affairs. The aim was to adapt the African tradition of bringing the village's 'sages' to talk together about the practical and moral questions concerning the community (Salon 1993). Other such councils have come into existence, but not just as the direct result of a policy decided at the national level. They have been born in a special context and have their own specific ways of operating. However, the objective is to enable older people to devote their free time to civic affairs. This sort of social usefulness s a response to the need felt by some retirees to be involved in local life and o acquire a place in society – not just a consumer statistic or a voice making demands.

These councils have been criticized as 'political gadgets'. The fact that they are near municipal authorities breeds suspicion about how autonomous heir actions can be. None the less they are, indeed, a new – though not yet widespread – phenomenon that reflects the determination to change the role and place of retirees in society. At this local level, older people may be able to transcend institutional or political affiliations. Unlike traditional retiree organizations, these councils have sprung up in various fields depending on he problems existing at the communal level. Their actions move beyond the polarity between pressing demands and the organization of leisure activities.

Unlike the interest groups in our typology these councils do not have the objective of advancing the interests of older people as an identified age group. On the contrary, they see retirement as a relation to others in civic affairs. The age criterion yields to a more intergenerational conception of social bonds. As our surveys in the field have shown, the retirees on such councils have shifted the focus of their preoccupations and interests away from the individual and towards the general interest (Argoud 1991). In this way their conceptions of old age change deeply. The older person's identity as a social actor is no longer defined as the unilateral beneficiary of services: retirees acquire civic rights by participating in social affairs. Significantly, the persons in these surveys define themselves not as 'older people' but as citizens'.

## The major barriers to political participation

At present, there are 11 million retirees in France: they make up 20 per cent of the population and a third of the electorate. This political potential leads us to inquire into the reasons accounting for this age group's apparent underrepresentation in political decision making. Withdrawal from the world of work marks the start of a period of participation in associations, especially among men (Gallard and Argoud 1995). Quite gradually, older people withdraw from the activities organized by associations: the pace of this withdrawal speeds up only after the age of 79. The problems related to dependence are the first cause of this withdrawal from social activities politics (Thomas 1996).

According to the statistics quoted in Subileau (1995), senior citizens go to vote in large numbers. In 1988, the percentage of persons not registered to vote was 9 per cent, ranging from 26 per cent among 19 to 20-year-olds to 4 per cent among persons over 65. Likewise, turnout at the polls varied from 32 per cent for 25 to 34-year-olds to 12 per cent for persons over 65. Turnout begins gradually to decrease only after the age of 75.

In fact, the impediments to political participation have less to do with older people's social characteristics than with the socially recognized place granted to them. According to a survey conducted by the councils of sages, 72 per cent of French people would like older people to be regularly consulted in local affairs. But only 26 per cent of local elected officials hold this same opinion (Michel 1990). For local officeholders, such councils could eventually turn out to be counterbalancing powers. Besides, older people are already present in local and national politics – not as an identified group but as officeholders. For instance, 32.5 per cent of mayors in France are between 60 and 69 years of age. After the age of 70, their ranks shrink to 9.3 per cent (Paillat 1995). Given their availability, older people are inclined to run for election. In fact, the percentage of older people among mayors has increased significantly: from 15.3 per cent following local elections in 1977 to 23.7 per cent in 1989.

The highest officeholders at the national level are over 60 years old: the president of the Republic, senators, the top justices in the judiciary (Cour de Comptes, Cour de Cassation and Conseil d'Etat). In fact, the members of the constitutional high court (Conseil Constitutionnel) are among the oldest officeholders: their average age is near 70 (Véron 1995).

## The future of old age politics

If we restrict the notion of intergenerational equity to equal monetary transfers between generations (or age groups), we clearly observe that older people in most developed countries have reached an average income level comparable with that of other age groups. This success is definitely attributable to the welfare state, particularly to retirement systems. But the price older people have paid for being well-off turns out to be their marginal dependent social status. To assess intergenerational equity, globally other parameters must be taken into account: static, synchronic ones based on age groups, as well as more dynamic, diachronic ones referring to generations (Guillemard 1990).

When one assesses intergenerational equity it is misleading not to take into account the ways work and free time – not just monetary resources – have been redistributed between generations. During the past 20 years in most developed countries, the labour force participation rate of persons over age 55 has dropped, and young people are entering the labour market later. Overall, we can conclude that working life is contracting to middle age. This trend sheds new light on the debate about intergenerational equity. Employnent policies, compensation for early withdrawal from the labour force, the integration of young people in both society and the world of work: these are the topics that should be the focus of any analysis of intergenerational equity. 'Winners' and 'losers' in such a focus are not likely to be the same as those in studies that have addressed monetary transfers between generations via the welfare state.

In fact, the increasing number of intermediate statuses apparently corresponds to a change in entitlement. First of all, the older wage earner's right to a job has been restricted. Second, the eligibility requirements for welfare benefits have changed. For instance, social security systems provide general coverage for universal risks. After contributing the required number of years and reaching a certain age, one is entitled to a pension. All French citizens know that they will automatically have a full pension, once they have contributed to the Old Age Fund for between 37.5 and 40 years and have reached the age of 60. In contrast, the conditions for admission to the intermediate statuses between 'wage earner' and 'retiree' are neither universal nor stable. Fluctuating with circumstances, they are continually modified. For instance, the status of 'unemployed' does not inevitably lead to retirement.

Under the intermediate early exit arrangements, beneficiaries have very restricted 'rights' in comparison with entitlement under social security. A person who falls victim to the covered risk is not necessarily eligible right away, but only if society decides to provide coverage. This trend in welfare makes us doubt whether today's young retirees are 'winners'. At least, they pay for this period of non-work through their precarious status. These fluctuating intermediate statuses have set off an identity crisis. Few 'early exiters' think of themselves as retirees. Instead, they claim to be jobless or, in many cases, 'discouraged wage earners', with no hope of finding an opening in the labour market (Guillemard 1986).

The end of people's working life also comprises intermediate phases in which they have no fully fledged status: they are neither exactly jobless, employed nor retired. Many older wage earners are dismissed and then go on unemployment benefit; some of them benefit from special arrangements. They may find an unstable job and then go back on unemployment benefit before being admitted into the retirement system. If benefits are reduced and the retirement age is increased, as is now happening, then 'pre-retirees' will fully join young people in the role of 'welfare recipient' or in the even more precarious position of being ineligible for any public support.

Deinstitutionalizing the end of the life course not only keeps people from foreseeing how their lives will evolve, but it also upsets the system of reciprocity between generations. Uncertainty encompasses both retirement and the underlying long-term contract. What are the prospects for this long-term contract, which binds successive generations together? One cannot count on the reciprocity of commitments across generations in a society where the life course no longer has a long run marked by standard chronological milestones. People still working are beginning to doubt whether the coming generation will pay for their pensions as willingly as they are now paying for current retirees' pensions. The temporal strategy underlying this transfer implies delaying compensation for the alienation of work in exchange for the right to rest at a later stage. But the motivations behind this strategy are weakening, because the life course no longer places individuals in a foreseeable continuum.

For younger generations it is no longer evident that retirement will continue to organize the life course and regulate social transfers. Young people are less likely than older or middle-aged people to be able to foresee a continuous career that ends in retirement. They also have the least secure position in the labour market, therefore they see more keenly than other generations the contradictions between (on the one hand) organizing social transfers on the basis of a stable wage-earning relationship and an immutable life course and (on the other) increasing flexibility, both in the life course and in labour management, as a response to changes in the labour market.

The intergenerational retirement contract should not be reduced to a mechanized demographic/economic explanation for arguing that the current system is too costly to sustain. Cultural changes in perceptions of time and of the future are just as important in explaining the prospects of this intergenerational contract. They also help us to understand why questions about the retirement system's future are now being raised in such bold terms.

The distribution of jobs between generations does not support arguments about intergenerational injustice. Although early exit has often been based on the principle of redistributing work as older wage earners 'make room' for unemployed youth, such policies have yielded meagre results. The middle-aged have fared best in the labour market, whereas more and more of the young and old are precariously covered under diverse welfare programmes.

## Note

1  The circular of 7 April 1982 provides for the voluntary establishment of regional committees for pensioners and older people (*conférences régionales des retraités et personnes âgées*) at the regional head offices of the health and social affairs offices.

# 7

# The politics of old age in Germany

GERHARD NAEGELE

n the past, neither political science nor social science in general have been nterested in the participation of older people in politics in Germany. However, in the past 10 to 15 years we have observed a noticeable change n public awareness concerning older people's political attitudes, voting behaviour and their overall participation in political life. In the wake of demographic change and the enormous change in the age structure of the population, the proportion of older persons among voters, members of political parties, trade unions or other political or semi-political organizations is constantly rising. Germany's senior citizens have risen to the ranks of a significant political power but – up to now – they have not been playing this role effectively. Today, their political power is more latent than active.

The demographic structure of the German population has changed enormously since 1900. The proportion of those aged 60 and over – approximately 8 per cent in 1900 – has increased to more than 20 per cent in the mid-1990s. Future models suggest that the German population, excluding migration, will decrease dramatically in the next few decades, with an increase in the number of older people to more than 30 per cent in 2020.

One consequence of the rising numbers of older people is the considerable and ever increasing pressure on the political elite groups in Germany. Yet the role senior citizens play in today's political life and in established political bodies stands in sharp contrast to their increasing latent political power as well as their demographic importance. There is a significant underrepresentation of older people in Parliament and executive boards of the political parties, with the figure dropping even lower among those over 70. Although those members of the different parties aged 60 and over now make up between 20 per cent and 29 per cent, the number of older people in parlia-

ment itself is decreasing. In 1994 for example, only 3 per cent of th
members of the German Bundestag (the lower house of Parliament), wer
aged over 65.

In the current discussion concerning demographic change in German
which affects nearly all aspects of daily life (Deutscher Bundestag 1994), th
low level of political representation of older persons is increasingly consid
ered to be unsatisfactory. More and more politicians, political scientists
gerontologists and other key figures who mainly represent Germany's intel
lectual elite, voice the critical opinion that the needs of older people are no
well represented in politics, given the percentage of the population made u
by older people. Thus decisions concerning older citizens are mainly mad
by younger politicians who are often criticized for their lack of sufficien
knowledge of the situation and the needs of older people. It also seems tha
political power among the older members of the population is only devel
oping quite slowly. Nevertheless, we still do not know whether thi
evidence is only reflecting a short-term effect or whether it is the beginnin
of a new stage in the role played by older people in the history of politics i
Germany.

However, at the same time one can see within certain groups of the polit
ical and intellectual elite a strong hope and belief that the so-called 'politica
exclusion of older people' will soon be confined to the past. One coul
assume that not only older people would benefit from this but that it woul
also be a step forward for society as a whole. However, since at presen
Germany's senior citizens themselves – with the exception of certain minori
ties – do not support this idea, it cannot be called a grassroots movement a
all. Despite this, the following arguments in favour of this notion are ver
often used.

First, the active political participation of older persons is regarded as
cohort effect. Presumably future generations of older Germans will be mor
experienced in democratic culture and thus more open minded in their polit
ical activities. Furthermore, they will show a stronger wish to represent thei
age-related needs and interests themselves, leading almost automatically t
an increasing desire for political self-determination. Among other things, thi
is also seen as the result of a higher level of knowledge and education, o
better economic resources and of improved health in general, compared t
preceding generations.

Second, increasing differentiation within society can be characterized i
terms of a differentiation of interests and needs. This also affects older persons
The more age-related needs and interests develop as a result of demographi
change and the extension of the retirement phase, the more older people loo
for adequate forms of representation in public and political life.

Third, older people's lifestyles are changing and life expectancy continue
to increase. Old age has been promoted to an independent phase of life in it
own right. These factors would not match up with the role of an older perso
as a politically inactive citizen. Furthermore, a new way of looking at old ag
is gaining ground: the 'active senior citizen'. This does not correspond to
person who more or less leaves it to others to pursue his or her political an
social needs and requirements.

Fourth, there is widespread criticism of the predominant practices of political representation in Germany. The established political bodies are supposed to represent the needs of the population as a whole, yet they primarily pursue their own economic interests or other demands. This is to the disadvantage of socially underprivileged groups, in particular, and thus also affects older people. Consequently, people are placing their hopes more and more in the self-representation of their needs and interests.

Fifth, in Germany, the increasing difficulties of the welfare state primarily affect older persons. Social services for all age groups are being reduced. This may perhaps provoke severe distributional conflicts within the population. As a consequence, it is feared that generation conflicts, as they are already known in the United States and which were previously completely unknown in Germany will be part of the future political agenda. This would inevitably lead to a build-up of resistance on the part of older people. In order to be successful, it would also result in a stronger desire to be represented more effectively by members of their own age group.

When listing these arguments, which are used as a whole to underline the necessity of more effective political representation of the needs and interests of older people, the social ambivalence of greater political power for this group must not be neglected either. In the last few years especially, the increasing 'silent power' of older people has been criticized by the younger and/or working generation in particular, who on the basis of the 'generation contract' would have to pay for the older population (Schüller 1995, 1997). Against the background of greater power among senior citizens, it is feared that the younger generations may be disadvantaged and thus become one of the losers in the process of the distribution of diminishing public resources.

In discussing the improvement in the participation of older people in politics, we must first look at the specific tasks and aims of policies for this group. In general, policies for older people can be understood as the sum of those public measures which aim at setting up adequate frameworks which allow older persons to live independently and autonomously according to their own personal needs and interests (Dieck 1996). In the past, policies concerning older people in Germany were primarily considered to be a part of social welfare politics. However, several recent publications define these policies in a broader sense. They are regarded as an independent branch of politics with their own rights which interprets the affairs of senior citizens in cross-sectional terms (Holz 1993). At least two significant dimensions of policies for older people should be mentioned in detail.

The first dimension concerns the question of who should make policies for older people. Here again, two distinctions can be made. First, policies for senior citizens in Germany have previously mainly been made by professional politicians or within responsible administration boards, as well as by the federal or county ministries for social and/or family affairs, local authorities, big welfare organizations and so on. As a rule, however, those making the decisions, even in politics, are not older members of the population themselves. As a matter of fact, older decision makers and makers of policies for older people in Germany are still in a clear minority. These types of 'policies for older people' can be described as 'representative policies' since, as a rule, older persons themselves are neither involved in the development of concepts and strategies nor in their implementation. A particular sub-type which has recently gained ground in Germany is the one of policy advisory services by experts. These experts very often come from the field of science and research (for example gerontologists, economists, sociologists) (Holz 1993); very few or none came from the group of older people themselves or their official representatives.

A more recent view is taken from the model of political self-determination and makes a plea for a more active role for older people in politics. The basic idea is that policies for older people should ideally be made by senior citizens themselves or at least by their official representatives because of their experience as those directly affected, i.e. 'experts in their own affairs'. In this context, we have to look for adequate and effective forms of participation for senior citizens (Evers *et al.* 1993). Since the end of the 1970s, special forms of representation for older people have been established, such as senior citizens' councils, parliaments or advisory boards. In the meantime, the larger political parties have also established special departments for senior citizens (for example the Senioren-Union within the Christian Democratic Union (CDU) and the working group '60+' within the Social Democratic Party (SPD)). A special party of senior citizens (Die Grauen, The Grey Party) was even founded in the late 1980s, which expressly claims to pursue the political interests of senior citizens. So far, however, with the exception of some spectacular showings, the party has had no noteworthy successes (see below). As a whole, only a very small minority of Germany's older population can be counted as evidence of the beginning of political power for older people.

The second dimension is the question of which target groups of senior citizens' policies should be aimed at. Some commentators believe – a view also shared by the author – that policies should not be aimed primarily at senior citizens or their needs and interests *as such* but should focus on those subgroups within the older population who, from a socio-political point of view, are exposed to age-related risks and social problems. According to this theory, significant target groups would be, for example, older workers who are excluded from the labour market, older migrants, impoverished women or those rising numbers of older persons in need of care (Holz 1993; Dieck 1996). The significant question here – and this is something which is currently being discussed in Germany – is whether the needs and interests of those vulnerable groups could be represented in a more effective way by the so-called 'representative model' or by the model of political self-determination (see below).

## Political behaviour of older people in Germany

As a rule, the political behaviour of the population can be defined as belonging to either conventional or unconventional forms (Olk 1997). The first group primarily covers the degree of political interest as such, namely voting behaviour and memberships of political parties, associations, executive boards, parliaments and so on. The second group covers, for example, active participation in demonstrations, strikes, the collecting of signatures or the public denunciation of social injustice. On the basis of this distinction, the predominant model of political behaviour can be described as one where there is polarization within the conventional forms and clear underrepresentation within the unconventional forms. With regard to the conventional forms, older people are characterized by a very high degree of clear political interests and a voting attendance which is well above average on the one hand, but by less active political commitment, even as member of a political party, on the other. As far as the unconventional forms of political behaviour are concerned, hardly any senior citizens, except for very small minorities, are politically active.

*Turnout at elections*

Germany's senior citizens show the highest turnout of the whole population. In 1994, the figure for those aged between 60 and 70 was 86 per cent, whereas the average figure for all those entitled to vote was only 76 per cent. Although there is a remarkable decrease in the case of voters above 70, the turnout of the very old is still higher than of those aged between 18 and 30. Bearing in mind that in Germany the entitlement to vote is given at the age of 18, older people currently represent nearly 30 per cent of all persons entitled to vote and more than 30 per cent of all those who voted. Against the background of demographic change, it is estimated that this figure will be 40 per cent in 2030 (Holz 1993; Alber 1994). In other words, electoral victories and defeats in Germany are being more and more decided by its senior citizens. The more the turnout rate decreases, as has been the case in Germany since 1992 – mainly due to the behaviour of younger voters – the more decisive the votes of older people become.

The high turnout of older persons in Germany is usually interpreted by political scientists as proof of their excessively strong belief that representative democracy is working. In turn, this is considered to be based on the fact that Germany's senior citizens have been able up to now to rely on their interests being represented (and realized) in the best possible way by the welfare state and, although to a far less degree, by the big welfare organizations. Therefore, at least in the past, Germany's older citizens did not need a particular 'senior citizens' lobby' because they could count on the efficiency and financial strength of the public authorities. Strong senior citizens' lobbies, comparable with the AARP in the United States, can usually be found in countries with inferior or less developed social security systems (Kohli *et al.* 1994). This, in turn, gives rise to two questions which will be taken up later. Are there any age-related needs at all, beyond the level of social security, which could one day also promote a particular 'senior citizens' lobby', in line with the US model? Second, is it feasible that a powerful 'senior citizens' lobby' is developing at present, against the background of the financial difficulties confronting the German welfare system and to a large degree affecting the social security of older people (for example the decision taken in 1997 concerning the considerable reduction in public pensions)?

*Party support*

Although representative opinion polls reveal a considerable proportion of 14 per cent to 25 per cent of older Germans who would welcome a particular party for older people (Kohli *et al.* 1997), the election results of 'Die Grauen', the only 'grey' political party in Germany (see below), have repeatedly shown in the past that there is a great discrepancy between voters' opinions and their actual voting behaviour: in 1994, 'Die Grauen' got a share of 0.8 per cent (400,000) of all votes, but the relevant data reveal that only about 1.5 per cent of the population aged 60 and over voted for the 'Grey Party'.

For nearly 40 years, all election results in Germany have shown that the majority of persons aged 60 and over regularly vote for conservative parties (Christian Democratic Union/Christian Social Union – CDU/CSU). The Social Democratic Party (SPD), Free Democratic Party (FDP) and Alliance 90/Green Party (Bündnis 90/Die Grünen) – with the two latter parties well behind in the list – regularly lose votes among the older population. An above-average proportion of older women, who make up about two thirds of all persons aged 60 and over in Germany, favour the CDU/CSU. Furthermore, older voters are characterized by strong party affiliation. They also change between established parties, whereas new political parties have had little chance up to now of attracting older voters. In East Germany, however, the situation is different: here, an above-average number of older men give their votes to the SPD (Holz 1993; Roth and Emmert 1994; Kohli *et al.* 1997).

Not only their actual voting behaviour but also their political opinions as a whole are evidence of a conservative-based attitude among older Germans. When looking for the differences between younger and older persons, the following basic values among older people can be found: financial security and wealth, internal and external security, economic growth and traditional virtues such as discipline or a sense of duty. The basic values of the younger German population differ quite considerably. For them, post-materialistic values such as the quality of life or environmental aims are predominant.

There are two opposing interpretations to explain the more basic conservative values of the older population in Germany, but on the basis of our research we are not able to say for sure which is the most reliable (Tews 1987, 1996). Political scientists answer 'both are as good as each other' when asked to decide between them. On the one hand, the cohort thesis considers the historical experiences of today's older Germans to be responsible. In extrapolating this assumption, it might be likely that future groups of older persons could change their conservative political behaviour as a result of a longer experience of democratic culture and may therefore also show more 'left-wing' attitudes. This is expected, in particular, when the so-called '68 generation', which claimed to democratize public life in Germany at the end of the 1960s, reaches old age. Consequently, we will have the opportunity in a few years' time to examine in greater detail whether the cohort thesis has substance or not.

By contrast, the life-cycle thesis states that basic conservative attitudes are naturally linked with the ageing process. In other words, when reaching the later stages of life, people quite naturally tend to become more conservative because they 'simply have more to conserve' (Tews 1987). A third explanation from the UK is also worth mentioning: according to the so-called selection thesis, conservative parties have more success among the older population since the traditional voters for left-wing parties, the male working class members, die earlier (Kohli *et al.* 1997).

Looking at the future there are good reasons to assume that tomorrow's older population might tend to be as conservative as older people living now, because there will be more women, a higher level of knowledge and education, and a further decline in the working class population. On the other hand, the younger population's party ties continue to decline, which could be considered as a sure sign of support for the CDU/CSU. This may then help to compensate for the above-mentioned cohort effects.

*Membership of political parties*

With the exception of the FDP and Alliance 90/The Greens, the proportion of older members in the five parties represented in the lower house of parliament (Deutscher Bundestag) is at present higher than the proportion of elderly persons in the population: today, about one third of CDU members, about 30 per cent of SPD members and even about 40 per cent of PDS (Democratic Socialist Party) members are aged 60 and over. However, as already mentioned, there is a strong contrast between membership and the active representation in the respective executive bodies or in parliament. Of the current members of the lower house of parliament, only 3.3 per cent are 65 years and older and only 10.9 per cent are 60 and above. On the other hand, however, clear underrepresentation of the younger generation can also be observed. The majority of members of all forms of German parliaments is aged between 35 and 60. This leads us to the question of whether the older members have been replaced or have left of their own accord. There is no research material available to provide an answer to this question. In any case, it seems to be an unwritten law in politics that reaching official retirement age means retiring from positions held up to that age. Sometimes, it is also assumed that leading figures of the parties pressurize older members into going, in order to make way for applicants climbing up the political ladder. In addition, one can see with older politicians, in particular, that the daily business is exhausting. The result is that many are forced to resign as a result of excessive stress and for health reasons.

*Senior citizens in trade unions*

Although trade unions traditionally do not like to be regarded as representatives of the needs and interests of older people, they have in fact – involuntarily – been promoted to one of the most powerful senior citizens' associations. In spite of demographic change and the enormous pre-retirement programmes in the past, a lot of union members are now pensioners, who are still entitled to continue their membership of their former trade union. Currently Germany's trade unions have more than 1.7 million members who are retired people, i.e. about 18 per cent of all union members. This figure is steadily increasing. The proportion varies widely among the different types of unions. There are very 'old' unions like IG-Metall, which represents the workers of the iron and steel industry, or IG Bergbau und Energie, which represents workers in the mining and energy industry. Each of these unions receives about a third of all shares of the vote from older members. There are also very 'young' unions such as the GEW (teachers and scientists), with a share of less than 5 per cent of members aged 60 and over (Ristau and Mackroth 1993; Kohli *et al.* 1997)

Hence it was just a question of time before the unions were forced to examine the issue regarding the future role retired people would play in an association which traditionally focuses on the world of employment and which usually pursues the aims of the working class. The issue is still under discussion. Following the example of the political parties, the trade unions do not grant their retired persons' organizations their own rights either. Some of them, in the meantime, have automatically established a seat and a right to vote in their executive bodies or in other significant bodies where union work is practised. Thus, for the trade unions, the term 'latent senior citizens' power' is used as well. The real policy making within the unions, however, even if affairs relating to older people are concerned (e.g. pension politics), takes place without the official participation of older members or their official representatives (Künemund 1994).

This, however, does not mean that union members who are retired citizens would not be involved in any practical work at all. For example, many political and very often socio-political events or conferences are organized by active, older union members; older members canvass new members, produce newsletters or look after members who are ill or in need of help.

In spite of all that, and despite a remarkable amount of latent power, the fact remains that the trade unions have not yet found an official answer to the contemporary demographic challenges confronting their associations. In this context, there are an increasing number of pleas from (mainly) scientists – who are emotionally linked to trade union work – to quickly take organizational measures to provide the opportunity for older members. If action is not taken quickly, Germany's trade unions may already lose ground in the initial phase of the development of real power for senior citizens in the future. Unless older members are integrated in a more effective way than is being done currently, it may well be seen as a historical fault – comparable to the difficulties Germany's trade unions faced when dealing with 'white collar' workers (Kohli *et al.* 1994; Künemund 1994).

## The political representation of older people in Germany

Older people in the Federal Republic of Germany have no genuine, active political power. However, there are examples and signs that the political interests of older people are beginning to become more noticeable in Germany too. Some authors are already speaking of a political activism of this group (Neckel 1993). The following section discusses whether these political initiatives and political patterns really do represent the new political power of older people – i.e. 'the older, politically active citizen' – or whether they actually stand for a 'political mobilization of this group from the top' rather than a mobilization from the bottom, as many of their representatives claim. I will examine the most important of the newest examples of the heteronomous political organization or self-organization of older people.

*Senior citizens' councils and representations*

Local senior citizens' councils and representative agencies were first formed in 1972 and are now rather widespread, mainly in the new German Länder. (The term 'SR' is used in the following text for all the various synonyms of senior citizens' representation.) At the beginning of 1997, there were more than 700 SRs in urban and rural communities, which, however, is still a notable minority when compared to the almost 15,000 cities, districts and communities (Schweitzer 1996). Due to the lack of legal foundations, communities in Germany are free to decide whether or not SRs are to be set up. The existing SRs are brought together in 17 senior citizens' representative bodies in the Länder, which in turn have been included since 1996 in the federal representative body for senior citizens (Mayer 1994). There is an estimated total of some 7,000 people involved in such activities, all of them on a voluntary basis.

Only in very few cases were local SRs founded by older citizens of a community. Usually, they are set up – if not appointed – by others, i.e. the local political elite, and often even by the local authorities, to serve older people (Tews 1987). This can also be seen in the forms of constitution, where we can differentiate between three basic types (Kühnert and Gloddeck 1996). *Direct election*: all senior members of the respective community are asked to elect their representatives. This form of constitution, however, is the exception to the rule. In the past only minorities participated in the relevant elections. *Election through delegates*: older people vote for their delegates in accordance with a special voting method. Delegates are appointed by all institutions for older people, such as voluntary welfare care, the communities, voluntary supporters, self-help groups or other meetings for older people. Every delegate is entitled to vote. The delegates organize a meeting where the senior citizens' representative body is elected. *Delegation through appointment*: the communities select older persons and appoint them as senior representatives. Associations of voluntary welfare as well as of the political parties, homes for older people, syndicates, etc. name their members, who can be appointed by the communities afterwards.

The second and third forms of constitution are the most common ones in practice. As a result, those working in SRs are mainly people who are already closely affiliated with the existing local political elite or organizations and syndicates anyway. This is also reflected in the members of staff who make up the SRs: retired politicians and syndicate officials or formerly full-time administrative employees, etc: that is, people with experience in local politics are highly overrepresented, while political newcomers are in a minority.

According to the SRs themselves, their aim is to represent the interests of older people in their area and to refer their wishes and claims to local governments and administrations – acting according to their self-designated status as experts in their own interests. At the same time, experts view this as an important motive for founding an SR. SRs are often seen as a reaction to the unsatisfactory representation of older people in local governments and committees. Consequently, their existence is often taken as a sign of the failure of local politics to represent effectively the interests and wishes of senior citizens.

The activities of local SRs can be summarized as follows (Reggentin and Dettban-Reggentin 1990; Kühnert and Gloddeck 1996): planning of activities in the field of leisure, culture and education; supporting older people who are in need of advice and help (e.g. senior counselling, organization of services and help, home visits, neighbour support); community work and information services (e.g. of new laws, local activities, new scientific discoveries relevant to older people); attempts to improve housing and living conditions in local older people's homes and nursing homes by representing the interests of the occupants; participation in the local planning of social affairs, traffic matters and building projects, also by representing the interests of older people involved; political participation in the sense of advising the decision-making local bodies as well as attempting to influence them (e.g. through parliamentary initiatives, inquiries concerning locally relevant subjects).

The actual political power of SRs depends to a great extent on the local conditions and opportunities, which can vary throughout Germany according to how willing communities are to set up SRs. Not only the forms of constitution vary considerably from community to community, but also the tasks appointed to them, their rights to act, their financial and infrastructural means (such as facilities, telephones and so on). There are, for example, communities which automatically involve senior citizens' councils – since they are 'well-informed citizens' – in social committees, which are generally in charge of the politics and work concerning older people. The by-laws of other communities state that SRs have to be invited to participate in meetings of all committees which deal with topics relevant to older members of the community, even if only indirectly. On the other hand, there are also communities to which none of the above applies and which are even run by the local administration (Schweitzer 1996).

Depending on the composition of members of the SR, their course of action is considered to be 'instrumental' in that they are focused on the cause and represent a functional approach to work concerning senior citizens. A style of politics prevails which aims not at representing the interests in an expressive and conflict-oriented way, but rather at 'low-profile politics' which avoids conflicts. It is not directed at pointing out scandals, but rather at 'co-operating with those in charge of political and administrative matters concerning the older generation'. According to this view, senior citizens' representatives from politics and the administration want to be accepted as legitimate representatives of the interests of older people. 'They strive for competence as experts in their own affairs' (Kohli *et al.* 1997: 20).

Local SRs usually work outside or alongside the established bodies representing the interests of older people and their practical implementation in public life. That is to say, they coexist beside local parliaments and committees, where the actual decisions important to local politics are made. However, the by-laws of the communities in Germany do not actually allow for a stronger right of participation and decision making. This right is retained by the representatives who were elected to parliaments and committees in proper democratic elections. Thus the SRs have basically the same rights of participation to which all citizens are entitled.

Many SRs will not content themselves with what in their view is the inadequate right of political participation, which among experts is regarded even as the main reason for their lack of efficiency. Therefore there are attempts currently being made by the amalgamations of SRs to change the by-laws in such a way that SRs are given more rights. However, the fact remains that the exclusion from decision making which is stated in the by-laws does not necessarily mean a *de facto* exclusion from the process of opinion forming in local politics. This is prevented by the 'natural proximity' of many members of SRs to the parties represented in the parliaments or local charitable organizations, which are equally strongly represented. Moreover, the by-laws offer numerous rights of participation which are open to the SRs as well, though seldom used by them. However, 'the greater the participation in the decision-making becomes, the more acute is the question of the democratic legitimacy of the persons involved' (Schulte 1996: 226). This is because, for reasons of democracy, only the ones elected through the SRs have the right to represent the interests of older people and put them into action on a political level. Yet even here the extremely low participation in the elections is seen by many as evidence of a lack of legitimacy.

At present, it is impossible to make an empirically safe statement about the practical function of SRs. There are no surveys available in the sense of a social-scientific evaluation of their practical work or the question of their actual achievements on the spot (alone or primarily). Reports issued by the SRs themselves are not regarded as suitable, partly because they do not always differentiate exactly between programmatic objectives and effects (Tews 1996).

Public discussion on this subject, however, is even more controversial (Deutscher Bundestag 1994). There are many examples of successful work, but there are also some which show laziness and lack of success. The main point of criticism is that SRs, due to their proximity to the established political bodies and administrations, are too deeply embedded in the dominant local structures. Hence they have been accused on many occasions of being merely 'the extended arm of local senior politics', of being superficial and not legitimate representatives of the interests of the older generation. Experience has also shown that it is not so much the formally safe patterns of action or regulation that count in the process of actually promoting these interests, but rather, success in pushing through rights for older people comes from making every possible effort, by making oneself heard, by being persistent and by doing public relations work. Many experts believe that the actual criterion for measuring the true meaning of SRs lies in their practical achievements and not in their wide area-coverage or numerous new foundations – as their official representatives like to emphasize again and again.

*Federal Associations of Senior Citizens' Organizations (BAGSO)*

BAGSO was founded in 1989 as a federal association of senior citizens' organizations. It is an amalgamation of independent organizations; it aims to do independent work for senior citizens on a federal level. In other words, its goal is to serve as a forum to bring together affairs concerning older people throughout the country, and to organize and represent them efficiently in public (Neubauer 1994). It sees itself as a 'forum of different approaches to working with older people and articulating their affairs in order to do advisory work on all levels of older people's politics' (BAGSO 1996: 4). BAGSO receives financial support in the form of government funds. Special features of its work are the organization of big annual conventions (Deutscher Seniorentag) and its own publication programme. Otherwise, their (political) statements are more confined to general discourses on daily political issues like 'independent living', 'voluntary work in old age', etc. In addition to its financial dependence on the federal Ministry for Families, Senior Citizens, Women and Youth, this is presumably a sign of the heterogeneous, non-party composition of its members, making it very unlikely that a real forum for the political interests of older people will be established, when anything more than just making political statements is required.

Today, BAGSO consists of 47 organizations, syndicates and institutions, most of them in the fields of health, social affairs, employment, culture and politics, which represent more than 8 million older people in all. Its organizations are extremely varied, such as for example, 'older vegetarians' or the 'federal association of older dancers' and organizations like the federal senior citizen representative body 60+, the Senioren-Union and the federal senior committee of the German Union of Employees (Deutsche Angestellten Gewerkschaft). As with the senior citizens' representative bodies, a systematic evaluation of BAGSO's work and its actual influence in senior politics is not yet available.

*Special sections within the political parties*

It has already been mentioned that both the CDU and SPD have established special sections for senior citizens. But so far they seem to be fighting more for better appreciation by the membership than actually influencing effectively the main party politics.

*Senioren-Union (CDU)*

In 1979, the Senioren-Union was founded in Baden-Württemberg and expanded to include the rest of the country in 1988. Membership of the CDU/CSU is not essential for becoming a member of the Senioren-Union, yet there are very strong ties of membership and leading positions shared between both of them. In fact, many of the Senioren-Union members used to be active party members and leading party figures who have resigned from active politics. At present, the Senioren-Union has between 50,000 and 65,000 members. Apart from the fact that there is no obligatory right for representatives of the Senioren-Union to participate actively in the process of policy making within the executive boards (Central Committee) of the CDU/CSU, they lack an effective infrastructure of their own and are thus dependent on the parent party's support.

Their own political aims are officially described as being the desire to influence the process of practical policy making within the parent party, according to the needs and interests of the older population. The representative model, based on the idea of political expertise concerning older people, characterizes its activities according to the official self-declaration. Despite this, neutral political scientists emphasize that the Senioren-Union has in fact no philosophy of its own but is more or less completely embedded in the political aims of its parent party. The Senioren-Union was therefore supposed to have been founded merely in order to attract older voters by showing the public that representatives of the older population were among their own ranks. Critics make the assumption that the Senioren-Union itself represents nothing more than an extension of the CDU without any profile of its own (Neckel 1993).

## 60+ (SPD)

In contrast to the Senioren-Union, the SPD hesitated for nearly 15 years before establishing its own group for senior citizens. Before 60+ was founded in 1992, so-called senior citizen commissioners had been responsible for the representation of the interests of older party members within all subsections of the SPD since the end of the 1970s. Until 1992, the general belief among leading figures of the SPD was that they should not establish their own senior citizens' department, in order to avoid separating older party members organizationally, and thus also in their political work, from the rest of the party. The senior commissioners were automatically members of all important SPD executive bodies. They represented an integrated policy concept. Its basic idea was to avoid a division of political interests which would neither tally with the idea of a people's party, nor would it be in line with the wish of most of the older party members themselves.

This basic attitude lasted about 15 years until active older party members themselves pleaded for a change of this status and for a department of their own, in the same as way young people (the Jungsozialisten) or women (Arbeitsgemeinschaft sozialdemokratischer Frauen) already had. One of the driving forces behind this was that there was also an insufficient number of older SPD members in the executive boards and in parliament, in proportion to their share of the vote. The foundation of such a special senior citizens' department was therefore considered as an instrument for improving the chances of older applicants of gaining leading positions in executive boards or seats in parliament. At the time, this was consistent with the great concerns of leading figures of the SPD that they may lose ground with the electorate as a result of demographic change, bearing in mind the success which the CDU/CSU had repeatedly notched up among older voters. Also it must be noted that the SPD was the first of the main political parties in

Germany to begin serious discussion on the social consequences of demographic change. It even established its own commission for dealing with demographic affairs which was ranked just below the board of the party. It would therefore have appeared strange for it to present itself to the public (and to the voters) as one of the leading groups in society while excluding older people from its ranks (Ristau and Mackroth 1993).

In contrast to the Senioren-Union, all members of the SPD aged 60 and over automatically become members of 60+, but even younger members are welcome to join. The basic political aim of 60+ is to guarantee that policies within the SPD are also made *by* older people themselves and not just *for* them. A further obvious contrast can be made here between 60+ and the Senioren-Union: 60+ does not deal merely with issues relating specifically to older people but tries to integrate the views of older people into all branches of politics, not just in the traditional domain of social politics. Furthermore, 60+ is said to be more effective in making publicity and organizing public campaigns, political events and conferences, publishing books and brochures (not only on issues concerning older people) and consistently campaigns for the right of political self-determination for the older population (Ristau and Mackroth 1993). Nevertheless, it is fact that also the SPD has now established its own department for older members and thus risks segregating them politically.

### The Grey Panthers and The Greys

The examples of political activity for older people in Germany shown so far can basically be regarded as instances of the political mobilization of older people 'from above'. Elements of a movement 'from the bottom' can, at best, be observed within the SPD with the foundation of 60+ or in the attempts of individual trade unions to increase participation of older members. This does not apply to the Grey Panthers and the party founded by them, The Greys. For many, both of them are a prime example of the political activism of older people themselves.

The older people's action group, the Grey Panthers, was founded in 1975 as a non-party self-help organization for older people. Data available on the number of members range from 20,000 (estimated by experts) and 100,000 (officially stated). The main aim of the Grey Panthers is to enable older people to lead an independent life as well as protecting them from any form of incapacitation. Accordingly, campaigns by the Grey Panthers aim at promoting the rights of older people by pointing out social problems such as poverty among older women (or other striking examples of particularly bad housing) and living conditions in old people's homes; this is often supported by spectacular actions. Moreover, they establish social political alternatives based on the principle of self-determination in old age (such as a general basic pension) (Schweitzer 1996). However, the Grey Panthers – like The Greys – do not restrict themselves at all to typical matters of old age, but tackle general political topics such as the environment or the peace movement. Their primary motivation, though, is 'increasing public awareness of the social situation and rights of older people by means of revealing scandalous cases of discrimination against older people' (Kohli *et al.* 1997). The number of members alone indicates that their success can only be regarded as very limited. But also their party, The Greys, founded a few years ago, has been leading a miserable political existence for years as a marginal party. In past elections they have never gained more than 2 per cent of the vote.

Contrary to the examples given earlier of the political activism of senior citizens, the political pattern of the Grey Panthers/The Greys can be classified as unconventional (Olk 1997) and aimed at the direct participatory representation of the interests of older people. It thus contrasts sharply with the otherwise prevailing 'representative model'. Internally, this political style is backed up by 'the ritual action pattern'. For instance, this group tends to stress the group identity and family feeling which exists, thereby suggesting elements of a 'sub-culture of old age' (Neckel 1993). This, however, stands in contrast to the fact that, according to their motto 'us today – you tomorrow', the minimum membership age of the Grey Panthers or The Greys is only 18.

## Conclusion

Kohli, Neckel and Wolf (1997) differentiate between three patterns of active political citizenship currently practised by older people in Germany, in which the examples presented above, however, can only partly be included. First there is the instrumentalization of the politics of older people, serving the symbolic purpose of higher-ranking organizations. This applies to the Senioren-Union, BAGSO and partly also to the senior citizens' representative bodies. Second comes the professional politics of interests by specialists and experts, with their limited willingness to face conflicts. This applies especially to the work of the SRs. Third, there is the expressive politics of moral minorities, combining a strong orientation towards the outside while closing ranks at the same time. This is typical for the Grey Panthers/The Greys.

The 60+ in the SPD as well as the senior members of the trade unions cannot be clearly assigned to any of the above. They could partly be represented in all three forms of participation. However, they show, in particular, signs of a clear movement away from their parent organizations and towards the more independent political representation of interests, although still under the same ideological roof. The Grey Panthers/The Greys are probably the best example of the independent political self-organization of older people. What applies to all three of the patterns is the fact that they clearly represent only a minority of older people in Germany.

A first conclusion on the political organization of older people in Germany is that one can observe a distinct discrepancy between the hopes and expectations fostered particularly by parts of the political and intellectual elite, namely that the 'political exclusion of older people' will soon find an end and that there will be actual political participation by this group. The examples given here and the minimal extent to which they are rooted in the older population as a whole make this end appear more unlikely than likely. The above-mentioned theory of a strong faith in the effectiveness of parliamentary democracy, and the belief that the specific concerns and needs of older people will be dealt with by the major political groups, seems to support this. Experience suggests that in spite of what many people hope for, there appears to be no realistic possibility, either in the short or long term, of the independent and autonomous political representation of the interests of older people by older people.

The low level of political activism in the older population itself reinforces the idea that there are obviously only few, if any, typical old people who could be referred to as political. Moreover, numerous surveys confirm that the vast majority of older Germans do not wish to be treated as a special group ('older people') and do not at all identify themselves in such a way, but see themselves instead as an integrated (though older) part of society.

The fact that political activism among senior citizens has been established (even though it seems rather modest when looking at the figures) does not contradict this in principle. With the exception of the Grey Panthers/The Greys, political activism is exercised within the established political opinion-forming structures, but not as an alternative to them. It can for now be explained by a cohort effect, new lifestyles and new role models which are sought by the older people themselves, though without any 'pressure from below'. Moreover, the considerable extension of old age suggests that it has an influence on this increasing search for new role models. It has to be noted, though, that the established political elite groups have actively supported this development and partly used it to their own ends.

What is striking, however, is that some members of the 60+ in the SPD and the older trade union members – but also more and more of the committed members of the new generation of the SRs – are beginning to oppose this instrumentalization and look for an autonomous space for action and rights, and sometimes even find it. However, these initiatives are still not usually directed against the 'parent organization', and never against the established political opinion-forming bodies in Germany. Their aim is, rather, to achieve more openness in the parent organizations or the political patterns which are predominant locally, and to gain more influence within established work structures. In this way, the actions of such groups and (especially) persons can be seen as a criticism of the current – inadequate participatory structures.

The same applies to the SRs. To focus on them as the primary form of representation of the interests of older people would be to disregard the whole range of opportunities within parliament and the parliamentary system. Yet this is the area where older people are underrepresented. SRs potentially isolate the interests of older people into a form of 'special representation', which does not necessarily represent their interests more effectively. Thus, political parties and trade unions should not commit themselves solely to SRs – the remaining local political structures continue to play a valuable role. Otherwise ultimately these local structures might become useless and break up.

Many 'old age activists' are not primarily interested in ensuring that the typical concerns of older people are given greater consideration in the aims and work of older people's organizations *per se*. On the contrary, they are increasingly opposed to representing only old age concerns. They prefer to participate in subjects *not* related to old age when they take part in organizations, parliaments, committees, syndicates, etc. The reason very often given for this is that there are only very few topics related specifically to old age which need to be represented politically (which, incidentally, also applies to federal social politics regarding old age in Germany, as a result of the current generational contract). Therefore, it is quite plausible that the political activism of older people, which has only just begun, could in fact soon come to an end, should the established opinion-forming structures offer their older members more concrete opportunities for access and participation. If this is not done, however, the political activism of older people within the established bodies may well damage these structures' long-term survival.

# 8

# The politics of old age in Italy

___ MARIA LUISA MIRABILE ___

The Italian population is ageing rapidly as a result of increasing longevity and declining fertility. This is confirmed by the statistics: from 1971 to 1995 there was a rise in the percentage of over-65-year-olds (from 12.8 per cent to 18.8 per cent), whereas young people between the ages of 0 and 14 decreased in the same period, from 23.4 per cent to 14.3 per cent.

Since the 1980s these figures have caused great alarm among social observers. On the one hand, experts on demography have highlighted obsessively the spectre of the ageing Italian society; on the other hand policy makers have been slow to adapt to the changing equilibrium in the labour market (between the employed, unemployed, 'informal' workers, 'baby' and old age pensioners). Therefore we are in a situation where policies on welfare reform have to be rushed through in order to meet the demands imposed by European unification while at the same time providing social protection for everybody.

Even though the debate between the government, political parties, trade unions and employers on how to implement pension reform was intense and hard, it seems that it has not undermined the social image of the older population. The basic infrastructure of Italian society, still very much centred on the family and its patriarchal structure, was able to soften the effects of the ageing population. Women are able to take on the burden of caring for both the previous generations and their own children (if they have them). On the other hand, it has been estimated recently that the contribution of older people's pensions in households is very high: in some areas of the country (Islands and the South), older people contribute more than 50 per cent of the income in households of two or three people (IRP 1997). It seems that confronted with the standstill in the welfare system, other 'adjustment' mechanisms have been put into action, which are awkward for everybody, both children and parents.

The first campaigns in favour of older people date back to the mid-1980s, with ministerial attempts to promote them as a social resource and, specifically, to launch local programmes (that were unsuccessful) to involve older people in community services. Already at this time there was a widespread opinion that the average contributory pension was not very high. Indeed in the case of illness or invalidity, these pensions were not sufficient to pay for treatment or care in nursing homes. However, only in recent months has Italy emerged from a political debate that virtually placed younger and older people at loggerheads in terms of public spending quotas. The direction for the reform of the welfare system (after the debate on pension reform, and since the 1998 finance law) is to create new (for Italy) mechanisms of social protection, whose principles of elegibility are no longer necessarily connected to previous working status or inability to work; the emphasis is on the creation of 'employability' for younger people and the protection of everybody from situations of need. The objective is a policy of larger and better services for older people (and future families).

Pension services received by those who are elderly today have derived from the Italian unions' powerful and progressive policy of protecting all workers and pushing the boundaries of this protection beyond the retirement barrier. Indeed, they succeeded in forcing previous governments to adopt pension criteria that were decisively advantageous for the 'retired', albeit the criteria centred on the profile of a 'typical' worker: male, breadwinner, with a continuous upward career.

However, this does not completely explain why older people seem reluctant to organize themselves politically. One explanation is the historical weakness of non-political and non-religious associations in Italy and the cultural simplicity of today's older people, whose average education level at the end of the 1990s was low: 3.5 per cent with a degree, 54 per cent with a primary school certificate and 15.7 per cent without any qualifications. Perhaps this explains why large numbers of ex-workers continue to be members of unions in Italy even after they have retired. Indeed, it has reached such a level that the unions' membership is largely made up of ex-workers rather than so-called 'active' workers.

## Associationalism, participation and representation

The most widespread form of association among older people is that of trade unionism. Indeed a study undertaken a few years ago (Di Francia 1992) estimated that about 20 per cent of over-65-year-olds were members of the main unions. Whether or not they are ex-workers, they belong (as pensioners) to trade unions, and by doing so lose their previous (employment) sector-related identity. Given that the unions have forged a role as political actors on many occasions in the past, they are thus able to intervene in the different areas that affect the lives of older people. At the end of the 1980s, the new type of actively participating older person emerged from the combination of the evolution of this type of 'general' unionism and the search for a solution to the welfare crisis. However, there has been a certain delay in this search because of the emphasis placed on voluntary work and the third sector, which are considered to be the bearers of high social-ethical values and therefore more capable of coping with the new social hardship. All these factors can be interpreted as an attempt to re-evaluate the position of older people in today's society.

Even though pensions have not been enough to allow all older people to have good or decent living conditions, the spread of a sense of general well-being among older people, combined with high rates of youth unemployment, has meant that a sort of competitiveness has emerged between the generations. In other words, a gap has developed between these two generations, because older people are guaranteed support, whereas young people are becoming socially excluded. It is perhaps for this reason that, at the end of the 1980s, experts on older people tended to highlight the image of older people as a resource that can contribute to the country's social economy. In fact, associations for older people and other deprived citizens have started to spring up everywhere. In some cases, these associations attempt to use the legislation on voluntary work (266/1991) and (to a lesser extent) on social cooperation (381/1991) so that they can apply for funding, even from the public sector. In other cases, they look for 'political' credit from the municipal administrations that are increasingly drawing up agreements with the self-managed organizations of older people in order to programme socially important activities and the management of places available for older people. This applies to the Centri Sociali Anziani (social centres for older people); more than 600 centres are located throughout the country and with the capacity for internal coordination.

Unfortunately, documentation on this issue is still rather scarce and fragmentary. The last official report on the condition of older people (1995) did not deal with this type of information – it only dealt with the initiatives undertaken by the various ministries and regional administrations in the area of social and health assistance. However, we know that at the end of the 1980s, the regional and municipal administrations set up consultation bodies on the participation of older people. Their set-up varies from one area to another, especially concerning their composition and organizational structure. The main common element, though, is that they have a consultative role and do not have the power to control or present proposals.

It can be said that the position of older people in Italy is rather uncomfortable. In fact there is a considerable difference between one welfare area and another, especially pension coverage for ex-workers and their capacity to influence the general orientation of government social policy, compared with the more general conditions in areas such as housing, political participation, health care and leisure, where awareness of the specific needs of older people has only recently been developed.

Social protection for older people in Italy reflects the more general structure of the national welfare system, characterized, as in other cases of Southern European family-based societies, by a preference for direct monetary benefits rather than the provision of services. This arrangement penalizes older people because they are forced to look for care services on the market. These services are costly and often older people cannot afford them, in spite of 'high' pensions. From this point of view, the wide variations in the economic and social circumstances of older people in Italy should be mentioned, as it is difficult to refer to a single reality. In fact, within this spectrum, there is a particular predominance of women receiving social pensions (about 80 per cent of total beneficiaries). This kind of benefit is so low that it is often an indication of poverty or hardship.

It is well known that there has been considerable growth in the pension system – faster than other items of expenditure – over the post-war period. It is possible to argue that there has in fact been two distinct versions of the social state (Sgritta 1993).[1]

The first version is characterized by economic growth that guaranteed the rise in employment or at least limited unemployment; at the same time, demographic growth contained the percentage of older people and the financing of benefits for the economically inactive. In the following period and second version, the relations between these two were inverted. Economic growth started to slow down drastically, unemployment (especially among young people) increased and (in the last 15 years) doubled. The age pyramid has been inverted and the benefit system has started to suffer, both in terms of financial cover and the reduction in the number of contributors and the rise in the number of recipients. Given that the social state and solidarity model, established in the post-war years, is not adequate to cope with new developments, it has produced unexpected effects on the equality of benefit distribution. More resources are concentrated among older groups of people who already have employment and those who have regular and stable jobs, whereas young people and the unemployed, without previous employment, find themselves in relative impoverishment.

On this basis, and because of the precarious financial situation, Italy is, for the first time, attempting to make a fundamental reform of the welfare state. Indeed, the government is currently debating this issue. The reformers want to save money *and* re-balance the system in order to re-establish equality between the generations. In actual fact, more money is spent on the pension system than on other parts of the welfare state.[2] However, most spending on pensions should be interpreted as an inappropriate and concealed substitute for other forms of benefit cover.[3]

Given that there are no additional resources for interventions in the areas of youth unemployment, unemployment in general, structured family policies, the establishment of a national minimum wage or measures to combat poverty, the pension system risks becoming the designated victim of this pointless game. During the early part of 1998 the trade union movement has been very cautious towards any attempt to change the pension status quo (and here it should be mentioned that the last reform, launched in 1995, had been due to come into force in 1998). On the whole, union action is dominated by an attitude that favours the 'gerontocracy of the labour force' (Paci 1996).

## Historical background

In Italy, the development of social associations and mutualism is strongly linked to the constitution of the state. However, the separation of these two aspects occurred at the very beginning. According to the reconstruction carried out by Paci (1984), the wide network of charitable organizations, credit institutions (for farmers and craftsmen), postal savings schemes and, above all, workers' mutual societies was developed in the middle of the nineteenth century without initially requesting public recognition, so as to avoid the risk of being transformed into mere charity organizations. However, the newly unified state exerted its disciplinary power on the network, thereby reducing its size. This came about in spite of the influence of the governing class, which wanted to develop a liberal system of social reform based on insurance, pension and cooperative institutions freely promoted by the citizens.

Therefore in 1886, after about 20 years of debate, the law recognizing the Società di Mutuo Soccorso (mutual society) was approved. The more class-conscious workers of this society formed resistance leagues and the first organizational forms of unionization. Yet, in 1898, when the principles of obligatory insurance were becoming widespread, the chosen institutional system did not take into account the reality of voluntary insurance. This privileged the Casse di Previdenza e Capitaliszazione (Provident and Capitalization Funds) because central government exerted some control over these funds (albeit illegally). In 1911, the state finally accepted the obligatory regime but only after certain resistance. The insurance system became totally obligatory in 1919. Contrary to what happened in Germany and England,[4] Italian social legislation did not involve the populace and their voluntary organizations in the management of the obligatory insurance system, not even during the fascist era or in the period after World War I. Indeed, the creation and management of the Enti Nazionali Autarchici di Assistenza e Previdenza (National Autarchic Assistance and Security Authorities) was an important factor of social control that outlived the fall of fascism and developed a particular kind of welfare system based on the exchange of favours and illicit (corrupt) practices.

The Italian social protection system, inherited from the fascist era, is characterized by sector and employment fragmentation. In other words, insurance cover was historically managed by a plethora of assistance, security and insurance organisms that dealt with the distribution of benefits on the basis of the characteristics of the individual in need (single mothers, abandoned children, people with various kinds of disability). Or the actual or previous working status of individuals affects those who have 'the right to receive benefit' because they are members of a recognized professional group and have paid the necessary contributions. In 1945, a ministry commission was set up to study work problems, and included a specific subcommittee dealing with social protection. Then, in 1947, the commission chaired by President D'Aragona was set up to examine forms of social protection, assistance and insurance, and aimed at carrying out a reform of the system. The interpretation that Ferrera (1993) gives to this sequence of events and decisional conflicts is that there was a subtle attempt to create a universalistic social protection system. However, this idea was rejected because of the financial situation and the desire to keep the pre-existent insurance arrangements and the principle of work as the inspiration for the new post-fascist constitution. This was also the main orientation of the parties – even those on the left –

and the unions. It should be noted, however, that in this phase of poverty the CGIL also represented the unemployed, those badly employed and the poor as well as being a general trade union. In fact, in 1950, Mario Belinguer, who proposed the pension reform project to parliament on behalf of the CGIL, stated that the condition of poor pensioners in Italy was 'distressing' and 'tragic'. He also addressed the issue from a Keynesian perspective, as particularly low pensions represent an economic limitation in terms of economic development through domestic consumption.

But let us go back to the history of the pension system, and once again Ferrara (1993) highlights that between 1950 and 1966, the phase immediately before the launch of the pension reform, there was the maximum development of the system based on the exchange of favours and corrupt practices: at this time period, ten pre-existent independent organizations were recognized and a further 11 were set up for different employment groups. Sometimes the recognition was accompanied by the establishment of a new pension authority, along with regulations concerning the contributions and benefits, and its own administrative structure. In contrast to this actual situation, the 1965 measure ('Introduction of pension reform') set up the so-called 'social pension' that partly took on board the results of a previous study undertaken by CNEL (National Economic Council) in 1963 that suggested extending pension protection to cover the whole population through a national arrangement not based on professions (Ferrera 1993: 248).

The actual reform of the Italian pension system took place in 1968–9 with the introduction of two laws. In the period between the approval of one law, 238/1968 and the other, 153/1969, there was great protest from the CGIL: they refused to sign the initial agreement with the government, calling a national strike of protest. In this way they managed to obtain an amendment of the first text. At the end of the two-year period, the social security system, based on employment, was much better because of the improvement in the ratio between pension and salary[5] and the introduction of the so-called 'sliding scale'[6] for pensions. In this framework, the social pension represents a means of support for older people who did not have a job that included the payment of contributions or those with incomes below the fixed thresholds.[7] Even the so-called 'minimum integrated pension' was introduced and was applied to cases where there had not been enough years of contribution payments (less than 15 years). A public quota was added to bring it up to a fixed sum. Today it is about double that of the social pension. Moreover, the reform also reorganized the old age pension, the cause of much controversy today, as it allowed the accumulation of pensions and income. Today this practice is heavily discouraged.

As mentioned earlier, since the beginning of the 1990s, the theme of pension reform, especially concerning the present 'early pensioners' and the benefit level for older people in the future, has returned to the forefront of discussions on the reorganization of public finance, financial integration for the so-called 'entry into Europe' and the reform of the welfare state. In fact, two laws have been introduced on the social security system, law 503/1992 and 335/1995. Moreover, in 1994, a further attempt was made to modify the social security system by the centre-right government, but it provoked such a backlash from the unions that it brought about the end of its term of office.

The greatest innovation, stipulated in the 1995 reform, concerns the introduction of the contributory method of calculating pensions, based on the individual's entire working career. It did away with the previous method of calculation based solely on the salary of the last working years as it had created a wide variation in pension benefits, and the state could no longer sustain this level of payment (April 1997). The retirement age was also extended to 60 years for women and 65 for men; changes were also introduced for so-called old age pensions (whereby retirement was allowed after 35 years of work, therefore it was possible to retire at 50 if he/she had started to work at the age of 15), by increasing the minimum retirement age to 57 and creating incentives to make individuals stay at work, such as a 5.7 per cent rise in pension if retirement is delayed by a year, with a 6.5 per cent rise for a two-year delay.

These changes are to come into force in the year 2008. There are still the 'special pension funds' for electricians, public transport personnel, pilots and stewards, employees from the postal service, private gas enterprises and the tax office, the clergy and people working in show business. However, they should be phased out once the social security authorities have been reorganized.

## Union associationism

Since the reconstruction period after World War II, older people have mainly turned to the unions for support. After the fall of fascism, one of CGIL's objectives was to 'prepare a plan to transform the social security system and institutes' taking its impetus from the 'Rome Pact' (1944). From this there emerged the associations of pensioners and older people. The CGIL, along with representatives from the National Civil and Military Pensioners' Association and the Italian Pensioners Federation of All Sectors, set up its 'pensioners' sections', thereby creating the only political associations in Italy for pensioners and older people.

The union's intention was to organize the coordination of pensioners from all the different working categories, so as to create the right conditions to protect their interests effectively. The union's action in this area can be interpreted as a form of united solidarity to counterattack the fragmentary particularism of interests that we have previously mentioned. The attitude of the unions has not changed over the years; in fact, even the other two main unions, CISL and UIL (formed after the break-up in 1948 between the three components of confederate unionism) have adopted the same viewpoint.

Coming back to the situation today, the considerable number of pensioners who are union members should be mentioned. There are about 5,000,000 members in the three unions, CGIL, CISL and UIL: 2,800,000 in CGIL, about 1,500,000 in CISL and about 400,000 members in UIL. The greatest increase in union membership occurred after 1968, the year in which the unions showed great commitment and success in reforming the law. In that year, there were only 400,000 pensioners who were CGIL

members; by 1978 membership had reached a total of 991,887 and showed
a tendency for growth that has not looked like slowing down.[8]

It is not possible to discuss the causes of such success in great depth but
certainly one of the main reasons is the influence of the demographic-social
mix on trade union strategies. The rise in the older population, (over-65-
year-olds) went from 9.5 per cent in 1961 to 15.3 per cent in 1991 (according to census data), has been accompanied by the decline in employment
for the young age groups. There has also been the complex organizational
transformation of enterprises and work that has undeniably produced a
crisis in union participation due to the greater difficulty in representing less
standardized jobs than in the past.[9] This trend can be borne out by the
statistics on regular employment (as a type of employment that allows
continuity of public pension payments) in the period 1984 to 1994 (Isfol
1996); there was more than a 1 per cent decline (–1.1 per cent) in employment among under 29-year-olds and an even greater decline among over-
50-year-olds (–2.1 per cent). The first age group have found it more difficult
to find support through trade union membership than the over-50-year-
olds, who remain attached to the union's pensioner representation structure – a structure that represents the interests of ex-workers, whether they
be physically old or considered to be so in the world of work, as well as
those of its employed members.

## Economic conditions

'Older families have lower income levels than the national average.' This is
a brief summary of one of the most important results of a recent study on
the consumer trends and living conditions of older people (CER 1997). Older
families in Italy have a monthly income of between 1.5 to 2 million lire, well
below the average of 2 to 2.5 million lire a month. Over-65-year-old families only represent 24 per cent of national expenditure, and most of it is
spent on groceries. Moreover, an interesting paradox emerges from the
study: in the centre-north of the country, the consumption of older people
is 0.5 per cent less than average, whereas in the south, older people consume
0.6 per cent more than the average rate in the same area. This can be
explained by the high level of unemployment (and the higher proportion of
income that is declared) in the south of Italy, sustained by the considerable
diffusion of false invalidity pensions that act as a substitute to unemployment benefit and/or income support. Indeed this explains why most social
spending goes on pensions. In effect, according to INPS (National Social
Security) data from 1996, the average monthly contributory pension was
1,127,000 lire (about 550 ECU) for male pensioners and 834,000 lire (about
415 ECU) for female pensioners.

## Rights and the protection of older people

There is no framework of principles and rights designed specifically to apply
to older people.[10] Therefore interventions in favour of older people derive
from the institutions of the pension, health and social assistance systems.

The Italian system is set up in such a multifaceted way that it includes a network of national institutions, dealing with different types of pension with assistance characteristics; then there are locally based institutions, regulated by the regions, provinces and municipalities, dealing with different forms of health, social-assistance and monetary interventions or services that support older people. The right to assistance and health takes different form and levels of payment depending on available financial and instrumental resources, service capacity (innovation of the services, relations between public and third-sector organization) as well as choices on the destination of funds in each area.

The types of pension assistance support distributed centrally are characterized by certainty and continuity, whereas other forms of help are much more uncertain. However, it should be mentioned that such uncertainty does not only concern older people. Indeed, at the local level, resources are channelled the same way to older people as to other sectors of the population.

The non-contributory or partially contributory pensions are:

- The minimum pension (law 218/1952) establishes that pensions, paid either direct or to the surviving members of the family, are not less than certain amounts, (periodically updated). The difference between the amount due, based on contribution payments, and the minimum fixed amount (today about 700,000 lire a month, roughly 350 ECU) is made up by INPS (Istituto Nazionale della Providenza Sociale – National Insurance).
- With invalidity and disability pensions (law 392/1984), invalidity pensions are allocated when there is a reduced working capacity, whereas disability pensions are distributed when work is totally impossible. The invalidity pension can be added to the 'accompaniment benefit' if the individual is not self-sufficient.
- Social pensions, introduced by the reform law 153/1969, are allocated to citizens who are over 65 with a level of income below certain thresholds (see note 6). This pension amounts to about 400,000 lire (about 200 ECU) a month.
- Pensions for surviving members of the family – set up with reform law 153/1969 – are allocated to the family members of deceased pension holders.
- Extra social benefit (maggiorazione) is allocated to those who receive social pensions and minimum integrated pensions and who are in particular conditions of poverty (the individual's income is below the amount of extra social benefit).
- Accompaniment benefit, introduced by law 18/1980, is allocated to citizens of any age who are in a condition of total invalidity and who are incapable of independently carrying out the normal necessities of everyday life. It amounts to about 700,000 lire a month (about 350 ECU).

Health and welfare interventions cannot be defined in the same way because the provision of services is rather different. Moreover, both the health and welfare systems (whose present structure is relatively recent and rather dissimilar in terms of the quantity and quality of the services offered may differ from one geographic and institutional territory to another.[11] Furthermore, these interventions are in a state of continual transformation.[12]

In cases where there are few controls, below-standard services are certainly a major defect of the system. However, such heterogeneity also results from positive social changes that have led to administrative decentralization and institutional democratization. Indeed, the Italian social welfare system underwent important and positive developments in the 1970s.[13]

Before that, welfare services for older people took the form of long periods of hospitalization. However, between 1977 and 1978, two decisive laws on the reorganization of the social welfare system were passed. DPR 616/1977 brought about the redefinition of the public provision of welfare: power was devolved from the central authorities to the local ones. This allowed a more accelerated and widespread development of initiatives aimed at the older population. In 1978, there was a law (833/1978) on the National Health Service that instigated the setting up of the local health boards (USL Unita' Sanitarie Locali) and gave guidelines on how to achieve the integration between social and health services. In this way, the foundations were established for the implementation of subsequent integrated interventions, created at the local level and aimed at coping with the needs of the older population. With particular reference to older people, the law is resolved to protect their health 'also in order to prevent and remove the conditions that can cause their marginalization'. That particular phrase was influenced by much pressure for the reform of the Italian social system, stemming from the widespread criticism of institutional care and assistance. The most important action (also the result of a strong expression of public opinion) was the famous law (180/1978) specifying the closure of mental hospitals. (The aftermath, however, was rather controversial, and still is, as no type of alternative solution to the mental hospital was offered.)

Following the de-institutionalization process after the introduction of law 180, it was not clear whether older people should apply to welfare or health authorities for care; the reciprocal unloading of responsibilities between welfare and health structures in borderline cases has only been partly resolved. The Progetto Obiettivo per la Tutela della Salute degli Anziani (National Project for the Protection of the Health of Older People), approved by parliament in 1992, set up a series of principles and measures that have never been applied: new rights for economic benefits, home helps for older people who are not self-sufficient, and sheltered housing for lonely older people. Today there are still deficiencies in these areas. In fact there is still much controversy about the hospitalization of older people. For example the Decreto del Presidente del Consiglio dei Ministri (decree issued by the Cabinet) in 1985 allowed welfare structures to be reimbursed by the health board for any kind of health intervention, whereas health reform in the early 1990s (laws 502/1992 and 517/1993) has put pressure on health structures to reduce spending. As a consequence older people are not hospitalized so easily.

As far as health benefits are concerned, over-65-year-olds are exempt from paying for medical treatment as long as their annual income does not exceed 70 million lire (about 35,000 ECU). Pensioners with minimum integrated pensions, however, are exempt from payment after the age of 60.

In general, the guidelines for health benefits concerning diagnostic-thera-
peutic needs for the entire population are also used for older people: older
people who are not self-sufficient can take advantage of long-stay hospitalization, rehabilitation services in day hospital structures, and health interventions in the form of home help or hospital care at home.

The social welfare sector has a similar kind of organization. In both cases
there are wide differences at the regional and/or municipal level, in the
quantity and quality of the supply; such differences are caused by the effect
of greatly decentralized legislative arrangements.[14] However, the welfare
sector is characterized by a low level of national legal uniformity because the
different municipalities have made their own legislation on these subjects
thereby reflecting different local administrative cultures, organizational
capacities, available expenditure, and so on;[15] they distribute the available
benefits according to their own priorities to people who are considered
needy or worthy. On the whole it can be stated that older people are usually
taken into consideration in the distribution of local assistance benefits.

At the local level, the type of welfare distributed to older people consists
of economic help (minimum income), the availability of community centres,
money for the use of transport services, home help, interventions for housing assistance through forms of allocation of council houses, and support
given to help pay the rent. There is also a range of services specifically aimed
at older people who are not self-sufficient, such as sheltered housing day
centres with rehabilitative services and integrated home help.

## Conclusion

The main aim of this chapter is to illustrate, by drawing on some historical
events that have had an effect on the present situation, how policies towards
older people in Italy are in a state of great turbulence. It has been necessary
to go beyond policies for older people and look at other connected topics
such as the Italians' historical unwillingness to participate in movements
unrelated to politics or religion. In fact, the only data available on the participation of older people in associations are derived from their membership of
the unions or from research conducted on voluntary work (that is mainly
religious). Significantly, the organizations of a consultative nature set up by
some local authorities to deal with policies concerning the over-65 population touch upon this point; their operation seems to be rather vague.

However, it seems that there *is* respect for older people in Italy, and this
can be traced back to the rural origins of Italian society. Even today, older
people who require assistance are still looked after by their families. Apart
from this, as far as the ordinary citizen is concerned, the break up of these
traditional values, the growth of private provision and questions about the
capacity of the family to give support to its weaker members (the family is
the main form of provision in some regions) mean that the real social risk
concerns those who do not receive high pensions. Often these pensioners
manage to cope well until confronted with serious illnesses or disabilities, a
distinct possiblility in the last phases of life.

The provision of pensions for older people, as ex-workers, was first of all fought for and then strongly defended by the trade unions; this accounts for the large membership of pensioners in the unions. In fact there is a reciprocal link: the union is the most popular association among older people, and they at the same time represent a large part of the union's membership. Therefore it follows that future ways to calculate pensions will have an influence on stable middle-aged workers.

We also wanted to emphasize that the 'demographic revolution' is a phenomenon that has been ignored for a long time, so that it has only been confronted very recently. Today the topic is the object of much discussion, especially concerning the modification of the present system of social protection. There are dual tendencies. One aims to give young people, ultimately viewed as the older people of tomorrow, greater capacity to survive in a labour market characterized by uncertainties and discontinuity (by designing a pension system capable of protecting the old age of those who have had a discontinuous working career). The other seeks to progressively modify the system for today's older people so as to transform it from a purely monetary benefit distribution system to that of a provider of services, thereby creating the prospect of greater autonomy at every age.

## Notes

1  Between 1951 and 1971, individuals who received pensions (of those entitled) went from 35.4 per cent to 85.1 per cent (and to 93.7 per cent if those who receive double pensions are also included) and continued to increase in the following years; at the same time, the level of the pensions increased in relation to the GDP. However, individuals who received benefits for accidents, total or partial unemployment and temporary inability went from 49.1 per cent in 1951 to 60 per cent in 1971, but then decreased to 47.6 per cent in 1986, even if the average annual benefit increased in proportion to the GDP. Lastly, those who received child benefit went from 35.5 per cent at the beginning of the period to 58.3 per cent in 1971 and then drastically fell to 36.1 per cent in 1986; child benefit has continued to decrease well below the GDP: 1.0 per cent in 1988 and about 0.8 per cent today, according to Eurostat data.

2  Based on the percentage of GDP of 1994, 15.6 per cent of social spending goes on older people, 7.3 per cent on illness and invalidity, 0.9 per cent on the family and 0.6 per cent on unemployment benefits (Eurostat 1996).

3  In particular invalidity pensions, distributed above all in the non-industrialized southern areas of the country, have acted as a form of income support, given the absence of benefits to support low wages (Boccella 1982). However, specific initiatives to check the beneficiaries' state of health have been introduced to combat this type of abuse. From this point of view, the age-old controversy concerning the criteria used to elaborate INPS (Istituto Nazionale della Previdenza Sociale – National Insurance) budgets should be mentioned. In fact INPS also runs the provision of welfare pensions, but if these structures were separated, the pension budget would follow more transparent criteria and would certainly be higher today. In our opinion, this controversy is justifiable, but it is less important than the more structured framework of the current debate on equality and the present and future funding of pension systems.

4  This refers to the choice made by Bismarck in 1883 when he abandoned his project to centralize social security and therefore chose to protect the role of the workers'

societies, transforming them into 'public right entities'. It also refers to the inclusion of the workers' societies as 'Approved Societies' in England.

5  Such a ratio went from the previous rate of 65 per cent to 74 per cent at the time of the reform, and 80 per cent to be introduced in 1975. These quotas are also to be applied to the three best working years out of the last five.

6  The 'sliding scale' is an automatic mechanism to keep salaries and pensions in line with increases in the cost of living due to inflation; it was abolished in 1993 and replaced by a contractual mechanism to make up any losses in value. With regard to pensions the sliding scale mechanism is still applied but not in such a rigid manner.

7  Social pension thresholds are: 15,446,200 lire (about 7,500 ECU) per year for an older person living alone and 20,338,100 lire (about 10,000 ECU) per year for an older couple.

8  There has been the following trend for CGIL pensioner membership: 1949, 244,237; 1958, 353,016; 1968, 401,733; 1978, 991,887; 1985, 1,388,441; 1988, 2,059,771; 1993, 2,668,867; 1995, 2,813,200.

9  In 1996, 33.3 per cent of the population were employed in 'atypical' work (any kind of work different from the usual 'standard', stable and full time, employment that lasts the individual's entire working life).

10 The Constitution refers to old age as a time of life when it is possible to assert one's right to have pension protection as an ex-worker and the right for protection for every citizen who cannot work, therefore this especially includes older people who are weakened or ill, through a general system of social security.

11 See Vicarelli (1988) on the type of variation in provision by territory promulgated by law 833/1978. At the moment, guidelines have been produced by the territorial authorities to help citizens use the services available at the local level, especially since people are more used to centrally controlled, standardized benefits.

12 The last health reform partly changed the organization of the health system by introducing territorial districts instead of the territorial unit previously defined by the USL; it also reduced the number of interactions between the structure and user. It also introduced considerable cuts in administration whose effects on the population have still not been estimated, although it is probable that they are great, especially for the older population, considering the scale of their demands on health services.

13 Some of the information in this paragraph has been based on the indications specified in the Guide produced by the Finney Foundation and Labos on behalf of the Cabinet (Presidenza del Consiglio dei Ministri/Fondazione Finney/Labos 1996).

14 There is a difference between the cases dealt with by the health system and that of social assistance, due to the fact that the former has undergone differentiated regional development (and this regional aspect became even stronger with the last national reform), whereas the latter is not regulated by national law.

15 Some studies on poverty and policies to combat social exclusion have highlighted the most interesting aspects of the differentiation of legal regimes caused by non-coordinated welfare policies. See Commission against Poverty and Marginalization (1996) and Negri and Saraceno (1996).

# 9

# The politics of old age in the Netherlands

THEO SCHUYT, LUCIA LAMEIRO GARCÍA
AND KEES KNIPSCHEER

Participation means 'being part of', or 'taking part in', but a second meaning is 'the exercise of influence', which could be described as a continuous scale with 'knowing/being informed' on one side and 'helping make the decisions' on the other. In the framework of this chapter on the participation of older people, we are concerned with both of these aspects of participation, 'taking part' and 'exercising influence'. The participation of older people and government policies concerning them are inseparably bound together. Older people in the Netherlands are politically involved. They vote *en masse* and, compared with other age groups, are often active members of political parties. None the less, they have less representation in the political power structures. Participation means more than participation in governmental structures or political parties. In addition to this sort of political participation, older people can participate in socially oriented organizations which determine the quality of life of older people: private pension funds, health care insurers, care institutions, employer and employee organizations, and so on. Accordingly, we also identify the participation of older people in the *social* structure as well as in the political structure.

By way of introduction we will begin with a brief characterization of the circumstances in which senior citizens in the Netherlands find themselves. In some aspects, these will be comparable to those of seniors in other European Community countries; in other aspects it will differ (Table 9.1). As of 1 January 1996, there were 3.5 million people in the Netherlands aged 55 or older. Of these, 2.1 million are over the age of 65 (Sociaal en Cultureel Planbureau 1996a) – over 13 per cent of the Dutch population. The Netherlands does not have a particularly high percentage when compared with other EC countries, but this percentage will increase markedly in years to come. The percentage of 65-year-olds and over in the total population will rise to nearly 17 per cent in the year 2015, and 23 per cent in 2035 (WRR 1996). In the

**Table 9.1**   The ageing of the Dutch population, aged 55 and older, between 1990 and 2020*

|  | 1990 (%) | 2000 (%) | 2010 (%) | 2020 (%) | 1995 |
|---|---|---|---|---|---|
| Males 55–64 | 95 | 111 | 151 | 166 | 718,000 |
| Males 65–79 | 94 | 109 | 129 | 173 | 671,000 |
| Males 80+ | 92 | 106 | 135 | 159 | 144,000 |
| Females 55–64 | 98 | 108 | 148 | 163 | 734,000 |
| Females 65–79 | 96 | 105 | 113 | 149 | 886,000 |
| Females 80+ | 89 | 106 | 127 | 135 | 332,000 |
| Total 55–64 | 96 | 109 | 150 | 164 | 1,452,000 |
| Total 65–79 | 95 | 107 | 120 | 159 | 1,558,000 |
| Total 80+ | 90 | 106 | 129 | 143 | 476,000 |
| Total 55+ | 95 | 108 | 134 | 159 | 3,485,000 |

*Source*: Timmermans (1997: 4)

* 1995 forecast; middle variant. Index: 1995 = 100

next 25 years this means an increase of about 60 per cent of the number of 55-plussers, a rapid growth caused by the high birth rates in the 1940s and 1950s (Timmermans 1997).

   The participation of Dutch older people in the labour market is remarkably low, with only about 25 per cent of people aged between 55 and 65 in paid employment (Table 9.2). Dutch older people have 'limited access to positions of social and political power' (Dekker and Ester 1993: 72). It is, for example, indicative that only five members of the Dutch Lower House of Parliament (3 per cent of all Lower House members) are 65 or older (Table 9.3), and all of them belong to one of the parties representing older people which only first took part in elections in 1994.

   The Netherlands also has a broad and well-balanced pension system, consisting of a basic segment, a public pension for which everyone living in the Netherlands between the ages of 15 and 65 is insured and which is financed by the 'pay as you go' principle. For retired people of 65 and older in any given year, this pension is paid for by the wage and salary deductions of those who are working in that same year. In addition, about 60 per cent

**Table 9.2**   The working population aged 50–64 analysed by gender, 1994 (per cent)

|  | Males | Females | Total |
|---|---|---|---|
| 50–54 | 81 | 32 | 57 |
| 55–59 | 55 | 20 | 38 |
| 60–64 | 19 | 5 | 11 |

*Source*: Enquete Beroepsbevolkig, CBS (1996)

**Table 9.3**  Persons aged 55 and over in the Dutch Lower House of Parliament after the 1994 elections

| | |
|---|---|
| 75+ | – |
| 70–75 years old | 1 (0.7%) |
| 65–69 years old | 4 (2.7%) |
| 60–64 years old | 7 (4.7%) |
| 55–59 years old | 13 (8.7%) |
| | |
| Total 65+ | 5 (3.3%) |
| Total 55+ | 25 (16.7%) |

*Source*: Information service of the Dutch Lower House of Parliament

of older Dutch people (80 per cent of households including older individuals: Timmermans 1997) have a supplementary pension for which they have contributed either individually or collectively through a private pension insurance company.

The Netherlands has an especially high percentage of people in older people's homes or nursing homes (together they house 8.5 per cent of all those aged 65 and over). Finally, in the context of 'the politics of ageing', it is important to point out the specific relationship between the Dutch government and private initiatives. There are numerous non-profit institutions such as hospitals or educational institutes, frequently with ideological backgrounds, which shoulder the major responsibility for realizing government policies. Many policies concerning older people in the Netherlands are carried out by private institutions, funded by the government within that policy framework (Baars *et al.* 1992; Schuyt and Van der Zanden 1994).

Compared with other European countries, certain characteristics of the Dutch situation can be termed unique, in particular the low labour market participation of older people and the high percentage living in residential care facilities. The situation as it has evolved is both cause and effect of the policies pursued.

## A theoretical framework

Government policy, including that affecting older people, is concerned with two problems: the question of legitimacy and the question of information, also referred to as the question of participation. The legitimacy question touches the very core of how government functions, in the sense that government steps in on behalf of and in the service of the general good, and in the name of 'everyone', the collective society. In order to do so, government must know what is happening in that collective body (information) and then involve that collective, or its representatives, in its policies (political, social participation).

Over time, because of exceptional demographic developments (the greying of the population and reduced numbers of young people), and because of the limited participation of older people and their underrepresentation in the political process and in social organizations, legitimacy has become a problem for the Dutch government. Over the last two decades, older people have become firmly convinced that their voices are not heard in national politics. This feeling is much stronger than among young people (Sociaal en Cultureel Planbureau 1996a).

When government policy loses its legitimacy, fertile ground is created for social movements (Jenkins and Klandermans 1996). One may argue that older people who experienced the economic crises of the 1930s and who worked to rebuild post-war society will in principle not take action against a government which guarantees an acceptable level of financial security (Mishra 1981). In contrast, a frontal attack such as that made by the Christian Democratic Party in its 1994 election campaign led to the establishment of political parties for senior citizens (the Algemeen Ouderen Verbond and Unie 55+) and to a number of nationwide demonstrations. The coming generation of older people are the more highly politically educated – their socialization included the protest period of the 1960s. It can be expected that in the future, this group will let the power of its numbers (the percentage of voters over 65) be felt in politics. On the other hand, research shows that the values, norms and attitudes of the coming generation of older people do not differ so much from those of today's seniors (Dekker and Ester 1993); although preparedness to take action has increased in the Netherlands over the last 20 years, the actual participation in the political process lags very much behind, and the social participation of the more highly educated has also decreased somewhat (Sociaal en Cultureel Planbureau 1996b). All this suggests that over-enthusiastically high expectations of greater (future) participation of older people should be brought back into perspective.

The detachment of certain categories of the population is a threat to social cohesion, and requires that attention be paid to achieving social integration. These are ideas that have resurfaced in Dutch government policy, but which have their source in the functionalist thinking which dominated Western Europe and the United States in the 1950s and 1960s.

Although social integration is the reference point for functionalist thinking, this theory also includes concepts which attempt to explain change and protest. Merton introduced the concept of 'dysfunction'. In his analysis of the welfare state, Mishra, an author whose work is based on group and action perspectives, none the less uses a number of concepts from functionalism to explain tension and conflicts. He refers to 'the problems of functional incompatibility between various institutional sectors, e.g. the social services and the market economy' (Mishra 1986: 23). He furthermore criticizes his own group and action perspective on the point that analysis through group and power relationships does not reveal enough of the institutional perspective: 'despite general agreement among social groups about the welfare state, institutional dysfunctions (the disequilibrium or contradiction between institutional parts) could determine the social compromise' (Mishra 1986: 24). We could further explain Mishra's analysis by saying that social tensions arise when laws and institutions no longer suffice, because the problem for which they were established has totally changed. Put simply, the gap widens between social problems and the arrangements of society as a whole. In social gerontology, we make use of Riley's concept of 'structural lag': society has neglected to create structures appropriate to the changing circumstances affecting older people (Van Rijsselt *et al.* 1994). Institutional dysfunctions and problems of government legitimacy reinforce one another.

A second important theoretical question concerns the future of the politics of ageing against the background of the changing welfare state. Indisputably, in the European Community countries a development has begun: although government remains essential for today's complex society, other social institutions fulfil a greater role in realizing collective or partially collective goals. Take, for example, industry, non-profit organizations and primary networks. Western European welfare states are developing towards welfare societies in which, alongside governmental welfare, there is greater space for individual and/or semi-collective insurances, for occupational welfare, for philanthropy and the caring role of personal networks (Schuyt 1990).

## Overview of the politics of old age

*A brief historical sketch of policy*

In the Netherlands, many government tasks are carried out by private institutions, financed through government funding. Hospitals, senior citizens' homes and nursing homes are all such institutions run by private initiative. They are responsible for carrying through policy on ageing within the guidelines set by the government, but they do have some degree of freedom in how they do it.

Since 1970, the Netherlands has had a specific seniors policy in the form of a government memorandum on older people. Prior to 1970, such a policy certainly existed, namely regarding income security, residential care facilities and policy concerning older employees, but these were not united in a single document. After 1970, the Ministry of Social Welfare published the 1970 Memorandum on Policy for the Elderly, whose theme was the problems of older people. The 1975 memorandum focused on the coordination of care and service facilities for older people. In 1982, the memorandum covered the financial problems of older people; in 1988, senior citizens as a power group. In 1990, the national government published *Ouderen in Tel*, or *Counting Older People*, in which participation by and for older people was explicitly adopted as a policy goal. The 1996 memorandum had a different objective. Here the concern is categories within the senior population: the very old, older women, older people of ethnic origins and older employees. The integral approach has gone. As far as there is any question of generally applicable problems, such as housing, labour market politics and so on, government solutions have been removed from the jurisdiction of the Ministry of Social Welfare and brought under the wing of other ministries (Timmermans 1996).

*Organizations and parties*

In 1988, as part of government policy on senior citizens, a Temporary National Council for Policy on the Elderly was set up; it was dismantled in

1996. The successor to this council is now the Council on Social Development, one which clearly has a more generally defined purpose.

In 1997, around 650,000 senior citizens were members of a senior citizens union or association. This is about 30 per cent of people over 65. Traditionally, the seniors' associations put considerable emphasis on recreational activities, certainly at the local level. More recently, supporting members rights has taken on greater importance. At the national level, the senior citizens' unions, which evolved from the original Protestant (PCOB), Catholic (KBO) and socialist (ANBO) socio-political blocs, have become federated in a national organization, the CSO (Coördinatieorgaan Samenwerkende Ouderenorganizaties), which now also includes the Islamic Senior Citizens Association (NISBO) and other smaller associations. The active roles in senior citizens' organizations management are generally filled by men.

Moreover, at the municipality level, whose importance for older people has been increasing, there are nearly 300 senior citizens' councils, which means that nearly half of all Dutch municipalities have such a council. These are advisory committees with the task of advising – whether consulted officially or not – on local policy on older people. They take one of three forms: advisory committees based on municipal law; advisory committees organized as foundations; and advisory committees with informal status. Though these committees are growing in number, it is not clear to what degree their advice has any influence on final policies. They lack the means of exerting power or the authority to pursue their cause further than offering advice, nor has that advice any binding strength.

In the early 1990s, two laws which were extremely relevant for the older population were brought under discussion at national government level. These were the Wet Bejaardenoorden (WBO) or the Senior Citizens' Residences Law and the Algemene Ouderdoms Wet (AOW) or General Law on Ageing. The discussions led to political action and a general politicizing of senior citizens. The results included the establishment of two political parties at national level, the General Senior Citizens' Union and Union 55+, which together won seven parliamentary seats (out of 150) in the 1994 elections. Although the large political parties in the Netherlands do not give the impression of taking the question of older citizens very seriously, except when it concerns the affordability of pensions or the expense of health care, it is very much in question whether seniors will still be represented in parliament after future elections. Persistent internal problems have decidedly not increased the popularity of the senior citizens' parties.

## Recent developments in the politics of old age

*Pensions, health and social services*

The Netherlands has an extensive public pension system. Everyone who has lived in the Netherlands between his or her fifteenth and sixty-fifth year has the right to an AOW pension, whether or not they were in paid employment. The AOW (originally established by temporary law in 1947 and permanent law in 1957, in the form of the General Law on Ageing) was brought to life for a relatively small population of older people who retired at age 65 and had an expected ten more years to live. The reality shows quite a different picture (Knipscheer 1995: 35).

The amount of the AOW pension can vary, depending on the nature of the household and other possible sources of income, between 610 and 700 ECU per month for individuals and 850 and 1,000 ECU per month for couples (this includes public health insurance). The AOW pension is a basic income, at 70 per cent of the minimum wage. About 15 per cent to 20 per cent of Dutch people aged 65 and over have to make do with this income and increasingly come into difficulties due to rising costs of living, local (municipal) taxes and utilities and increasing patient percentage fees for care, care equipment and services (Timmermans 1997). The problem of poverty is affecting more and more elderly people, especially women. Because women were in the past not given the opportunity to build up their own (supplemental) pensions, two thirds of the population of older people comprises women with low incomes.

Municipalities have the means to do something about the financial status of older people through special social welfare benefits and exemptions from tax and utilities payments. In actual fact, because people do not know about these options, through embarrassment or the inaccessibility of the services, older people do not take enough advantage of these possibilities (Timmermans 1997).

In Western Europe, the Netherlands has long had the highest percentage of older people in residential care or nursing homes. In 1975, 9.3 per cent of all those aged 65 and over were in a home for older people and 2.2 per cent in a nursing home. One reason for this is the fact that from 1963 to 1965, when the General Social Security Law (ABW) came into effect, many private anti-poverty organizations invested their remaining funds in building homes for residential care. This effect was further strengthened by sectarianism, because each ideological group wanted to create such facilities for their own adherents. Government policy has changed drastically since 1975. By 1993, 6 per cent of people aged 65 and over were in older people's homes and 2.5 per cent in nursing homes. In addition, about 5 per cent live in a self-sufficient home with some associated care, for instance in the form of a service flat or semi-detached home, 6 per cent make use of meal services and 26 per cent receive care from an institution providing care in the home (Sociaal en Cultureel Planbureau 1996a).

The management of policy for older people has increasingly concentrated at the regional level, the same level at which financiers operate: health insurers, care planners, traffic planning, consumer organizations, patients interest groups, and so on. Local municipalities are also assuming increased authority when it comes to their own input to policy in this field.

### Changes in the nature of political participation by older people

Where political participation is concerned older people are the most active voters and members of political parties (Tables 9.4 and 9.5). Within those political parties and party structures, however, they occupy few positions of

**Table 9.4**   Voting turnout by gender and age at the 1994 elections for the Dutch Lower House of Parliament (per cent)

|  | *1989* | *1994* |
|---|---|---|
| *Gender* | | |
| male | 75 | 76 |
| female | 85 | 82 |
| *Age* | | |
| 18–26 | 63 | 65 |
| 27–41 | 76 | 73 |
| 42–55 | 88 | 84 |
| 56–70 | 91 | 89 |
| 71+ | 84 | 91 |

*Source*: Van Holsteijn and Niemöller (1995)

**Table 9.5**   Membership of different types of associations, 1995 (per cent)

|  | *Political party* | *Union* | *Library* | *Sports club* | *Hobby association* | *Total (=100%)* |
|---|---|---|---|---|---|---|
| *Age* | | | | | | |
| 18–24 | 2 | 9 | 44 | 46 | 12 | 383,000 |
| 25–34 | 3 | 18 | 39 | 42 | 16 | 932,000 |
| 35–44 | 4 | 24 | 50 | 42 | 18 | 860,000 |
| 45–54 | 8 | 27 | 44 | 38 | 19 | 621,000 |
| 55–64 | 7 | 25 | 36 | 28 | 25 | 493,000 |
| 65–74 | 9 | 13 | 34 | 18 | 22 | 482,000 |
| 75+ | 10 | 8 | 25 | 10 | 15 | 257,000 |
| Total | 5 | 19 | 41 | 36 | 18 | 4,038,000 |

*Source*: Centraal Bureau voor Statistiek (1996)

power. If we look at their social participation, we see a comparable picture. Either older people are not represented or they are underrepresented in the management of those social structures which decide on matters of concern to them, such as income, housing, care services or facilities and transportation. Senior citizens do take part in volunteer work and recreational activities (Table 9.6) as well as in primary relationships. We could phrase it in a different way: older people are relatively well represented in the management levels with the least power. They are not – or to a far lesser degree – represented in decision-making or executive structures. Age discrimination and the process of increased professionalization form two of the causes underlying the removal of older people from public management (Köbben and Nelissen 1989; Van den Berg 1991).

**Table 9.6**  Participation in voluntary work by age (per cent)

|  | *1980* | *1986* | *1992* |
|---|---|---|---|
| *Age* | | | |
| 18–29 | 48 | 48 | 36 |
| 30–44 | 56 | 57 | 52 |
| 45–59 | 43 | 45 | 46 |
| 60–74 | 36 | 36 | 41 |

*Source*: Sociaal en Cultureel Planbureau (1994)

## Measures to increase participation

To increase the influence of older people in society, the Dutch government has taken a number of steps. First of all, pension funds are now required by law to give seniors a voice in their management. The government has also set up a national agency on age discrimination, and seniors have officially gained places on the committees that implement the Hospital Facilities Law at regional level. These committees comprise representatives from munici-palities, financiers (health care insurers), care providers (institutions) and care consumers (senior citizens' associations represented either autono-mously or through patient or consumer interest groups). On a local level, roughly half of all municipalities have set up a senior citizens' council. These advisory bodies are not required by law, and they vary in social effectiveness from one municipality to the next.

Although older people do have means of influencing government policy through their unions and the senior citizens' councils, these bodies are simply advisory and consequently can only have indirect influence on policy. In order to actually increase older people's influence it is necessary to increase their participation in executive and decision-making structures. In this sense, some effect can be expected from legal measures to prevent age discrimination. However, the government could go much further by setting up legal requirements about age spread in certain official bodies. In addition more could be done through government channels to encourage participa-tion in various educational courses so that they can develop the skills to keep up to date with the demands of modern society.

In 1993 the Ministry of Social Welfare began the Increasing Social Partici-pation of the Elderly project, resulting in the *Seniors Help Decide* handbook. This was distributed free of charge to local senior citizens' initiatives. For the 1997–2001 period, national organizations (unions, the national associations of older people, the Association of Netherlands Municipalities, the National Women's Federation, and churches) agreed that their policies, with the hand-book as a guide, would encourage the increased participation of older people.

## Barriers to political participation

Our argument is not limited to political participation: social participation must also be taken into consideration. Barriers are often of a political, structural nature, but they can also exist within the individual (education, health, and so forth). The political participation of older people is chiefly curtailed by restricted access to political office and the political power elite, and limited possibilities for exercising influence on government politics. Not only is the number of seniors in important political functions negligible, it has decreased sharply over the course of the years. A review of the line-ups of lists of candidates for discussions surrounding the leadership of the Lower House of Parliament makes it particularly clear that seniors are being consistently pushed out of the arena at a progressively younger age.

The most important structural cause of limited participation of older people in political and social policy-making bodies is age discrimination, whether established by rules and regulations or not. Seniors are expected to step aside when they reach a certain age. A second structural cause is the lack of means of power. For instance, although seniors are formally represented, they are hardly at all party to the regional debate on hospital and care facilities. And even should they be included they do not have the means to put up a show of force. This lack of the means of power can primarily be ascribed to the absence of group consciousness, the so-called 'we-feeling', among 55 plussers. A third structural cause is the undervaluation of volunteer work as compared to paid work. As long as top priority and value is placed on paid work, while volunteer participation in associations and organizations continues to get second-class treatment, large segments of the population – whether older or not – will feel totally disinclined to offer their services in this direction. Furthermore, older people are confronted with the problem of how to deal with modern technologies as well as financial difficulties (participating takes money): this especially besets older women.

Besides structural causes, some hindrances to political and social participation lie within older people themselves. In today's meritocratic society (and this applies equally well to participatory politics and social interaction), education, employment and income are extremely important resources (Sociaal en Cultureel Planbureau 1996a). It is exactly in these areas that seniors lag behind.

Other factors hindering seniors from social participation, often mentioned in publications in the field, are the care for others, declining health, loss of memory, or a changing perception of time (the awareness that time is running out and the concomitant need to set priorities can mean that older people spend more time on things which never got done in the past or on things that they really like doing). Research shows that seniors also suffer more from feelings of powerlessness and incompetence (factors, incidentally, that are closely related to socio-economic status), causing a lack of the self-confidence necessary to take on social positions.

Moreover, there are other factors assumed to contribute to the excluded situation of older people, although as of yet they have been insufficiently substantiated. For example the supposedly traditional attitudes of older people, said to be especially evidenced by a tendency towards more hierarchical or formal modes of thought and a reduced inclination to change, causes seniors to be less often asked to assume duties, or bars them from office. It is also argued that there is a lessening of ambition: achieving success is said to become less important than things like the pleasure gained from an activity, whether or not this is combined with a larger need for recognition (which is particularly important in relation to voluntary functions but often not forthcoming). Older people may have more realism and wisdom through experience, or a sense of perspective, so that they are less likely to jump into a project which does not show a clear chance of success.

More generally, the loss of paid work not only has consequences for the level of income, but also for the possibility of participation in collective activities (because of a reduced social network, more difficult access to information, and so forth, which goes with not having a job). As a result, retirement soon leads to more private and individualized, home-bound activities.

## The future politics of old age

A notable aspect of future governmental policy towards older people is that from 1996 onwards there is no mention of a specific policy for senior citizens. Seniors have become just one aspect of a more general policy concerning the labour market, public housing and social benefits. This seems insufficient, especially considering the rapidly changing demographical situation. The fact that the national political parties in Holland hardly include any older people in their ranks is equally worrying – and this is happening when the number of older voters will soon increase drastically. In the future, seniors may very well exercise substantial political clout. Intergenerational solidarity could come under pressure when public pensions for the senior citizens – who will comprise more than 20 per cent of the population in 2020 – will have to be financed by the work force via the transfer system.

The Dutch government, in anticipation of these financial difficulties, is putting aside a considerable amount each year in a public pension fund. It is very possible that in the future seniors will again work until a much older age, thereby lessening pressure on the public pension system. Although this might be brought about by governmental labour market policy, it is not inconceivable that employers, because of the tighter labour market, and employees, because of the expected decline in income, will both press for extended careers. Another (theoretical) possibility is the social revaluation of unpaid work done by seniors, both in the form of voluntary work for the general good as well as the care of near relations.

In any case, following Mishra's example, we can characterize the current – and future – situation of older people as one in which different social sectors are 'functionally incompatible' and in which the cohesion of Dutch society is threatened by 'institutional dysfunctions'. Sweeping demographic changes will lead to labour market and payment problems in the economic sector, which will be reflected in the social sector, where the income guarantees for seniors, the expensive intramural medical facilities and the many home and care facilities will be brought under pressure. The tensions in and between the economic and the social sectors will create problems in the political sphere. At the core is the decreasing legitimacy of government. The question of participation should accordingly remain high on the social agenda.

Much, but not everything, will depend on the politics of old age in the future. The present Western European states are indisputably developing further in the direction of welfare societies, or welfare-capitalistic societies. Seniors are individually or collectively insuring themselves against expected reductions in security provided by the government. The business community will also provide facilities for seniors in the form of occupational welfare. The support of primary social networks will strongly increase, just as will the contribution of philanthropic organizations. At the beginning of this chapter we divided participation into political and social participation. Because the future politics of old age will also be present in the age of non-governmental politics, the increase in social participation of older people will be one of the challenges of the first half of the twenty-first century.

# 10

## The politics of old age in Sweden

SANG-HOON AHN AND SVEN E. OLSSON HORT

The power structure of modern Swedish society is primarily rooted in the institutionalized class divisions and interests generated by the advent of capitalism in the late nineteenth century. Until very recently the parties have remained almost the same since the introduction of parliamentary democracy after World War I. This pattern was reinforced in the 1930s with the advent of majority governments and the defeat of the small Nazi element. In general, party identification is still anchored in the social stratification of Swedish society. Among the parties, the Social Democratic Party has been a rigorous supporter of the welfare state. The Social Democratic Party has been in government since 1932, except for the two short periods of 1976–82 and 1991–4. Their stability in power has been possible because of the support of a strong labour movement and the party's strategic alliances with other groups in society.

The role of farmers is crucial to an understanding of Swedish welfare state development, especially during the formative years. In addition, middle class voting has become one of the key factors in electoral results: about 40 per cent of white-collar employees have voted for the Social Democratic Party in the post-war elections. Social Democrats could have successfully remained in government by making alliances (Esping-Andersen 1985; Baldwin 1990) first with farmers and then with the urban middle class. In the unanimous choice in 1913 of an all-encompassing, universal basic pension scheme instead of a workers' insurance, the balance of power was held by farmers and rural smallholders. In contrast, the unanimity behind the pension reform in 1946 was more intricate, although conventional wisdom holds that this was basically a Social Democratic affair. The Social Democratic victory in the general election of 1936 – with the pension issue as a main focus – was a turning point (Olsson 1993). Obviously the introduction of an incomes-related national supplementary pension (ATP) in 1960 was made possible by the Social Democrats' alliance with white-collar employees, who became politically important due to their increased proportion of the electorate.

In the post-war period, the process of interest articulation has gone beyond the conventional corporatist configuration of pure party politics, the labour market and the old popular movements. Today, the logic of collective action is applicable to most sectors of contemporary Swedish society. Pressure groups, primarily in the form of voluntary national associations with local and regional branches, have mushroomed. In many respects, these postmodern type of social movements[1] can be regarded as responses to welfare state developments. Most of them enjoy financial support from the state, but they ought to be seen as independent social forces. Most associations participate in one way or another in decision making and the implementation of social policy, but the present-day interaction between organized interests and the welfare state is far from the traditional corporatist mode of societal representation. There is a mixture between old and new institutional representation.

As for major interest groups which are more conventional in terms of the class-based corporatist power structure, we can put them into an ideological spectrum of party preference, from left to right: the Trade Union Confederation (LO) is a major supporter of the Social Democrats; middle level salaried employees' organizations (TCO: lower middle; SACO/SR: upper middle) are internally divided in their electoral preferences; the Swedish Employers' Confederation (SAF) is a major supporter of the Conservatives. The farmers' organization (LRF) supports the Centre Party (Farmers' Party), which is in the middle of the political system.

Concerning pensions, organizational efforts have proved successful, even though their political influence on *de facto* decision making has been small. Pensioners have been split along the political-ideological lines between two major national associations: between the social democratic PRO (Pensionärernas Riksorganization – National Organization of Pensioners), with more than a quarter of all old age pensioners, and the non-socialist SPF (Sveriges Pensionärsförbund – Swedish Organization of Pensioners), with relatively small but recently increasing numbers of members (Andersson 1983; Sparks 1994).

To repeat, the development of the welfare state in general and actual programmes for older people in particular during the post-war period was mainly determined by the ideological struggle and compromise between labour and capital; the Social Democratic Party has been highly influential, owing to the party's long period of office. It is therefore a relatively new phenomenon, that cannot be ignored any longer, that Swedish older people's own 'old age politics' are beginning to play a significant role, especially as a response to the downsizing of the Swedish welfare state, namely, the crisis in the welfare state. In this change of politico-economic climate, pensioners' organizations can now be situated at the very centre of welfare politics, where interests are divided according to the different socio-economic positions, welfare recipients versus taxpayers.

In the following analysis, we will first decipher the general structure and the history of social welfare programmes for older people according to Social Democratic notions based on class politics. We will then discuss recent changes in the political and economic situation, looking especially at the implications of the general welfare state crisis, which has made possible a counter-tendency, namely *de facto* political mobilizations and the campaigns of pensioners' organizations.

## Development of welfare programmes for older people

The state, counties and municipalities share the tax-levy rights and tasks of social welfare provision for the older population, especially after decentralization in the 1980s. Social insurance is mainly the task of central authorities and is administrated by the Social Insurance Board via regional insurance offices. These include sickness insurance, pension insurance and housing allowance.

As we can see from Figure 10.1, 'Employer' is currently the biggest source for the total welfare expenditure because the Swedish social insurance is chiefly financed by the insurance contribution.[2] Table 10.1 shows that employers are still the biggest source of pension revenue even when we consider solely the pensions of older people. Also note that the local authorities spend more than the state as a result of a Social Democratic strategy of decentralization in the 1980s, the aim of which was to avert the governmental budget deficit. While social insurance is mainly controlled by the central authorities, the elected county councils are responsible for the administration and performance of health and medical care.[3] The task of providing personal social services is traditionally the duty of the 288 elected municipalities.

Under the Social Services Act, the municipalities are responsible for providing their residents with services in the areas specified in the Act. The

**Figure 10.1** Financial sources for social welfare expenditure (per cent of total)

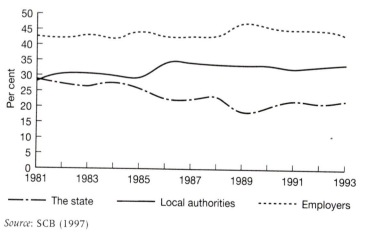

*Source*: SCB (1997)

**Table 10.1**   Sources of revenue for older people's pensions in 1994 (million SEK)

|  | Basic pension | Supplementary pension | Part-time pension |
|---|---|---|---|
| Employer | 36,388 | 82,684 | 1,303 |
| The state | 42,939 | – | – |
| Local authorities | 3,656 | – | – |
| Fund interest | – | 36,473 | 322 |

municipalities are given relatively great freedom to design their programmes according to local needs and the goals stated in the Act. Care of older people is the most important task. Care services for older people by the municipal governments span every form of services, from residential homes for the very old to home help services; the latter has been expanded since the late 1960s in terms of variety of activity and now benefit some 300,000 pensioners. Municipal pensioners' dwellings are an intermediate form of housing care which presuppose a high degree of self-help. About 60,000 of the country's 1.4 million retired persons live in residential homes, and about 80,000 live in pensioners' housing. Since the end of the 1960s the numbers of beds in residential people's homes has hardly changed; instead local authorities are now constructing service buildings or ordinary apartments with access to social services.

*Golden era growth*

Pension programmes and related services for older people are the core provision of the welfare state. Universal pension rights are a governing principle in Sweden dating back to the beginning of the century. The three main political parties at that time – the Liberals, Conservatives and Social Democrats – emphasised the need to establish a system of social security that guarantees each individual a basic minimum income. Older people were the first to benefit when a universalistic and contributory old age basic pension programme was introduced in 1913. Pensions, however, were very meagre and had to be supplemented afterwards. In 1946, Sweden became the first country to establish a universal and relatively generous flat rate pension financed solely out of government tax revenues. In 1948 the real value of the old age pension was tripled, enabling pensioners to live on pensions for the first time, though at a low standard of living. The decision meant that the universalistic principle adopted earlier – pensions for all citizens, not just employees – was maintained. Means-tested elements were abolished and a flat-rate pension introduced, though it differed for single persons and couples. In the following years several improvements were made: indexation was introduced in 1951, and income-tested municipal housing allowances became available on a nationwide basis in the mid-1950s.

In 1963 the national supplementary pension (ATP)[4] came into effect; being an earnings-related benefit, the pension level is calculated on the basis of previous earnings and years of employment. The new pensioners of 1979 were the first to receive a full supplementary pension from the ATP system. The national supplementary pension was built up, financed both by contributions from employers and the self-employed and by the interest from the accumulated funds.[5] Since the late 1960s, there have been several reforms in the pension system: a special pension supplement for pensioners with a low or no ATP benefit was introduced in 1969; and from 1976 the retirement age was lowered from 67 to 65, with a flexible retirement option at any time between the ages of 60 and 70.

Following the 1948 reform, all basic pensions with the exception of housing allowances were paid out of central government revenues, including an 'earmarked' amount added to personal income tax. Until 1975, taxation was the main source of revenue; in the late 1950s and early 1960s the earmarked contribution from the insured increased. The supplementary pension became more and more financially important, while social services for older people have constituted a minor expenditure item throughout the entire post-war period.

Apart from the pension, there has been a continuous increase in social care for older people by local government. Expenditure on housing allowances for pensioners financed by municipal governments has increased steadily in real terms. Until 1963 local government expenditure on basic pensions was totally absorbed by housing allowances. Housing allowances were a particularly important source of income for pensioners between the mid-1950s and mid-1970s, but with increasing supplementary pensions the proportion of pensioners receiving these allowances has declined from 57 to 44 per cent. After 1963 these allowances have only been partially financed by the municipalities. Besides, other types of social services for the old have been implemented by the municipal governments, although the exact nature of the service is different in each case.

*Changes after crisis*

After the successive oil shocks in the early 1970s, Western welfare states started to face serious economic difficulties, which in turn led to reductions in welfare provision. This was accelerated by the declining rate of Fordist capital accumulation. The formerly applauded Keynesian interventionism began to be blamed, as every country began to follow the new trend of neo-liberal economic reconfiguration and sought to create a so-called free market economy. This seemed to be a critical defeat of the labourist politics that had been the main sponsor of the development of the welfare state.

The Swedish welfare crisis caused by economic difficulty and political change came later and more superficially than in any other Nordic countries. In 1976, the first bourgeois, centre-right coalition government in almost half a century came to power. However, this was not because of people's disapproval of excessive welfare expenditure but because of the nuclear energy issue; people voted in favour of a 'clean and safe environment' (Olsson 1993). During this period, the centre-right government introduced a few minor austerity measures supported mainly by the Employers' Confederation although the government announced its adherence to the traditional redistributive policy in the run-up to the general election of 1982.

The right wing saw the public sector as being too big and as an obstacle to economic growth. There was a change in the general indexation of pensions: the base amount, previously linked to the consumer price index and adjusted with a two-month lag each time the index had moved up by 3 per cent, was changed to only once a year as of 1982 and became no longer influenced by changes in energy prices (1981 and 1982), indirect taxes and food subsidies (from 1981). This affected both the basic and supplementary pensions. The benefit level of part-time pensions was reduced from 65 to 50 per cent of the previous wage rate; between 1980 and 1983, the percentage of those eligible decreased from 27 to 20. In 1982, the government aborted a minor, complementary housing allowances programme for pensioners. However, the changes during the period were marginal, and the right wing lost in the election of 1982 in which 'welfare and social rights' were major issues.

Some scholars assert that Sweden experienced a consolidation of its welfare state, not a serious crisis or backlash (Olsson 1993). However, the Swedish economy also had to be changed in a post-Fordist way by means of a labour market strategy that entails fragmentation of the labour class; this in turn diminished the power of the solidaristic labour movement and stimulated the decline of unanimous support for the universal and general type of welfare programmes. This means that it is now accepted by Swedes that they can no longer afford to expand the welfare state and that they have to restructure the distribution of existing resources. The subsequent austerity of social policies in general and social services for older people in particular has produced many changes. More importantly, this has coincided with a 'decorporatization' of decision making and a decentralization of social policy administration. In Sweden, as in other Western countries, the concept of care of older people has changed: the earlier belief that escalating needs within the older population could be satisfied by the provision of more residential places has been replaced by a new belief, namely, that by reducing dependence on institutional residence in favour of older people remaining at home, both humanitarian and economic benefits can be reaped (Thorslund *et al.* 1991). Concealed by rhetoric, this change has resulted in older people paying more for services, and is thus the result of the financial problems encountered by medical services for very old people. As is well known, age naturally has a strong correlation with health problems, which are significantly more common in the older age groups; they are more likely to be exposed to serious health problems; and as a result they sometimes do not leave hospital and rarely leave residential care, once registered (Bernadotte af Wisborg *et al.* 1996; Lundberg and Kåreholt 1996). In the 1980s and 1990s, several attempts have been made by the authorities to get older people to pay a greater share themselves, for example, through the elimination of the pensioner's 'free year' paid by social insurance to hospitals. Unsuccessful though they were, it reflects the likelihood of unfavourable change in the future. Besides, older people have suffered considerably as waiting lists for hospital treatment have become longer. However, the basic problem was due to long term geriatric care, where in-patient turnover is too low for hospitals to be prepared to transfer people quickly to a lower level of care, such as nursing homes or their own homes. To solve these problems, several alternatives were planned.

The intended solutions happened at the same time as the increase in the 'home help' service and the decrease of institutional care covering the very old with low health care needs. The municipal social service agencies have been responsible for providing home help services to those older people living in their homes who cannot cope with their own household chores, including shopping, cleaning, cooking, washing, and even personal hygiene. Up until 1978 the number receiving home help has increased greatly, but has subsequently diminished appreciably. Between 1990 and 1992 alone, the number receiving home help decreased by 26,000, or 11 per cent. During the 1980s, it was mainly women and the poorly educated who were affected by this reduction in help. There are possibly several reasons why municipalities are recently cutting down on home help: new forms of services such as security alarms and distribution of cooked meals; stricter need assessment; older people with incomes above a certain level must buy services for themselves; increased charges for help are deterring some people from applying for help (Daatland and Szebehely 1997; Szebehely *et al.* 1997)

In general, services for older people are provided by the municipalities, but the county councils are also involved in them.[6] Today, county councils actively supply pensioners with visiting nurses in order to avoid hospital treatment. It is the long term institutional care of older people that health administrators are trying to restructure. A lot of older people worry about this threat to the quality of health care because the trend implies there will be more community-based health care, instead of the formerly much vaunted comprehensive medical care; pensioners fear because they have much to lose in Sweden.

Now it is evident that there is a trend in welfare cutbacks, whose inevitability is accepted even by the Social Democrats, the traditional supporters of generous welfare provision. The 1994 election campaign falsified the standard thesis of public choice theory in the sense that Swedish political parties were competing with programmes that were aimed at 'cutting benefits or increasing taxes'; this opened a new era of welfare-cutback politics in Sweden. The Social Democratic Party issued an election programme about a month before the election which outlined a number of measures that were designed to deal with the rapidly increasing budget deficit, and it included benefit cuts as well as tax increases. The proposals for benefit cuts were in some cases specified in terms of procedures while, in other cases, the amounts were given (Palme and Wennemo 1996).

In 1994, the Swedish parliament took a decision about 'guidelines' for the future of the public pension system, in which the notion of cutbacks was broadly accepted. The reform guidelines had been laid down as a political compromise between the right-wing parties and the Social Democrats. Reform involves both continuity and change. For the sake of continuity, the universal and publicly administered system should provide for both basic and income security; besides, the present systemic mixture of public and occupational programmes will be maintained. As for the actual contents of the reform, there are several fundamental changes as well. Earnings-related benefits will be the first tier of the pension systems, and the basic benefit will be utilized only as a supplement; in other words, the pension system will change from being 'benefit-defined' to 'contribution-related'. In addition, a new element of the compulsory system is an individual and fully funded benefit to be based on contributions equivalent to 2 per cent of the gross wage. This programme implies a shift of the control of pension funding from the public to the private sector. There was also a change in indexing of pension benefits. A number of measures have been taken to cut expenditure on the housing supplements for pensioners. Married persons will receive the lower rate of basic pension even if they are not married to another pensioner (FKF 1997).

As is evident, social welfare programmes for older people in Sweden face a big challenge which will affect the standard of living in old age. Despite the egalitarian and humanitarian orientation of former legislation, there seems to be a new long term trend of downsizing welfare. In this new situation older people's own interest organizations should actively try to protect their vested interests which have previously been sustained by passively supporting the political parties. Their political response can now become the centre of the present reform process because older people comprise the largest beneficiary group of the Swedish welfare state, and their relative electoral power resource is increasing in terms of age-consciousness and organizational mobilization. However, the possibility of a new solidaristic movement of Swedish older people seems to be somewhat unlikely if we remember their passivity or acquiescence in old age politics until now (see Chapter 2).

In addition, there are many reasons why Swedish older people cannot be defined as a homogeneous group; there are internal divisions among older people, for example, in terms of class and sex. This raises a very interesting question: what then are the crucial divisions, in terms of welfare programmes for older people? The answer to this question will lead us to grasp the present structure of old age politics in Sweden. In the next section, we will firstly discuss the demographic elements and welfare expenditures that generally determine the characteristics of the welfare politics of old age. Then we will look at the nature of expenditure distribution that causes the existence of fissures in the Swedish population as a political whole, with each interest group fighting for a larger share. Based on the results of such a discussion, we will reach a conclusion that a new politics of old age is emerging, where the interest organizations of older people are starting to play a significant role in the policy-making process, at all levels of Swedish welfare politics.

## New politics of old age

*Divisions rediscovered*

It is said that the current Swedish politics of the welfare state are not solely to do with pure class politics. If we accept this as true, what are the characteristics of new interest divisions in the battlefield of Swedish welfare politics? As mentioned earlier, the main split seems to lie in the division of role in the welfare state, that is, welfare recipients versus taxpayers. However, this dichotomy, which is usually utilized by neo-liberal theorists when they criticize the welfare state as being an unfair distribution mechanism, cannot explain the phenomenon completely when almost all members of society belong to both groups at the same time. Due to various income maintenance policies, almost all recipients are automatically included *de facto* in the Swedish tax system. Therefore the dichotomy does not exactly fit the Swedish case – hence we will look at the welfare division of labour in (albeit vague) terms of 'winners and losers'. 'Winner' is here defined as one who gains more welfare benefit, in comparison to their current contributions; 'losers' are necessarily the opposite.

Sweden's life expectancy is among the highest in the world; consequently, the Swedish population is among the oldest on the globe. According to an estimate by the Swedish Statistical Bureau, the percentage of people over 65 will increase, though only slightly, as we can see in Table 10.2. This fact is also reflected in Figure 10.2, showing the relative size of the expenditure structure of Swedish social welfare.

Overall, the number of people over 65 has more than doubled in the post-war period, from almost 800,000 in 1950 to well over 2 million several decades later. Pensioners as a group are key welfare clients – traditionally winners (in our terminology) in Sweden due to their relatively large proportion of the total population. Today, pensioners comprise more than 100 per cent of the population over 60 because of multiple pension ownership. There are various subgroups, the largest being the old age retirement pensioners, whose number rose from 600,000 in 1950 to well over 1.5 million in 1996. For a long time, this group made up around 60 per cent of the total population aged over 60, but by 1980 its share had risen to 75 per cent as a result of the lowering of the general retirement age from 67 to 65 in 1976, together with the introduction of a flexible partial pension system permitting retirement from age 60 onwards. During the period between 1960 and 1996, there was a rapid growth in the number of recipients of old age supplementary pensions, and this is the biggest expenditure item of the Swedish welfare state.

In the Swedish pension system, the retired generation wins and the working generation loses when we consider the intergenerational redistribution effect of the system (Ståhlberg 1991). As can be seen from Table 10.2, from about the year 2010, a reduced number of economically active persons will

**Table 10.2** The age composition of the Swedish population (per cent)

|  | 1970 | 1980 | 1994 | 2000 | 2010 |
|---|---|---|---|---|---|
| Age 0–15 | 22.1 | 21.3 | 20.0 | 20.6 | 18.6 |
| Age 16–64 | 64.1 | 62.5 | 62.5 | 62.4 | 63.1 |
| Age 65+ | 13.8 | 16.2 | 17.5 | 17.0 | 18.3 |

*Source*: SCB (1994)

**Figure 10.2**  Subsectors of social welfare expenditure in million SEK (constant price, 1980 = 100)

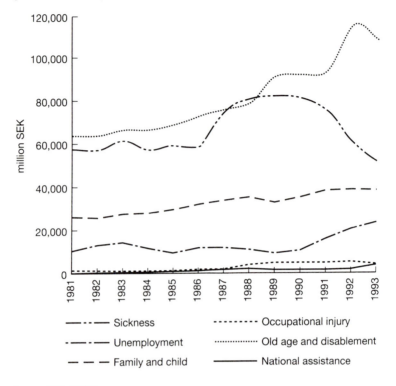

*Source*: SCB (1997)

have to support a growing number of economically non-active persons. In its forecast, the Swedish Statistics Bureau foresees a higher fertility rate and greater immigrant input than in the estimate above. However, this is of marginal importance in relation to the systematic problems being discussed here. An increased dependency ratio will of course place a great strain on pension politics in the future[7] (Eriksen 1988; Ståhlberg 1991).

In examining differences between pensioner groups – that is, intragenerational redistribution – we have to rely on data on individual incomes taken from tax statistics. Pensioner incomes vary greatly according to programme membership, previous economic activity, age and sex; among them, the division along class lines is the most important. Basic pensions are progressive while the ATP is regressive in its redistributive aspect: in total, private sector white-collar employees receive the highest pensions, followed by central government employees, private sector workers and local authority employees; those receiving the combined supplementary/basic pension are the second-lowest group, the worst off being those receiving only a basic pension. More and more women become eligible for ATP as more women work and earn pensionable incomes. However, women's ATP is on average still lower than men's. Under the scheme, the individual pension rights for any year are equal to the present value of that year's contribution to future pension benefits. Formally, everyone is treated equally in the ATP. Men and women are subjected to the same rules. Women's lower wages are therefore one reason why in practice women's earnings-related pension benefits differ from those of men. Besides, women's labour market behaviour is different from that of men, so that the rules concerning qualifying years and pensionable income have other consequences for women than men (Ståhlberg 1990).

As to the question of 'winners and losers' in the arena of welfare for older people, we can now answer that there exist certain divisions along the line of occupation and sex. These can, however, be subsumed in the more significant struggle between the generations (pensioners versus the others) if we consider the on-going current political debates. This is true especially when we consider that the old age pension is the biggest part of Swedish publicly administered welfare programmes. The growing number of older people is the more decisive factor affecting future old age politics in Sweden; these traditional winners will become losers if more cutbacks are made. This is also true when we look at the current trend of downsizing in the welfare state. This damages older people's standard of living and the job security of public employees, although it is concealed by complicated techniques and political caprice under the liberal slogan of 'reduction of unfair social burden'.

In addition to this, another sector of the Swedish population is relevant to the issue of welfare cutbacks and old age politics: people who are working for older people in the public sector. In 1994 there were 1.04 million municipal and county council employees. They comprised 29 per cent (municipalities 21 per cent and county councils 8 per cent) of gainfully employed people in Sweden. State employees accounted for 6 per cent of all jobs in the same year. The municipality or county council is often the largest single employer in its area. In 1994, 54 per cent of municipal employees worked in the social services, including child and elder care, and 19 per cent in the educational system. A clear majority of municipal employees (80 per cent) are women, many of them working on a part-time basis. Of county council employees, 82 per cent were women in 1994. The largest personnel category at the county council level is health care employees (Gustafsson 1988; KF 1994; LF 1995). Working women in the public welfare field (many of them dealing with older people's issues) therefore will be another big loser when there are more welfare cutbacks.

We can thus see that older people's interest groups and the public employment unions are important factors to be considered in terms of their organizational and, especially political, efforts to influence the policy-making process. In the following section, however, we only comment briefly on the pensioners' organizations because the welfare state cutbacks in Sweden are not as severe as in other EU countries, and the subsequent responses from the affected groups are not yet that strong.[8] In addition, public sector unions are less interesting here because they reflect existing class politics, at least so far.

*Bring the old age politics back in*

Now let us look more closely at pensioners' interest organizations in the context of policy-making. Because pensioners represent one of the most important sources of demand for welfare state services, their political mobilization and activities are likely to have repercussions for many other areas of public policy in general.

Sweden is often described as a corporatist state, in which public policy is worked out through a process of consultation and negotiation between organized groups representing major interests in society. The state, business and trade unions are usually seen as the three major voices in a corporatist state, but many other interest groups also exist.

For our purposes here, pensioners' organizations can be defined as the representatives of older people's common interests. Substantial numbers of pensioners have worked together in a more or less organized fashion to improve their living situation through quasi-formal contacts with state and market organizations (Andersson 1983; Olsson Hort and Sparks 1993). To participate in the preparation of social welfare policy, an organization needs to be selected for co-option under the Swedish corporatist decision-making mechanism. The state Ministry of Health and Social Affairs is responsible for deciding who is going to be chosen and for financially supporting the selected organizations. Policy is finalized after a democratic and time-consuming process through state commissions of inquiry (SOU)[9] and *remiss*,[10] where pensioner groups participate. As for implementation, a seat on lay boards governing certain public agencies is offered to selected insiders, but not to pensioners' organizations. Under this process, Swedish pensioners are represented chiefly by two major groups, invited to SOU or *remiss*. Both selectively invited organizations claim to act as interest groups for their members and (among other things) lobby policy makers to promote their views on important social issues.

There are at least five major pensioners' organizations in Sweden. The two largest are, as already mentioned, PRO and SPF. In addition there is a religious association (RPG) and two organizations for former public sector employees, one at state (SPRF) and the other at municipal level (SKPF). The latter is open to pensioners in general and recently became bigger than RPG and SPRF. In addition, SPRF decided to open its membership to the public in 1994. Although politically unsuccessful as yet, we can find some pensioners' political activity in Sweden, especially at the municipal level, for example, SPI (Swedish Party for Pensioners' Interests) and SVP (Pensioners' Unity Party). Of those organizations and parties, PRO and SPF will be discussed in the following section because they have been selectively invited to take part in the decision-making process at state level, regarding welfare programmes for older people.

Both PRO and SPF call themselves politically independent, but both identify themselves with the country's two largest political parties. The Social Democratic PRO is the larger of the two, with 375,000 members in 1992. The Conservative SPF had about 159,000 members in the same year. Both have similar goals: in addition to organizing leisure and educational activities for their members, they seek to influence public policy at all levels of government in order to improve pensioners' living conditions. They are currently developing several alternatives to public social services as well, for example 'organized friendly services' (older people helping each other) and so forth. In this sense, pensioners' organizations are distinctive in terms of membership and goals compared to other types of major interest groups, for example, LO or SAF. On pensions they are ready to ignore conventional class-based allegiances and fight solely for the pensioners themselves (PRO 1990; Olsson 1993; SPF 1997).

PRO was established in 1942 on the initiative of active members in trade unions and other associations. Officially, it is an independent voluntary organization, not connected with any political or religious group or party. The organization receives no financial support from Social Democratic Party, and although it analyses and publicizes each party's position on key issues before elections, it does not officially endorse any party, nor does it adopt a viewpoint on political issues such as Sweden's entry into the European Union. At the same time, PRO officials and members do not disguise the fact that the vast majority of the group's membership is Social Democrat. As a voluntary organization, PRO receives some support from the government at the national level, and in most cases at the county and local levels as well. However, the bulk of its revenues comes from membership fees. Among the eight main goals that PRO lists in its information booklet there are two of particular relevance: firstly, to take an active part in creating progressive policies that provide welfare and economic security for pensioners; and, secondly, to influence decision making and legislation concerning pensioners by means of communications and negotiations with authorities and political bodies. During its 1989 Congress, PRO further underscored its self-defined mandate to protect members' interests in the area of social policy by including social benefits and services on the agenda (PRO 1990).

SPF was established in 1939 and had about 190,000 members in 1997 (SPF 1997). There has been a steady increase of membership, which is attributed to a more aggressive stance by the organization, both towards recruitment and on political questions like fees for care. Like PRO, SPF claims to be politically independent, but the great majority of its members identify with a major political party, in this case the Conservative party. However, the group's spokesman at the national level insisted that 'SPF criticizes the Moderate-led government just as much now as it did when the Social Democrats were in power', and that 'we make no distinctions between governments when arguing the pensioners' cause'. It does appear that SPF's links to the Conservative party are less strong than those between PRO and the Social Democrats, for the simple reason that the Social Democratic tradition of grassroots organization means that many key members of PRO are longstanding party activists, well schooled in the jargon and organizational demands of sustained group action. Among its seven major goals, SPF stresses the monitoring of political questions related to pensioners; if listed according to their relative importance these are pensions, personal care, housing fees and so on. They are also against the increase of fees and contribution to the programmes; on this point, the two major pensioners' organizations share a common stance. More importantly, even if SPF has a pro-Conservative tendency, it is opposed to discrimination against pensioners (SPF 1997).

At all levels of organization, officials and members state that the two groups cooperate rather than compete when it comes to lobbying for the social and economic welfare of pensioners. They are purely organizations for older people and they do what is best for older people in spite of different perceptions on many issues (Sparks 1994). Such differences are apparent with regard to privatization of social services such as home help. PRO is absolutely opposed to this kind of change, claiming that it jeopardizes 'social rights' and is blatant 'profit making'; while SPF is more open minded, seeing it in terms of competition for better services. Representatives from both groups, nevertheless, have been united in their concern that the privatization of home helps would increase the cost. The campaign against prohibitive fee increases appeared to be a central challenge for both PRO and SPF in the first half of the 1990s, as fees for social services were raised, often drastically, throughout the country.

### The paradox of decentralization and decorporatization

The organizational structure and activity of both pensioners' organizations suggests that they should be seen as voluntary movements, with all the historical and political implications that this term carries in Sweden. The pensioners' organizations play a formal role in attempting to negotiate and discuss with government officials on issues that affect their members, although they have no formal power to oppose the government's decisions. The structures for the interaction of pensioners' organizations and government exist at all levels of government. Discussions on more stable contacts between government and the PRO began in the late 1970s when the forms of pensioners' consultation were first raised (Michelletti 1995). As a result, a research commission into pensioners' influence was initiated in 1981 and its report was published in 1988; during this period, the PRO and SPF were regularly consulted by the commission. The report's first recommendation to the Ministry of Health and Social Affairs was that 'a negotiated right to deliberation (överläggningsrätt) should be introduced at the national level, initially for a five-year trial period' (SOU 1988). This was realized in 1991 as the PK (the Pensioners' Advisory Committee). Priority at the national level could then be put firmly on formal rather than informal channels. Also overall status of grey issues rose on the political agenda. PK has become a focal point for the work of interest groups at the national level, and a means of raising awareness. To become a member of PK, an organization must be open to all pensioners and have a certain number of members (SOU 1988). PK members get an exclusive state subsidy. Currently, PRO and SPF are regular members of PK, while SPRF and RPG are invited to *remiss* and participate in the forum, named PSK (Pensioner Associations' Committee for Cooperation), through which pensioners' organizations have discussions on their views prior to PK meetings. This is a clear sign of closer relations between interest groups at the national level (Blake 1997).

The 1991 Local Government Act provides a framework designed, among other things, to strengthen local democracy. Strong emphasis has been placed on the importance of providing local inhabitants with opportunities to monitor and influence the decision-making process. Although the specific nature of the local committees differs from one place to another, it has become more possible for pensioners to participate at the local level of decision making, where personal social services for older people are dealt with. According to the Act, the task of the executive committee is to supervise the administration of municipal affairs and to keep itself informed about the activities of all the other, specialized municipal committees; its main tasks are budget drafting and coordination of the municipality's overall operations. There are executive committees with similar functions at the county council level. The executive committees are elected by their respective municipal and county councils.

The Local Government Act now allows municipalities and county councils to decide their own organizational structure. Most local governments have a special committee for older people's welfare services. In addition to this, most counties and municipalities have established advisory boards of pensioners (pensionärsråd) as the forum for formal interaction (PRO 1990; Sparks 1994; SPF 1997). However, county and municipal government levels are not clones of one another, with differences including levels of 'party support', money provided to each elected group, and differing political opportunities. Most of the existing LPR (County Pensioners' Advisory Board) and KPR (Municipal Pensioners' Advisory Board) were established in the 1980s and have no formal function other than as 'expert' consultation bodies. They are more evidently information sources (SOU 1988). As with PK at the national level, the LPR and KPR are the focal point for lobbying from respectively county and municipal pensioners' organizations. Here we will focus on the municipal level, since this is primarily where policies regarding personal social services for older people are determined and older people's participation seems to be more active under the slogan of 'consumerism'. In nearly every municipality, there exits a KPR where representatives from the pensioners' organizations and local government sit. The regulations governing KPRs vary to a degree among municipalities. According to a survey conducted by the Association of Swedish Municipalities Kommunförbundet), most KPRs meet four times a year. It is, in most cases, the only formal forum for communication between pensioners and municipality, although informal contacts also occur. Most responses felt that the KPRs' activities were not satisfactory and wanted them to be changed. In recent trend of 1996, however, the decision to have a KPR lies in the government's hands; the board can be abolished when the government wants. In this context we can say that pensioners' political power is still weak and nominal (Sparks 1994).

As mentioned earlier, the increased opportunity for pensioners' political participation in the decision-making process was reinforced by the decentralization trend at that time. Nevertheless, their greater participation does not seem to be totally effective due to the change in Swedish politics in general, i.e. the 'decorporatization' of the political decision-making mecha-

nism. Major attacks on the corporatist model can be traced back to 198?
when the SAF withdrew from centralized wage negotiations (Michellett
1991). Decorporatization then became a popular trend which affectec
sectoral policy-making networks. According to Streck and Schmitter (1991)
formerly distinct European politics may now be moving in the direction o
American-type 'disjointed pluralism'. The usage of social welfare policy
commissions has declined, and is regarded as an example of the break-up o
the consensus-oriented political culture which governed throughout the
golden era. This coincides with the time that pensioners' organization
appeared more active and were invited into the corporatist type of decision
making system. Hence we conclude that pensioners' recent active participa
tion in decentralized political decision making is therefore mitigated anc
marginalized by the phenomenon of decorporatization. Now what we car
observe is the repluralization and resurgence of Swedish civil society ir
which pensioners' political activism is undergoing an examination. Becaus«
decorporatization means fewer insider roles for pensioners' interest groups
they need to make more efforts to influence public policy as outsiders – fo
example by demonstrations on the streets or debates on the mass media –
(Michelletti 1993, 1995) or to become *de facto* policy makers themselve
through the elections.

## Conclusion

Regarding the current guidelines and reform proposals for the future of the
Swedish welfare state and the trend towards less government, it is clear tha
we will see more privatization and cutbacks in the future although they
might be less acute than those of other countries. In this situation, Swedis!
pensioners' organizations will form a united front to protect the social citi
zenship earned during the golden era of welfare state development. It will b«
more possible for Swedish older people to respond more actively by mobiliz
ing their electoral power resource within these organizations because of thei
higher level of equality in old age life in comparison to other countries. Ir
this sense, Swedish older people are more homogeneous as a social grou|
than their counterparts in other countries.

Pensioners out on the streets demonstrating has become a more and mor«
common sight; sometimes protests are organized nationally. This type o
outsider action in a way acknowledges that hitherto participation o
pensioners' organizations in the decision-making process was merely advi
sory and ineffectual. This is also connected to the general political change.
summarized as the decorporatization of decision making.

In step with new political phenomena such as distrust of establishe«
parties, rising electoral volatility and the emergence of new parties ir
Swedish politics (including the older people's SPI and SVP), the general elec
tion of 1998 is therefore very interesting. In addition, other types of organi
zation, for example public sector employees, most of whom are women
might form another political pressure group and join the front line backin;
the pensioners' groups when the degree of 'downsizing' becomes unaccept
able. Everything is unclear yet, but there is one visible trend, the increasin;

political radicalization of pensioners, as the crisis of the welfare state deepens.

## Notes

1 This trend of new social movements encompasses all the postmodern issues such as old age, gender, ethnicity, environment and so forth, in terms of 'diversification of interests'.
2 In addition to the payroll tax, most employers also set aside money to finance non-statutory insurance schemes as part of nationwide negotiations with the major trade unions. As a result, in recent decades a system of occupational welfare benefits has come into being, which complements the statutory system, but also creates problems of coordination between the two (Olsson Hort 1993).
3 Except for a small number of private hospitals, the county councils own all the hospitals in Sweden. However, three municipalities – Göteborg (Gothenburg), Malmö and the isle of Gotland – are not part of county council areas and are responsible for running their own medical care systems. The county councils are also responsible for outpatient medical care at hospital clinics and district health centres. This care includes maternity and child health centres. The county councils are also responsible for public dental services, psychiatric care, vaccinations and X-ray centres (Gustafsson 1988; LF 1995).
4 Employees are currently expected to receive an old age pension which is equivalent to roughly 60 per cent of their average income of the best-paid 15 years after a minimum of 30 years employment.
5 In the mid-1970s, employers' social security contributions were introduced and soon became the major source of finance, covering two thirds of total finance. As a system which accumulates capital, not only contributions but also revenue from interest are important for its future fiscal balance. This programme is administered by four extra-budgetary funds, and their contributions now account for approximately one third of total ATP finance (see Table 10.1).
6 In addition, some pensioners receive regular support from sickness insurance, for example, part of their in-patient hospital treatment costs, travel costs to hospitals and outpatient centres, reimbursements for pharmaceutical outlays and so on.
7 It is, however, the structure of the programme itself which is its worst enemy. The method of inflation protection, the rules for earning ATP, the programme's conception as a pay-as-you-go system, etc. are all characteristics which were hotly debated before the 1960 Bill. The results are now, three decades later, evident to see.
8 This is evident when we compare the Swedish severity of cutbacks with those of other European countries.
9 In Sweden, SOU are important because they are regarded as influential institutions which produce policy recommendations on the basis of their specific researches on certain issues.
10 This is a process in which invited interest organizations write responses to public policy proposals.

# 11

# The politics of old age in the UK

JAY GINN AND SARA ARBER

Britain's welfare state – so crucial to older people's well-being – was conceived in the turmoil of war and constructed in the difficult economic circumstances of the 1940s and 1950s. Designed by Beveridge, a Liberal, and implemented by the Labour government elected in 1945, the welfare state gained acceptance among all social classes. Yet while Beveridge identified five giants – Want, Disease, Idleness, Squalor and Ignorance – as the foes to be vanquished by collective insurance, the welfare state itself now stands accused as a public enemy, charged with undermining individual self-reliance and national economic competitiveness.

The paradox of the current retreat from state welfare, after 50 years of improvements in national productivity, highlights the need to take account of shifting political forces, as well as economic and demographic developments, in understanding changes in welfare policy. Conventional accounts which explain the privatization of welfare as determined by the ageing of populations need to be challenged from the perspectives of political and moral economy.

This chapter considers the political context in which Conservative governments since 1979 have reduced state welfare provision for older people. The main features of the post-war welfare system will first be outlined, focusing on state pensions and access to health and social care. Recent moves to privatize welfare for older people, and the arguments used to justify cuts in state provision are then examined. Finally, the effectiveness of organized resistance to this trend is assessed.

A key question is the extent to which older people have acted as an age-interest group, using electoral power, campaigning or consultation processes; or whether interests based on class or gender exert a predominant influence which crosscuts and outweighs identification on the basis of age (Walker 1986). Related to this issue is the differential impact and significance of state welfare for different population groups and generations, eliciting their support, indifference, or opposition to public spending on welfare for older people.

## Post-war welfare for older people

The 1942 Beveridge report on *Social Insurance and Allied Services* marked a decisive ideological shift in favour of state planning, a change stemming from the unifying effects of national struggle and from the evident success of wartime state control of the economy. The principle of state social insurance was accepted by most trade unions and employers, pre-war opposition having been muted by the wartime experience. Although doubts lingered in the Treasury, no serious argument was made that pensions and health care should be left to the market (Harris 1981). We outline, for the state pension and the National Health Service (NHS), the nature of the class compromise reached in the 1940s.

*State pensions*

The pension system introduced by the 1946 National Insurance Act was intended to be based on a funded, actuarially balanced, state pension scheme. National Insurance (NI) contributions by employees and employers would accumulate in a fund from which pensions would start to be paid after 20 years. For reasons of political expediency, however, the pension was set below subsistence level and was paid in full immediately, leading to a Pay-As-You-Go (PAYG) scheme. The basic pension was meant to provide a flat-rate income adequate for those lacking other resources but low enough to encourage voluntary additional saving. The NI pension scheme was intended to achieve both redistribution over the life course (or compulsory saving for later life) and a measure of intragenerational redistribution according to class, gender and marital status.

Middle class interests were reflected in the relatively low NI contributions from employer and employee, while the flat-rate pension ensured some redistribution towards the lower paid. Nevertheless, the low level of the pension perpetuated reliance on means-tested benefits for many working class pensioners. Occupational and other private pensions attracted tax relief for contributing employees, mainly middle class men, and for employers operating a scheme.

The interests of married men were served by the fact that a married man's contributions bought pension benefits for two – his own and a reduced (60 per cent) pension for his wife. In terms of opportunities to gain their own state pension, women were ill-served by the new scheme, due to the assumption that most would be financially supported by a husband. For example, married women were handicapped by the notorious 'half test', whereby those paying contributions for less than half their working life since marriage lost the value of all their contributions, and were discouraged from building a pension by the right to opt for reduced contributions. No insurance credits were available for periods of caring for children or parents-in-law.

One advantage for women, which also benefited married men, was

conceded in 1940 following representations from two quarters (Thane 1978)
First, the National Spinsters' Association argued that single women deserved
a pension at 55 because many cared for dependent older relatives, they
earned lower wages than men and they were often forced by employers to
retire in their fifties. Second, complaints of poverty among retired couples
were made to the government; because husbands were on average five years
older than their wives, a couple had to manage on only one pension until the
wife reached 65. Granting all women an earlier pension age at 60 was
deemed a cheaper solution than increasing the level of the basic pension.

The National Federation of Retirement Pensions Associations, founded in
1939 and now known as Pensioners' Voice, represented working class interests and was one of the earliest organizations to campaign for a higher state
pension. The value of the pension did increase slightly, as a proportion of
male manual earnings, from 19.1 per cent in 1948 to 21.5 per cent in 1975
(Johnson and Falkingham 1992), yet for most of the post-war period it has
remained below the level of means-tested benefits.

The low NI pension fostered a rapid expansion in occupational pension
coverage, from 13 per cent of the workforce in 1936 to 47 per cent in 1967
falling slightly to 46 per cent in the 1970s (Hannah 1986) and rising to 49
per cent in the 1990s (ONS 1997). British trade unions' aim to share in this
middle class 'perk' rather than campaign for better state pensions contrasts
with the long resistance, until 1993, of Danish manual trade unions to
participation in occupational pension schemes. British employers' welfare
payments, as a proportion of total remuneration, doubled between the mid-
1960s and the 1980s (Green *et al.* 1984), improving benefits for the minority of the population belonging to an occupational pension scheme but
exacerbating the social division of welfare. The social division was along
gender lines as much as class, with women's membership remaining well
below men's.

Because of the reciprocal relationship between state and private provision,
in which low provision in one tends to stimulate the other, Beveridge's
recommendations had 'furthered the conditions within social security for the
growth of a multi-billion-pound enterprise of private pensions' (Shragge
1984: 33). The introduction of the state Graduated Pension in 1961, extending an earnings-related scheme to those excluded from occupational
pensions, was too little and too late to stem the demand for private provision
(Hannah 1986). With the interests of large employers, pension fund
investors, non-manual employees and organized male manual workers
served by occupational pensions, the political basis of the defence of state
pensions was seriously weakened in the 1950s and 1960s.

For the first time, in 1975, under a Labour government the Social Security Pensions Act specifically addressed the pension needs of women, potentially broadening the base of support for the principle of state provision.
Home Responsibilities Protection (HRP) allowed years of caring to count
towards eligibility for the basic state pension while the new State Earnings
Related Pension Scheme (SERPS) based benefits on the best 20 years of earnings. This pension package, which promised to minimize the adverse effect
of women's family caring responsibilities on their pensions, also indexed the

basic pension amount to national earnings. The 1975 improvements were thus shared across generations, benefiting both current pensioners and working age people, as well as giving women a new stake in state pensions. The reinvigoration of state pensions was short lived, and was overtaken by the neo-liberal reforms of the 1980s (discussed later).

## Health and social care

The NHS Act of 1946 committed the state to funding a comprehensive health service based on the principles of collectivism and equality, free at the point of service. In spite of the radicalism of this approach, the medical profession retained its considerable power and independence: hospital doctors were persuaded to accept salaried status but remained free to supplement their income with private practice, while payments to general practitioners (GPs) were based on capitation.

Thus the new NHS, a 'compromise between the state and the profession' (Allsop 1984: 12) proved popular across the political spectrum. Although coexisting with a small private sector of health insurance which grew in the 1950s and 1960s, and suffering some erosion of free access through small but increasing prescription charges, widespread support made any major attack on the founding principle of the NHS politically unthinkable. In addition, the NHS proved remarkably cheap, costing 5.2 per cent of GDP compared with 5.6 per cent average in the OECD, with only Japan, Portugal, Greece and Turkey spending less than Britain (Hills 1993). The phrase 'from the cradle to the grave' encapsulated the all-embracing aim of the NHS and its basis in intergenerational solidarity.

However, some evidence of ageism in the NHS emerged in the low status and lack of resources accorded to geriatric specialists and to facilities such as psychogeriatric hospitals; in the way older people in institutional care were treated (Townsend 1962); in discrimination against older people in the provision of health care and exclusion from screening programmes (Henwood 1990); and in the frequent exclusion of older people from medical research studies (MRC 1994).

Moreover, the social care often required by older people (that is, support and assistance unrelated to medical conditions) was provided not by the NHS but by local authorities. Local authority residential homes, which charged on a means-tested basis, were covered by separate legislation, the National Assistance Act 1948, and were specified as for 'infirm' (not ill or disabled) older people. This distinction, intended by Bevan to ensure that old people's homes were not used to undermine the principle of free health care, remained until 1990.

The British welfare state, lacking the strong social democratic foundation of the Nordic countries or the corporate statist tradition of Germany, emerged as a class compromise. The mixed economy of welfare was sufficiently popular to withstand challenges from the right until the late 1970s, when the more solidaristic elements of welfare began to be undermined. The next section examines the political shift underlying the changes in welfare for older people from 1979 to 1997.

*Reducing state welfare for older people*

With the election of a Conservative government in 1979, an individualistic competitive ideology gained ascendancy, accompanied by monetarism marketization and privatization (Walker 1991). State welfare was attacked a breeding a 'culture of dependency' and stifling wealth-creating enterprise while public sector institutions were castigated as inherently inefficient. The ensuing spate of reforms was wide-ranging, including curbs on local government, anti-union measures, closure and privatization of nationalized industry as well as restructuring the welfare state. The latter reforms included cutting state pensions and reducing the role of the NHS in caring for the chronically sick and disabled, mainly older people. The main changes since 1979 are briefly outlined.

Indexing the basic state pension to prices instead of national average earnings has eroded its relative value since 1980 from 20 per cent of average male earnings to 14 per cent by 1993 (Commission on Social Justice 1994), well below the level of means-tested benefits. As a result, by 1994 a third of pensioners required means-tested benefits (Johnson 1994), while those with small additional pensions (less than £40 per week in 1993) faced a poverty trap, receiving little financial benefit from them (Hills 1993: 28).

The second-tier State Earnings Related Pensions Scheme (SERPS) although not abolished as planned in the early 1980s, was scaled back in the Social Security Act 1986. The accrual rate was reduced, giving a maximum pension of 20 per cent (instead of 25 per cent) of average revalued earnings and the calculation was based on earnings over a working life of 44 years for women and 49 years for men, instead of the best 20 years. This change will substantially reduce the amount of SERPS pension for those with periods out of employment or on low earnings. From the year 2000, widows will inherit only half their deceased husband's SERPS, instead of the whole amount.

The 1995 Pensions Act brought a further cut to state pensions in the future, affecting women only; their state pension age will be raised from 60 to 65, phasing in the change from 2010 until 2020. This will substantially reduce the amount of basic and SERPS pension received by women born after 1950, except for the minority who are able to continue in full-time employment until the age of 65 (Hutton *et al.* 1995). Among those who have a SERPS pension, women's income from SERPS is already only two thirds of men's on average (Davies and Ward 1992). Raising their pension age to 65 will magnify the existing gender inequality.

Since 1988, the government has provided financial incentives to opt out of SERPS; millions have taken the bait, providing lucrative business for the personal pensions industry but dubious benefits to most premium payers especially the low paid (Davies and Ward 1992). Although the government claimed that opting out would reduce public spending, the net cost of the incentives to the NI fund from 1988–93 was estimated as £6,000 million (1988 prices) (National Audit Office 1990). This example illustrates the more general practice whereby private welfare subsidies tend to be less visible than welfare spending. Treasury expenditure on tax reliefs grew dramatically under the Thatcher administration, from £1,200 million in 1979 to £8,200 million in 1991 (Wilkinson 1993). The cost of tax relief, rebates and incentives for personal and occupational pensions reached £20 billion in 1994/5 (Glennerster and Hills 1998).

Because private pensions are less accessible to women and the low paid (Ginn and Arber 1993, 1996), the switch in resources from state to private pensions has a disproportionate effect on these groups, magnifying the effect of inequalities in the labour market. Income inequality among pensioners has widened considerably since 1979 (Hancock and Weir 1994).

The main change in health care provision affecting older people has been the development of community care. British governments since the 1960s have highlighted the advantages of care in the community for frail or mentally ill older people, compared with long-term institutional care (Henwood 1990). Despite the political consensus on the desirability of community care, there has been confusion as to what this means (Walker 1982): care *in* the community supported by statutory domiciliary services or care *by* the community, that is, by family, friends and neighbours. The Conservative government favoured increased reliance on the latter (DHSS 1981).

In spite of the Conservative government's advocacy of community care, their 1980 Social Security Act fuelled the expansion of private residential and nursing home places during the 1980s by providing social security incentives in favour of institutional care (Audit Commission 1986). The escalating costs to social security in meeting the private care charges for older people on means-tested benefits reinforced and legitimated the government's preference for family care of frail older people (Department of Health 1989) and the subsequent major reforms in long term care funding.

The NHS and Community Care Act 1990, implemented in 1993, placed responsibility for assessing and arranging care packages on cash-limited local authorities. As a result, frail, chronically ill or disabled older people were increasingly charged for domiciliary services which had previously been free or heavily subsidized. Moreover, services have been restricted: a survey of local authorities showed that 70 per cent of older people who would have received services before 1993 would not be eligible after the reforms (AMA and ACC 1995). It also became more difficult to obtain local authority-funded residential care (Walker 1993). This, with the 33 per cent reduction of NHS beds for older people between 1976 and 1994 (Harding *et al.* 1996), has forced older people who are too ill to be cared for at home into private nursing homes charging from £350 to £450 per week. Whereas in the mid-1970s a quarter of older people receiving long term care in a residential setting were paid for by the NHS, only 10 per cent did so in 1995 (Harding *et al.* 1996). Nursing home and residential care fees are subsidized by local authorities for those with insufficient income and under £16,000 assets but some 40,000 older people each year are forced to sell their home to pay residential care fees (Hamnett and Mullings 1992).

Thus the founding principle of the NHS – free health care to all who are sick – has been preserved for acute illness but breached for chronic illness, a change which overwhelmingly affects older rather than younger people. The overall effect of the community care policy has been to transfer much of the cost of care from the state to individuals, mainly older people.

The British government's welfare cuts have been more radical than elsewhere in Europe. Although opposed by organized labour and by a mushrooming of new pensioner organizations, the trend to welfare retrenchment has shown no sign of slowing. Before turning to the question of resistance to the attack on welfare for older people, the next section examines how the government presented the issues to the public and assesses the validity of their arguments.

### Legitimating the shift to private pensions and health care

In justifying reductions in state welfare for older people, the government, the media and other commentators have relied on two kinds of argument: economic/demographic and moral/ideological.

The rise in the number of older people and in the gerontic ratio – the proportion of the adult population over state pension age – has created a sense of crisis about the sustainability of state welfare (DSS 1991, 1993). Media reports have raised alarm about a 'grey time bomb' or a 'rising tide' of older people, frequently referring to older people as a 'burden' on society. An academic version warns of 'a large, growing and possibly unsustainable fiscal burden on the productive populations in developed nations' (Johnson *et al.* 1989: 9), while a World Bank report (1994: iii) predicts 'a looming old age crisis': examples of 'apocalyptic demography'.

In Britain, challenges to the demographic determinism implied by these forecasts has come not from the political 'opposition' but from pensioner organizations and academic analysts. Writers have pointed out the uncertainty of demographic projections and of economic activity rates in the working age population (Falkingham 1989) and Britain's modest projected increase in the gerontic ratio compared with past increases that proved manageable (Hills 1993; Vincent 1996). Hutton, Kennedy and Whiteford (1995: 15) note that 'the UK pension system is currently one of the "cheapest" of all OECD countries', costing less than 7 per cent of GDP, that state pensions provide the lowest earnings replacement rate in the EU, with the exception of Ireland and that the rate of the British increase in pension costs is low compared with most OECD countries. The affordability of improved state pensions has been amply demonstrated (Townsend and Walker 1995; National Pensioners' Convention 1998).

Predictions of unsustainable health care costs based on rising numbers of older people have ignored evidence from the US showing compression of morbidity into a shorter period among later cohorts of the very old (Manton *et al.* 1995). The idea that the British welfare state is facing a financial crisis has been comprehensively assessed and rejected by Hills (1993, 1997).

A related debate has concerned the merits of pay-as-you-go versus funded pensions, respectively associated with state and private pensions. The previous Conservative government has been joined by the New Labour one in arguing that funded second-tier pensions, in which contributions are invested until retirement, are preferable for the individual and avoid intergenerational inequity arising from a numerical imbalance between generations. Examination of the chief economic arguments for private funded pensions – a higher rate of return for the individual and increased investment funds benefiting the economy – has shown them to be unconvincing (Mabbett 1997), or to apply only in certain circumstances (Lloyd-Sherlock and Johnson 1996). Nor can funded pensions protect individuals from the effects of an ageing population unless 'the rate of return on contributions exceed[s] the rate of economic growth by a sufficient margin to counter the effects of the rising dependency ratio', a condition unlikely to be met (Mabbett 1997: 30). As Hills (1993) points out, privatizing pensions does not remove pensioners' claim on resources but merely switches it from the tax system to dividends; the growing private pension funds have been taking ever-higher dividends from company profits, reducing funds available for investment in British industry and threatening competitiveness.

The economic arguments for reducing state welfare for older people have been reinforced by an appeal to equity: a 'welfare generation' of older people were taking an unfair share of public resources, jeopardizing the intergenerational contract in which contributions paid during working life create an entitlement to resources in retirement (Johnson *et al.* 1989). Turning the traditional stereotype of needy pensioners on its head, the British media invented a new form of ageism in which older people were portrayed as affluent, enjoying a jet-setting lifestyle on their occupational pensions. Politicians claimed that pensioners were no longer poor, had a diminishing need for state pensions and could afford to pay the economic cost of domiciliary care provided by social services (Falkingham and Victor 1991).

Creating an image of older people as affluent and privileged relied on quoting mean income rather than median, thus giving undue weight to the minority of very wealthy younger pensioners. Gender differences in income in later life and, in particular, older women's lack of occupational pensions (Ginn and Arber 1991, 1994) were ignored or obscured. For example, the previous government's (Lilley 1992) statement about occupational pensions coverage – 'Nearly 70 per cent of those now retiring in the UK will have supplemented their income in this way' – is true only for men; 68 per cent of men aged 55 to 69 had entitlement to an occupational pension in 1988, but only 29 per cent of women in this age group did so (Bone *et al.* 1992: Table 6.2). Misleading statements of this kind, repeated uncritically in the media, helped to bolster the impression that the majority of pensioners were wealthy.

Comparison of the lifetime welfare contributions and receipts of successive cohorts in Britain indicates that each generation born after 1921 will tend to break even. Scaling down the welfare state, far from alleviating intergenerational inequity, will make future generations net losers on average (Hills 1996). However, the lifetime gains or losses resulting from retrenchment and privatization differ according to class, gender and family circumstances.

The weakness of the arguments for cutting state welfare for older people has led some analysts to conclude that a crisis has been socially constructed in order to present a political choice as an economic imperative (Walker 1990; Vincent 1996). An ideological opposition to public welfare, rather than economic reasons or the danger of intergenerational conflict, has motivated welfare retrenchment: 'Political ideology has distorted and amplified the macroeconomic consequences of population ageing in order to legitimate anti-welfare policies' (Walker 1990: 377).

Apocalyptic demography has been less strident in Britain than in the US, where the complaint that older people received too large a share of federal resources was spearheaded by Americans for Generational Equity (AGE) (Minkler 1991). Significantly, this pressure group was financed by banks, insurance companies and health care corporations whose aim was to reduce state welfare and expand private insurance (Quadagno 1990). In Britain, too, the pensions, insurance and finance industry constitute a powerful lobby supporting private pensions.

Although demographic concerns had been raised in the 1950s, the legitimacy of the intergenerational contract came under more sustained scrutiny from the 1970s onwards (Walker 1993). This change, with the 1980s cuts in state welfare for older people, stimulated a growth in pensioner organization. In the next section, the mobilization and political influence of older people after 1979 is assessed.

## Older people's organizations

Campaigns and lobbying by older people's organizations for better state welfare have received remarkably little media attention. Their influence on political parties has so far been very limited, in spite of a growth in membership, level of activity and national coordination. In contrast, the media and the Conservative government responded to middle class concern over having to sell their homes to pay for long term residential care.

Older people's organizations in Britain vary widely in their objectives, activities, membership composition, structure and size, but they can be grouped into five types according to their aims and functions. The main types are: pensioner organizations whose concerns include national issues, especially improved state pensions and health care; a more middle class body promoting social activities and employment opportunities for older people in addition to a concern with welfare; a small political party promoting pensioner interests; charities providing information, advice and local services; and local older people's forums. Charities and some forums are primarily organizations 'for' older people rather than 'of' older people. There is inevitably some overlap in functions among the five types.

### Pensioner organizations

These reflect a trade union orientation in their aims, focusing on the needs of those without private pensions or health care insurance. They emphatically reject the notion that pensioners are a burden on society, pointing to the NI contributions and taxes paid by pensioners throughout their working life. Local pensioner groups, which take up a wide range of local issues of particular relevance to older people, are organized into national bodies.

Pensioners' Voice, the oldest national organization with over 350 branches and some 25,000 members, has maintained its longstanding campaign for an adequate basic pension. Officers of the organization meet regularly with government ministers and with the All Party Parliamentary Group for Pensioners (Age Concern 1996), although evidence of any positive influence through this route is lacking.

The British Pensioners and Trade Union Association (BPTUA) has 32 national trade unions affiliated and estimates it has over 100,000 retired trade unionists and their partners in 400 branches, grouped into regions. Founded in 1972 to mobilize trade unions in support of pensioner causes, the BPTUA aims to defend and improve universal state welfare. It produces a lively campaigning quarterly newspaper, *British Pensioner*. Its 1992 British Pensioners' Charter, which formed the basis of a petition to the government with 200,000 signatures, demanded a basic state pension worth one third of national average earnings for each pensioner and free health and community care as needed. The Pensioners Rights Campaign, founded in 1989, subsequently affiliated to the BPTUA, as has the Greater London Pensioners Association.

The National Pensioners Convention (NPC) was formed in 1979 following a Trade Union Congress (TUC) initiative and reconstituted in 1992 as an independent umbrella body. It has coordinated the policies and actions of a wide variety of pensioner organizations, including the BPTUA, other Trade Union Retired Members Associations (TURMAs) and Pensioners' Voice. County Pensioners Associations, Pensioners Liaison Forums and charities concerned with older people are represented. The total affiliated membership has been estimated at about 1.5 million pensioners. Member organizations support the Declaration of Intent, which includes the demand for an adequate basic pension indexed to national average earnings, as well as free health care and domiciliary services when needed. Although none of the major political parties has supported these demands, campaigning by pensioners helped to defeat the government's plan to increase VAT on fuel in 1995. A TUC Pensioners Committee, formed in 1988, advises the TUC on matters relevant to pensioners. Its aims differ little from the NPC's although occupational pensions have a higher priority.

A notable omission from pensioner organizations' agenda has been the structured disadvantage of older women and minority ethnic older people, although the main policy aims, if achieved, would disproportionately benefit those relying most heavily on the basic state pension – women and other low paid groups. Older women in the UK have not yet matched the success of older women in the US in raising the profile of gender issues. For example, the (unsuccessful) campaign in the early 1990s against legislation to raise women's state pension age was led by the Equal Opportunities Commission, the Fawcett Society and women trade unionists, not by pensioner organizations. Similarly, lobbying for legislation to allow courts to split pensions on divorce and to make sex-based actuarial tables illegal has been left to working-age women.

## Association of Retired People Over 50 (ARP)

Members of the ARP are younger than in other older people's organizations and many have occupational pensions. The ARP, founded in 1988 and claiming 125,000 members in 1991, undertakes political lobbying and maintains links with EU pensioner bodies but is not affiliated to the NPC. It is less concerned than other pensioner organizations with defending the basic pension, emphasizing instead the need for adequate regulation of occupational pensions as well as promoting discount services and social and leisure activities for members.

### Political party for pensioners

The only pensioners' organization to attempt to influence policy through the electoral route is the Pensioners Protection Party (PPP) formed in 1989. With 3,000 members, the PPP supported candidates in the 1992 general election, but made little impact, indicating that older people do not vote as an age-interest group. It became the National Pensioners Party in 1995 and the UK Pensioners Association in 1996 (Age Concern 1996).

### Charities

The main national charities aiming to further the interests of older people include Age Concern, Help the Aged and the Centre for Policy on Ageing. These bodies have moved towards a more active role in advocating policy change on behalf of older people. Ethnic minority older people are represented by the Standing Conference of Ethnic Minority Senior Citizens (SCEMSC), which in 1991 represented nearly 60,000 older people, including Afro-Caribbean and African (134 groups), Asian (82), South-East Asian (19), Mediterranean (14) and Latin American (3). SCEMSC has no formal links with the NPC and its main role is as a resource and advice centre for statutory and voluntary agencies. A major concern of ethnic minority older people has been the need for health and social services appropriate to their culture (Askham *et al.* 1993).

### Older People's Forums

The requirement in the NHS and Community Care Act (1990) that local authorities must develop a Community Care Plan in consultation with service users and informal carers has stimulated the spread of local Older People's Forums (OPFs) to facilitate such consultation, although many have a wider remit than this. Most OPFs have been initiated by the voluntary sector – pensioner organizations or charities – although local authorities have sometimes funded OPFs (Thornton and Tozer 1994). Coverage of OPFs in Scotland, Wales and Greater London is good, but is sparse in the remainder of England and in Northern Ireland (Carter and Nash 1992). Many OPFs have links with the NPC, supporting its campaigns, but forums vary in their independence (the extent to which older people run the organization themselves) and in the influence they are able to exert on local authorities.

There are several obstacles to effective consultation through OPFs. First, older people's heterogeneity, in terms of age, gender, race and class, means that their ability to attend meetings and articulate their views is socially structured (see Chapter 2). Physical and mental functional capacities, access to and cost of transport, as well as the daunting nature of large formal meetings, all affect the ability to contribute views and the representativeness of OPFs. Moreover, some local authorities are keener than others to ensure genuine involvement of older people in planning and evaluating community care or to hear older people's voices on other issues. Consultation may be cursory, limited to selecting 'representatives', and there has often been no feedback to OPFs on how their views have affected services (Thornton and Tozer 1994). Regional or metropolitan OPFs such as the Greater London Forum for the Elderly play a pivotal role in assisting the consultation process, for example by translating Community Care Plans into a more accessible form for local groups and highlighting issues of concern to older people. A variety of initiatives have been developed by the voluntary sector to inform and consult housebound older people (Thornton and Tozer 1994).

Given the inadequate funding of community care by central government, consultation on services resembles inviting the *Titanic's* passengers to comment on the design of the lifeboats, ignoring the dangerous shortfall in provision. However, the growth of OPFs may raise awareness of the political origin of cuts in local domiciliary services and in local hospitals' capacity to cater for chronic illness.

In contrast to the hitherto small impact of mass pensioner campaigns on government policy, protest from traditional Conservative supporters at the prospect of having to sell their homes to pay for long term care in a private nursing home received a great deal of media coverage. The Conservative government responded in 1995 by allowing more assets to be protected from means-testing, and in 1997 proposed providing additional asset protection for those with private long term care insurance, a reform which, however, would benefit only the most affluent.

The pensioner organizations' campaign to defend and improve state welfare was consistent with the moral economy of ageing – or the widely shared beliefs regarding older people's entitlement to a decent standard of living (Minkler and Estes 1991). Indeed, people's willingness to pay for improved state welfare grew through the 1980s, as shown by the British Social Attitudes Surveys, in spite of the media's apocalyptic demography. For example, the proportion of respondents saying the government should increase taxes and spend more on welfare was 32 per cent in 1983, 46 per cent in 1986, 54 per cent in 1990 and 65 per cent in 1991 (Jowell *et al.* 1992: 42). Most notably, the government made no headway in turning public opinion against spending on older people: respondents' consistent priority for increased benefit spending was retirement pensions. The view that the state pension was inadequate to live on was held by 70 per cent in 1986 and by 77 per cent in 1989, proportions which increased slightly when the actual amount of the pension was revealed (Jowell *et al.* 1990). Analysis of the British Social Attitudes Surveys showed nearly two thirds of respondents in all age groups thought the basic state pension should provide more than enough for basic needs, although younger people were more likely to see a role for private provision as well (Hancock *et al.* 1995).

Although those on higher incomes were as keen on welfare spending as the population as a whole, they were less likely to prioritize retirement pensions for extra spending (Jowell *et al.* 1990). Class differences in the opportunities to obtain private welfare are likely to colour perceptions of the value of state welfare and are reflected in the somewhat divergent aims of the NPC affiliates compared with the ARP. In particular, the middle class stake in state pensions is small compared with other EU countries, due to the low value of British state pensions and the prevalence of private pensions.

In sum, energetic campaigning by pensioner organizations to restore and improve state pensions and other forms of welfare, even though widely supported as fair, largely failed to influence policy. Middle class discontent, in contrast, prompted a modification of asset-testing designed to benefit the well-off. Middle class incorporation in the welfare state, never as strong as in Scandinavia or Germany, has further weakened since 1979. A stronger cross-class pensioner movement, combined with militant trade union action in defence of state welfare, may have prevented or moderated the welfare cuts, as in Italy, France and Germany. Re-election of a Conservative government in 1987 and in 1992, in spite of anti-collectivist policies endorsed by a diminishing minority of the public, raises the question of how voting relates to class, gender or age interests.

## Older people's electoral preferences and political activity

Older people are at least as likely to vote in general elections as younger people; older age has long been associated with Conservative voting. This relationship cannot be explained by cohort differences or by selective survival of older middle class women, with their high rate of Conservative voting (Abrams and O'Brien 1981). Thus it is suggested that there is something in the process of ageing itself which increases the likelihood of voting Conservative, even where policies seem particularly hostile to the interests of the majority of older people. Indeed, if people voted for the party whose policies served their material interest, older women would have disproportionately voted Labour or Liberal Democrat in 1992, both having promised a substantial increase in the basic state pension.

Whatever the reason for the apparently counter-rational voting by older people in 1992, the claim that older people have used, or will use, their growing numerical power in elections to further their own interests at the expense of younger people is misconceived: 'It is unlikely that grey power has any chance of succeeding in the foreseeable future' (Midwinter 1992: 23). In the US, a similar conclusion, that there is no evidence of an age-based voting bloc, has been reached (Binstock 1992; Street 1998).

Political participation by older people through other actions, such as presenting a view to the local authority or MP, attending meetings, making a speech to an organization or helping in fundraising were less common than among younger people, as were taking part in demonstrations, pickets, marches or sit-ins (Abrams and O'Brien 1981). Marsh (1975) found a sharp decrease with age in approval of 'unorthodox political behaviour'. A high 'protest score', where unofficial strikes and rent strikes or blocking traffic and occupying or damaging property were approved, applied to only 12 per cent of people over 65, compared with 28 per cent aged 46–65 and higher proportions of younger people. Women were less likely to approve such actions than men.

Thus internalized prohibitions are a major barrier to older people's political participation. A further barrier may lie in the dominant role of charities. In discussing why poor people's voices are unheard in debates on poverty, Beresford and Green (1996) observe that when well-intentioned charities take a leading role this excludes the poor from participation, citing as a contrast disabled people's success with anti-discrimination legislation. Representation through conventional channels may be a poor substitute for self-organized direct action in winning media attention and influencing policy.

## Future politics of old age and intergenerational relations

Both the major British political parties plan pension reforms which are likely to increase class and gender divisions among pensioners. Policy on pensions is at a crossroads. The route of increased privatization at the expense of state pensions beckons not only the Conservatives but also the Labour government.

The Commission on Social Justice, apparently mindful of New Labour's 'modernizing' agenda, failed to recommend measures to restore the value and centrality of state pensions; its political dilemma may be inferred from its devastating condemnation of means-testing followed by the recommendation of a partially means-tested Minimum Pension Guarantee (Commission on Social Justice 1994).

The Conservative government, before its demise in May 1997, proposed to replace state pensions with private funded pensions (Basic Pensions Plus) early in the twenty-first century; and the New Labour government have proposed a new private funded second-tier pension (the Stakeholder Pension), further marginalizing the State Earnings Related Pension. Since state pensions would still need to be paid during the transition period, the plans of either party would impose a double burden of taxation on working people for about 45 years. Younger people would become net losers in terms of lifetime transfers into and out of the welfare state, increasing resistance to taxation. Moreover, because private pensions magnify the effect of inequalities in the labour market during the working life, the numbers of older people reliant on means-tested benefits could be expected to rise. The latter would, Flora (1981) argues, increase the visibility of redistribution and hence the likelihood of a tax revolt. Far from 'averting the old age crisis' (World Bank 1994), privatizing British pensions could contribute to a weakening of the intergenerational contract at the macro level. It would also exacerbate inequality of income in later life according to class and gender.

An aspect of intergenerational reciprocity which is sometimes overlooked is the pension cost of reproducing the next generation. While good state pensions, especially arrangements such as Home Responsibilities Protection, acknowledge the value to society of raising children, private pensions increase the opportunity costs of reproduction, parenting and eldercare.

Fertility rates are already low in most EU countries and further decline will exacerbate population ageing unless compensated by increased immigration (Vincent 1996). Family members, especially women, have always provided the bulk of care needed by frail older people but the withdrawal of state welfare for older people may place intolerable strains on carers, increasing tension within families. The growing marketization of social welfare services means that chronically sick or disabled non-married older people will increasingly have to purchase care services, spending down their heritable assets, or rely on a child to provide care, to the detriment of the latter's own employment, earning power, pension acquisition and general well-being.

Although intergenerational solidarity remains strong, as indicated in attitude surveys, threats to the social contract between generations in the future seem more likely to arise from government policy than from population ageing, especially if accompanied by a continued stream of official and media accounts based on the 'public burden' model of welfare (Walker 1990, 1996). Given the political will, the intergenerational contract in Britain could be strengthened. A renewed commitment to state welfare for older people would restore confidence among working age people that their contributions will bring worthwhile benefits in their own old age.

The extent of the middle class stake in defending state welfare is likely to be a crucial factor in the future politics of ageing. Universal benefits unify the middle class behind the welfare state (Esping-Andersen 1990; Quadagno 1991), but middle class interests in defending state benefits decline as the latter become a less important source of pensions and health care relative to private welfare. Campaigns have been most successful when middle class interests, especially those of men, have been threatened. While benefits targeted on the better-off through tax relief go largely unnoticed, benefits targeted on the poor 'undermine political solidarity by fragmenting citizens' interests' (Street 1997: 120) in state pensions and health provision and tend to be resented by the better-off. As noted above, middle class incorporation has been undermined, most notably since 1979, by the (over)development of private welfare in Britain and increased emphasis on means-testing. In spite of the difficulties of designing state pension systems which provide an adequate standard of living for all, which are more equitable between women and men and which also attract sufficient middle class support, examples which have stood the test of time can be seen in the Nordic countries (Palme 1990).

The possibilities of organizing campaigns which unite generations have been shown by the Gray Panthers in the US, whose aims include a more equal distribution of power and wealth across society, improved state welfare for low income families and cuts in military spending. In Britain, a common interest in maintaining universal, rather than means-tested, benefits could form the basis for an intergenerational campaign in defence of Child Benefits, unemployment benefits and the basic pension.

Although the increase in welfare costs due to population ageing is small in Britain until 2030, costs could be reduced by making voluntary later retirement more attractive and tackling age discrimination in employment as well as increasing employment more generally; health promotion through improved material conditions and opportunities for sociable exercise could reduce health care costs. Possibilities for reducing public spending in the future include cutting defence spending to the average EU level, raising corporation tax and employers' social insurance contributions to the EU level, curbing the increased tax expenditure of the last two decades and restoring inheritance tax to the 1960s level.

## Conclusion

The ideological and legislative attack on the welfare state by the previous Conservative government has eroded welfare provision for older people and betrayed the pension promises on which people planned their lives. The construction of increasing longevity as a fiscal problem and of older people as a burden has been used to legitimate reforms which have been driven by political ideology and the interests of the private finance industry. 'A matter of political choice and social justice has been hidden in fragile pretensions to economic soundness and virtue' (Mabbett 1997: 1).

Sustained and often massive campaigning by pensioner organizations throughout the 1980s and since has not succeeded in influencing policy on pensions or community care. Public attitudes, however, continue to be supportive of state welfare for older people, more so than for other population groups requiring state benefits such as unemployed people and lone parents not in paid work. This suggests that the alarmism of apocalyptic demography has been misplaced: intergenerational solidarity remains strong in Britain in spite of media accounts suggesting older people are to blame for poverty among younger people (Walker 1993, 1996). A political and moral economy perspective based on stratification of interests provides a better explanation of the politics of welfare for older people than one based on age-interest (see Chapter 2).

The policy agenda of privatization and individual responsibility for welfare may itself jeopardize the intergenerational contract on which the welfare state has been built, by decreasing the middle class stake, and confidence, in state welfare (Walker 1996). New Labour's enthusiasm for privatizing second-tier pensions implies abandonment of the possibility of achieving middle class support for revitalized state pensions. Yet a reassertion of the advantages of state pension provision could be popular, especially since the drawbacks of private pensions, potentially affecting all social groups, have become increasingly apparent.

Britain has moved further towards the individualization of risk and marketization of welfare than elsewhere in the EU, in spite of facing more modest population ageing. The example of Britain provides a warning to other EU countries of the levels of pensioner poverty and inequality to be expected if the private pensions industry is allowed to replace state welfare for older people.

# 12

# The politics of old age
# in Hungary

ZSUZSA SZÉMAN

Since 1970 the population of Hungary has aged continuously in both the biological and social senses. The rate of natural increase which was 3.1 per thousand in 1970 fell to the reverse, –3.1, by 1995 (KSH 1996: 37). Between 1989 and 1995 this deteriorating ageing trend went together with a slowdown in economic growth which imposed ever greater pressure on the pension system. From 1989 unemployment emerged as another problem. Between 1989 and 1995 1.5 million persons left the labour market, and unemployment soared from between 1 and 2 per cent in 1990 and 1991 to reach a steady 10.9 per cent in 1994–5 (KSH 1996: 48), thus creating chronic unemployment. The situation of an ageing and not entirely healthy labour force deteriorated substantially. For this reason, as a form of defence many people opted for withdrawal from the labour market before reaching retirement age through pre-retirement,[1] anticipatory retirement or retirement on a disability pension. This trend accelerated between 1991 and 1995 (Table 12.1).

The proportion of those leaving the labour market through non-conventional retirement channels grew by 11 per cent between 1991 and 1995 and exceeded two thirds of all retirements. There was also a considerable change within the different withdrawal channels.

**Table 12.1** Proportion of those leaving the labour market through non-conventional retirement (per cent)

| Year | Pre-retirement | Anticipatory retirement | Disability pension | Total |
|------|----------------|-------------------------|--------------------|-------|
| 1991 | 22.4 | 0.2 | 34 | 56.6 |
| 1995 | 7.8 | 16 | 42.8 | 66.6 |

Source: Országos Nyugdíjbiztosítási Főigazgatóság (1996: 49)

The use of pre-retirement fell to one third, indicating that businesses were making steadily less use of this 'humane' means for shedding their surplus staffing either because they had become entirely profit-oriented, or because they had already sent their ageing workers into retirement in this way. However, parallel with this there was an 80-fold increase in the numbers taking anticipatory retirement, i.e. those who became unemployed three years before retirement age, remained chronically unemployed and could not be retrained. The rate of disability retirement increased in direct proportion with the restriction in the possibility of pre-retirement. This points to two things: the poor health status of the ageing workforce; and, in the absence of appropriate employment policy strategies at macro level, ageing workers increasingly sought refuge in disability retirement (Országos Nyugdíjbiztosítási Főigazgatóság 1996: 49) despite the considerable difference between pension levels, depending both on pension types and gender.

The average disability pension was 90 per cent of the average old age pension (17,325 HUF [Hungarian Forint] = 105 USD [US dollars]) and, in the case of pensions before retirement age, was only 82 per cent, while the widow's pension was only 70 per cent (Országos Nyugdíjbiztosítási Főigazgatóság 1996: 31).

As regards gender, women's old age pensions amounted to only 76 per cent of men's old age pensions, while in the case of disability pensions they were only 82 per cent. These figures faithfully reflect the less favourable labour market situation of women (such as lower wages, shorter duration of employment) (Országos Nyugdíjbiztosítási Főigazgatóság 1996: 32).

One of the biggest problems for the retired population was that the average pension was always largely equivalent to the subsistence level. In other words, the great majority of pensioners faced the problem of poverty.

## Main organizations and actors in affairs concerning older people

The three national organizations representing pensioners, the National Pensioners' Representation, the National Federation of Pensioners and the National Association of Agricultural Pensioners, were established before the change in political system; in the early 1990s, however, they did not represent their interests, either separately or together, as powerfully as similar organizations in Western societies. They were unable to take effective action against the poor social conditions of pensioners. Nor did they have any real say in the different reform proposals affecting pensioners.

At the local level, immediately following the systemic change, numerous foundations and associations for pensioners were set up but in the early 1990s their activity was restricted to providing emergency social aid, such as distributing clothing and food parcels for older people, campaigning for free medicine, and struggling for recognition.

Nevertheless, due to the growing expenditure on pensioners, older people increasingly became the focus of political attention. Already in the 1980s there had been a broad consensus among the experts that fundamental changes were needed in the pension system. After the systemic change, in 1991 Parliament traced the main outlines of the reform, a pension system based on three pillars (see below). One of the basic elements of the implementation was the creation in 1993 of a Pension Insurance Self-management and Health Insurance Self-management Board.

The new pensions board was faced with a difficult task since, parallel with the growing unemployment, there had been a further acceleration in the ageing of society. By 1995 pensioners made up 30 per cent of the population (Országos Nyugdíjbiztosítási Főigazgatóság 1996: 5, 31). At the same time, the number of contribution-paying active earners fell by 20 per cent (1.2 million persons) between 1990 and 1995.

As a result of this trend, the expenditure of the Pension Insurance Fund – which financed pensions from the contributions paid by employers and employees – within a very short space of time (between 1993 and 1995) grew by 150 per cent, and this was not matched by a corresponding growth in receipts. The balance of receipts and expenditure showed a rapidly growing deficit. In 1995 the deficit was 2.5 times greater than two years previously (Országos Nyugdíjbiztosítási Főigazgatóság 1996: 20, 21) and by 1997 reached 0.5 per cent of GDP.

To halt this negative trend various restrictions were introduced within the pension system, namely a different method of calculating the service period and a higher retirement age for women. This affected principally the younger age groups of pensioners. This led to a paradoxical situation in which recent retirees aged 55–64 received the lowest average pensions within the pensioner population – only women over 80 were in a worse situation (Országos Nyugdíjbiztosítási Főigazgatóság 1996: 33).

Despite the stabilizing effect of the wage-linked compensation system, because of the lower initial pensions awarded to younger pensioners, by 1995 the average pension amounted to only 62 per cent of the net average wage, compared to 66 per cent in 1990 (Országos Nyugdíjbiztosítási Főigazgatóság 1996: 2, 6).

Overall, welfare expenditures rose to 19 per cent of GDP by 1994 (Magyarország, Szegénység és Szociális támogatások 1996: 29). Among the main cash benefits, 55.2 per cent of households supported received a pension (Magyarország, Szegénység és Szociális támogatások 1996: 33). Since the dependency rate per 100 active earners rose from 57 in 1990 to 73 in 1995 (Table 12.2), measures for the reform of the pension system were speeded up.

**Table 12.2**   Unemployment rates and dependency ratios

| Country | Year | Unemployment (%) | Dependency ratio[*] |
|---|---|---|---|
| Hungary | 1994 | 10.9 | 148 |
| Poland | 1994 | 16.4 | 125 |
| Slovenia | 1994 | 14.5 | 116 |
| Czech Republic | 1994 | 3.3 | 99 |

[*] Number of people receiving pensions per 100 active earners

## Developments in the politics of old age between 1990 and 1996

*The pension system in the early 1990s*

In 1991 Parliament resolved to carry out a pension reform resting on three pillars: a basic citizen's pension with automatic entitlement; a compulsory work-related pension linked to earnings and the period of contribution payments and based on the classical principles of social insurance; and optional forms of insurance based on voluntary savings. Although the Health Insurance and Pension Insurance Funds were set up in 1993, for years this resolution was not followed by legislation providing for the full implementation of the principles adopted. Only one element of the second pillar was set up. In 1993 the retirement age for women was raised in steps to 60 years. This was followed in 1996 – out of context for the system as a whole – by a uniform increase in the retirement age to 62 for women and men.

Both measures were met with strong resistance from society. This resistance was related to a number of factors: the very poor health status of the ageing labour force; the average life expectancy at birth which is exceptionally low by international comparison; the sharp deterioration in recent years of the labour market chances of ageing workers and the rise in unemployment among this age group; the lack of a suitable link between unemployment benefits and the pension system to handle long term unemployment. People were afraid that if they did not receive a pension, they would be eliminated from all forms of welfare. In connection with the third pillar, an Act enabling the establishment of voluntary pension funds was passed. After the acceleration of reform in 1995 two solutions had crystallized by the end of 1996.

*The proposal of the Pension Insurance Board*

The Pension Insurance Board basically retained the resolution adopted by Parliament, namely the operation of a pay-as-you-go model within the three-pillar system. First, the basic pension was shifted towards the neediness principle. Second, the main element was the so-called point system work-related pension. According to this, the pension point in any year of the insurance period is a basis of reference expressed as a percentage of national average earnings. Payment for one year of a contribution corresponding to national average earnings results in one pension point. Higher payment means more points; lower payment means fewer points (within the set income limits). The insurer provides information each year on the points acquired in the given year and accumulated since entry into employment. This system makes the payment of contributions over several decades transparent and measurable.

According to the proposals, the average pension level should be 60 to 65 per cent of average earnings. In the case of a full work career of 42 to 44 years, this would be 75 to 80 per cent. During military service and maternity, the central budget would pay the insurance contribution. The minimum period of service is 20 years. The retirement age is 62 for both men and women. The insurance obligation would extend from the minimum wage to between 2.5 and 3 times average earnings. When the new system is introduced, the benefits of those already retired would be converted to pension points, so that there will not be old and new type pensioners. The pensions already awarded would not be reduced as a result of the conversion.

The third pillar of the proposals was voluntary supplementary insurance. Long-term savings could be used at least partially for pension purposes, based on the discretion of the individual. These savings could be given preference through the taxation system. It was the basic position of the Pension Insurance Board that the pay-as-you-go system could not be maintained in its present form, but a modernized form could be financeable over the long term if a point system (additional to the work-related system) was introduced; the conditions for awarding disability pensions were made stricter; it was combined with health and employment rehabilitation; the regressive calculation reducing pensions in the pension system was terminated; the elements of solidarity within the system were reduced but not entirely terminated – the pension system treats men and women uniformly, regardless of their differing life expectancy at birth; and the retirement age at 62 was treated flexibly.

*The proposal of the Ministry of Finance and the Ministry of Welfare (the government)*

By December 1996 the Ministry of Finance and the Ministry of Welfare elaborated a pension reform fundamentally differing from the above ideas, which they intended to present to the government in early 1997 but submitted for public debate only at the end of December 1996. The main features of the proposed new system were the following: a social insurance pension, which forms two thirds of the compulsory old age benefit and operates as a pay-as-you-go system; a compulsory private pension, which forms one third of the old age benefit; voluntary pension insurance; and an old age allowance.

In practice, the first two elements of the new four-pillar system cover the compulsory old age benefit. Within the social insurance pension element the longest service period was 42 years (1 per cent annually) and the contribution to be paid was based on gross earnings, consequently the pension too would be gross and taxable. The basis of the pension is twice the average earnings at the given time. The regular annual increase in the pension is based on the gross annual earnings for the previous year combined with the change in the consumer price level, giving a combined indexation. The sum on the basis of which the pension is awarded is adjusted to the second year of the three years preceding retirement. Retirement between 2 and 5 years before the age of 62 is possible in the case of a service period of between 35 and 38 years. Retirement before the normal age results in a 19 to 30 per cent reduction in the pension. The minimum service period is 20 years.

The compulsory private pension system means that participants in the new system pay one third of all pension contributions into their individual accounts in private pension funds (and two thirds to the social insurance system). These sums remain in the private ownership of the insuree until retirement and may also be inherited under certain circumstances. In order to set up this system, it is intended to create a new, modern system of records by November 1997, capable of keeping an individual record of those entering the new system and of those who continue to pay contributions in the present system. The voluntary insurances represent the well-known forms of self-provision.

The old age allowance would be paid to older/disabled persons who were unable to achieve one third of the average earnings at the given time in the compulsory pension system (the present minimum pension), and whose social, family and financial situation does not ensure this level either. (It would be funded 30 per cent by the local authority and 70 per cent from the central budget.) The Social Welfare Act provides for the old age allowance.

According to the government proposal, the present and the new pension system would exist side by side for between 40 and 50 years, but up to the year 2009 retirement would be allowed only under the present rules. Those entering the new system could first receive a pension in 2009. Entry into the new pension system would be compulsory for those entering employment for the first time.

The two proposals were based on different pension philosophies and values. They coincide on only three basic points: the retirement age, the voluntary supplementary insurance, and the close link between pensions and contribution payments. The Pension Insurance Board retains the principle that the contribution-payer should receive a pension proportionate to the contribution made towards covering the pension expenditures for those already on a pension. The government has abandoned this principle for one third of the pension. One third of the contribution to be paid would constitute savings which the contribution-payer will eventually receive (together with the yield, minus administrative costs). The proposed solution means that two pension systems would have to be financed simultaneously: benefits have to be paid to those already on pension and those retiring in the near future, and funds must be accumulated for the new type of benefit.

In the first year this would require additional funds of around 100 billion HUF (60 million USD), and this would continuously increase for between 25 and 30 years. There was no state guarantee for that. The government's intention is to guarantee these additional funds by raising the retirement age, lowering the level of pensions, continuously reducing the real value of pensions already awarded and drawing credit (increasing the state debt). The board's proposal did not involve such additional expenditure.

## Changes in the participation of older people

The proponents of radical reform argued that, through the funded element, capital would be injected into the economy, stimulating it, doubling the possibilities for businesses to draw credit, thereby speeding up economic growth and achieving a positive effect over the long term. However, in December 1996 the Council on Elderly Affairs formed at that time acquired an especially important role in the political debate. Although the Council was set up by the government its members included, in addition to the

National Pensioners' Representation, the National Federation of Pensioners and the National Association of Agricultural Pensioners, representation of the Health Insurance Board, the Pension Insurance Board, the country's biggest and most efficient charity organization (the Hungarian Maltese Charity Service), the Hungarian Federation of Practising Physicians, numerous independent experts dealing with a wide range of problems concerning older people (a gerontologist, a sociologist, a demographer, a pharmacist) and, very importantly, leaders of the Federation of Local Authorities. As a result the Council represented broad strata of society. Right from the outset it was able to act more effectively in the interests of older people and had greater influence than the organizations devoted exclusively to the protection of the interests of older people.

The Council on Elderly Affairs questioned many points of the reform proposals made by the Ministry of Finance, regarding them as unacceptable because of the attitude on gender, the intergenerational impact and so on. (The other important organization, the Conciliation Council grouping the trade unions, also attached great importance to discussion of the government's Pension Reform Proposal and their objections coincided almost exactly with those of the Council.) These objections can be briefly summed up as follows. First of all, the reform depends on 55 years of continuous growth of GDP and declining inflation. It assumes a 5 per cent growth of GDP up to the year 2000 and from then to 2020 3 per cent annually. The state budget deficit is put at 3.5 per cent after 2005 and the debt:GDP ratio is predicted to stabilize at between 55 and 60 per cent. At the same time, the proportion of savings accumulated in the funded part will amount to 2 per cent of GDP by 2010 and 4 per cent by 2013. Such a rosy picture would be questionable even in an economically strong society. In addition, the proposal calculated low running costs of between 4 and 5 per cent for the funded pension funds, although in other countries the private funds have between 8 and 14 per cent operating and maintenance costs. The combined indexing places the current 3 million pensioners at risk. In the 55 years needed for the new system to reach maturity, the value of pensions compared to national average earnings would fall from the present 61 per cent to 42 per cent for those not wishing to enter the new system. Even the first two pillars of the new mixed system would result in only 54 per cent, which is lower than the present level.

The deficit of the Pension Insurance Fund, which has been running at between 30 and 35 billion HUF, would increase to 100 billion a year under the new system. This would have to be covered each year from the central budget – without state guarantees – through credit, according to the proposal which in turn would have an inflationary effect. The level of pensions would substantially decline for those remaining in the old system too, due to introduction of the gross calculation and the linear scale.

While stricter conditions have been imposed for the disability pension system, the corresponding rehabilitation and employment policy system has not been elaborated. There are no calculations concerning the cost to society of employing and 'supporting' the large number of persons forced out of the labour market but not entering the pension system because of the stricter disability pension system. At present 28 per cent of all pensioners are disability pensioners. Because of the health status of the population and the present inadequacies of the employment policy and unemployment system, a considerable proportion of ageing workers have made use of the disability pension.

The new proposal acted against equality of the sexes by discriminating against women. Given an identical, compulsorily accumulated sum, men would receive a higher benefit than women. Women's life expectancy is longer and this is not accepted by the market principle. This principle can be accepted in the case of the freely chosen voluntary funds, but not for a compulsory system. The new pension unfavourably affects all those who pay contributions for less than between 25 and 30 years. Because of their life cycle – the years spent looking after a family – women are again at a disadvantage. Most firms are reluctant to employ women with young children, with the exception of a few predominantly female occupations. This is not counterbalanced by calculating one year of service for each child.

In contrast with previous practice the years spent at university are not counted in the period of service. This means that with the expected rise in the level of schooling, there will be a greater decline in the attainable period of service for university graduates. In other words, the pension prospects of this stratum will deteriorate. Those who are not sufficiently well informed to choose a good pension fund are at risk. It seems probable that the funds will soon become differentiated and that there will be funds operating well for those with higher earnings and others operating poorly for those with lower incomes.[2]

The reform magnifies the inequalities within the population above retirement age. The shift favours those continuously paying a higher contribution and with a longer period of service. Under conditions of chronic unemployment, the service period of 20 years (instead of the present 15 years) required to attain the (partial) minimum pension appears to be very long. The proposal emphasizes the responsibility of the individual and evades the state guarantee.

*The consequence of the debate*

The proposal outlined above, recommended by the government for adoption, reflects the state of affairs in 1997. It has already undergone certain amendments as a consequence of the public debate. As a result of the pressure that can be felt from all levels of society, further concessions can be anticipated. Recent amendments include: the postponement to 2000 of the introduction of the combined indexation planned for 1998; only one fifth of the pension contributions, not one third as originally proposed, would be placed in compulsory private pension funds; university students have been given the possibility of purchasing their years of study as service years after they enter employment; in place of one year per child as originally proposed, two years of service will be calculated for the period of maternity; in the new system, spouses (mainly women) will be able to receive 20 per cent of the pension of their deceased husband or wife, together with their own pension, to help cover the costs of their housing. The Council on Elderly Affairs accepted that certain elements of the pension reform must be introduced in 1998, provided that a new information technology system could be set up. By 1998, after further curtailment, Parliament passed the proposed changes which were already flawed as a result of numerous compromises.

## The future politics of old age

According to demographic forecasts, the proportion of persons over 65 in Hungary will rise from 14 per cent in 1994 to 22 per cent by 2025, while that of persons over 80 will double from 3 per cent to 6 per cent. (This places Hungary high among the countries of Central Europe in the ageing process – Hojnic-Zupanc 1996: 18.) By then the present middle generation will be pensioners. It is unacceptable for them that, despite the latest changes, preliminary calculations show that, up to the year 2050, while wages and earnings will increase 30-fold from the present level, the average pension will rise only 15-fold. This would cause a major shift in the equilibrium between generations. It is also unacceptable that the proposal promises a higher pension than at present only for men aged between 20 and 25 at the beginning of their careers, with high earnings and stable employment, while for all other strata of society, even at the level of promises, the prospects are worse.

The conditions applying to those not willing or able to transfer to the new system have the general effect of encouraging those concerned to flee from the 'old' system and of weakening discipline in the payment of contributions. This in turn makes the financing of future pensions uncertain, both for those unable to transfer to the new system and for those making the switch. The new system will be compulsory for some and optional for others; a third group will not be allowed to join. The large deficit that will be created for a long period in the general government budget will be a financing constraint creating unfavourable conditions for the economy.

## Conclusion

The decentralization of social policy, the termination of universal entitlements, or linking them to insurance (health care), together with two-digit inflation, have all been accompanied by the impoverishment of society to produce drastic regional and social inequalities in access to basic services as early as 1993.

The first democratic-liberal government (1990–4) tried, unsuccessfully, to create a kind of social safety net. The Social Welfare Act was introduced only in 1993 but a Non-profit Act was not drafted parallel with it. Moreover, this Social Welfare Act had the great flaw of placing greater emphasis on forms of aid rather than entitlements. Foreign financial agencies – World Bank, IMF, European Union – which have influenced the government, operated with the concept of absolute rather than relative poverty.

The second, socialist government (1994–8) in response to external pressure further weakened this already inadequate safety net. In addition, even in early 1996 there was no uniform legislation. Experts were debating the third draft of the Non-profit Act. At the same time, when preparing the Budget Act (which was also still at the drafting stage), the financial experts did not take into consideration the principles already elaborated in the Non-profit Act.

The government further reduced welfare elements, affecting the majority of society, with the so-called Bokros package in 1996. Increased expenditures was put forward as justification for the measure. The 1996 Bokros package thus meant another termination or transformation of universal entitlements into various forms of aid – such as the termination of childcare allowance, the introduction of a means test for family benefit and childcare aid – in such a way that a very low maximum income threshold was set for eligibility. This weakening of the welfare net was especially dangerous because the health status of the population was continuously and alarmingly deteriorating, and this situation was not improved by the transformation of the health care system. The reforms launched there have not brought a real reform in the health status of the population either.

In these circumstances the new pension is particularly dangerous. It will not provide adequate security in old age for broad strata of the population and will cause discrimination between the sexes. The present health status of the population prevents many people from holding jobs for long periods. At the same time, there is still no social safety net adequately connected to the pension system, to guarantee social security for these people. The new pension creates a society with dangerously dwindling welfare provision and no suitable safety net.

## Notes

1  Businesses could offer their workers retirement five years before the normal retirement age if they undertook to pay the pension of their former employee until he or she reached retirement age.
2  In Chile, for example, the number of members regularly paying contributions was 73 per cent in 1983 and 53 per cent in 1990. The contribution rate changed according to the income level: in the case of funds serving workers with lower earnings it was between 45 and 55 per cent, while for those with higher earnings it was between 80 and 90 per cent (Ferge 1997).

# 13

## The politics of old age in the United States

If Americans received all of their information from government reports and projections, they might be forgiven for concluding that the country's ageing population was less a triumph of the health and welfare improvements of the twentieth century than a looming crisis threatening to mortgage the futures of coming generations of younger persons. America's major public retirement system and its health programme for older people[1] – hardly generous by the standards of other developed nations – account for more than one third of the federal budget (US Congress 1997: 33), and the baby boomers have yet to reach retirement age. Even more ominous-sounding are the projected expenditures for Medicare, Medicaid[2] and Social Security reported in the 1997 Economic Report of the President, which could rise from under 9 per cent of GDP to 19 per cent in 2050. Given that federal revenues have been hovering around 18 per cent of GDP for the past several decades, these three programmes could, all things being equal, 'consume all government revenues by 2050 and exceed them thereafter' (Economic Report of the President 1997: 97).

The average American does not typically sit down with a copy of the federal budget or Economic Report of the President, but the popular press has been diligent in keeping readers informed about the potential cost implications of an ageing population and bombarding them with questions about whether America can afford to grow old. 'Will Social Security be there when you need it?' is a frequent refrain that serves to heighten anxieties about future well-being, foster intergenerational tension, and undermine confidence in the country's ability to provide for its older people. Though Social Security has never missed paying benefits on time, defenders of Social Security worry that unless confidence is restored, calls to privatize Social Security could succeed in fundamentally restructuring the country's most successful income-transfer programme.

Until fairly recently, Social Security was widely viewed as the 'third rail' in politics: touch it, politicians believed, and you are dead, a statement that might be regarded as a testament to the perceived power of the older voter. Indeed, lawmakers tended to steer clear of Social Security unless they were inclined to expand the programme. For decades after the passage of the Social Security Act of 1935, modifications to the Social Security system were virtually all improvements. Dependants' and disability benefits were added; coverage was extended to increasing numbers of workers; health care for older people became available with the enactment of Medicare legislation in 1965. Still, older people remained especially vulnerable economically: as of the late 1960s, the incomes of one in four persons aged 65 and older fell below the official poverty level. The poverty rate for this age group was also over 10 percentage points higher than it was for persons under the age of 18. That older people were viewed, in the words of Binstock (1991: 12), 'as poor, frail, socially dependent, objects of discrimination and, above all, deserving' fostered public support for programmes and services to assist them. The politics of age were shaped by the perception of need and worthiness. Sympathy could translate more readily into generosity because, again as Binstock notes, 'public resources for addressing social problems were perceived to be plentiful'.

One of the responses was an especially sizeable (20 per cent) one-time increase in Social Security benefits in 1972. That same year, Congress legislated automatic cost-of-living benefit adjustments (COLAs), effective as of 1975. From then on, Social Security recipients could rest assured that their benefits would keep pace with inflation, a promise not accorded to workers in relation to their wages. In addition, more and more workers were reaching old age with some form of private pension protection. As a result, poverty rates among older people plummeted during the 1970s, and more modest declines continued thereafter (Figure 13.1). Among children, on the other hand, poverty rates rose, eventually exceeding those of older people, a development that, though it may not have been clear as it began to happen, augured ill for old age programmes, despite the growing numbers of older people who might be expected to lobby for the expansion of those programmes.

Even 20 years ago, a few voices were beginning to warn of potential trouble ahead. In the late 1970s, for example, Hudson expressed concern about the impact that rising expenditures might have on older people, predicting that 'the widespread public sympathy and narrower political calculations which have been featured in the passage of many old-age policy enactments [would] increasingly give way to competitive and cost-based pressures' (Hudson 1978: 428). Binstock (1991: 11) has since written that it was about that time that

> the expansive social policy context in which the [Older Americans Act] was created . . . came to an end . . . Since then, social policy retrenchment has been in vogue, and the general political environment – previously supportive of almost any policy proposals to benefit aging persons – has become increasingly hostile to older people.

**Figure 13.1**   The poverty status of children and older people<sup>*</sup> in the United States, 1959–95

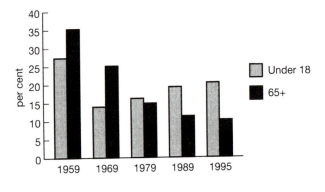

*Source*: Lamison-White (1997)

\* Children are defined as being under 18, older people as 65 or over

While one might quibble over the use of the word 'hostile' to describe the response of lawmakers to proposals to expand programmes for older people – 'less receptive' might be more precise – there is no question that cost constraints have pressured lawmakers to scrutinize spending programmes for older people to a degree perhaps inconceivable to all but a few prescient types in the 1970s. To be sure, it is doubtful that many lawmakers relish the prospect of reducing Social Security and Medicare benefits; none the less, it is certainly the case that older people and their advocates today have a far tougher time convincing legislators to fund new programmes or to continue support for some existing programmes than they did two decades ago, despite the recent and projected increase in the number of older persons.

No longer are older people automatically and unquestioningly regarded as deserving, an attitudinal shift that has occurred in part because older people are increasingly portrayed as so much better off than other groups, in part because younger people question the return they will get on their Social Security contributions, and in part because of a campaign by some groups to exploit younger workers' uneasiness about future well-being. It doesn't help that reputable newspapers and magazines convey the sense that the politics of old age is fraught with intergenerational conflict when they highlight articles with headlines such as 'The Coming Conflict As We Soak the Young to Enrich the Old' (*Washington Post*, 5 January 1986); 'Consuming Our Children?' (*Forbes*, 14 November 1988); 'Burden for Grandchildren' (*Wall Street Journal*, 9 April 1991); or 'Payments to the Retired Loom Ever Larger' (*New York Times*, 30 August 1992). Hence it is perhaps not surprising that means-testing is no longer unmentionable with respect to the two largest, most popular, and most important programmes for older people, Social Security and Medicare.

## Political participation and representation

*Older people as an 'interest group'*

Nor are the causes of older people aided when one of the country's largest organizations for older people is referred to as an '800 pound gorilla,' a sentiment equating numbers with heavy-handed political clout. But while it is the case that older Americans and their interests are represented by a large and diverse number of organizations, it cannot be said that in United States, at least up to now, they speak with a single voice.

For illustrative purposes, Binstock and Day (1996) single out 36 old age interest groups, among which can be found membership, advocacy and professional associations; however, they note that there are actually more than 100 national organizations dealing with old age policies and concerns. Thousands of local chapters of national older people's organizations have been established. Some of these organizations focus primarily on the needs or concerns of selected groups, such as women (Older Women's League) or minorities (National Hispanic Council on Aging or National Caucus and Center on Black Aged). Others serve professionals in the field of ageing (such as the Gerontological Society of America or National Council on the Aging), while still others are mainly issue-oriented (like the American Association of Homes and Services for the Aged). Size varies from the very small to the 32-million member American Association of Retired Persons (AARP).

Singly or in combination, these groups are perceived as having the wherewithal to get their way, with perhaps deleterious consequences for the rest of society. Former US Senator Alan Simpson has complained that if one of the larger older people's organizations managed to get what it wanted, 'it would bring America to its knees' (in Birnbaum 1997), as if programmes for older people could survive if the rest of the country were 'on its knees'. Statements such as this one assume, on the one hand, that what these organizations want is only good for older people, and, on the other, that a unanimity of outlook and purpose exists. Both assumptions are open to question – as parents, grandparents and great-grandparents, older people have an interest in intergenerational issues and the well-being of the young. Furthermore, the young eventually stand to benefit from the preservation and expansion of old age programmes (Day 1990: 132).

The latter assumption – unanimity of outlook – is especially hard to verify, at least with respect to the larger multipurpose organizations. The 32 million members of AARP, for example, range in age from 50 upwards; over half the members are women; incomes differ. Members are not even all retired: in fact, as many as one third remain in the labour force. Priorities are as varied as the members themselves, who may join AARP for a number of reasons, for example its lobbying efforts, its publications, its volunteer opportunities, the local chapter activities, and/or the numerous benefits and services that membership gives them. The majority are not active advocates on behalf of older people or old age issues. Yet AARP has been described as 'the most fearsome force in politics' (Birnbaum 1997: 122). Granted, the Association can mobilize many thousands of its members to voice their opinion on issues to members of Congress, a costly undertaking that it sometimes engages in. But while Congress may listen, it does not alway take heed.

Moreover, not everyone views numbers alone as a sign of power (Stree 1993; Douglass 1995). The larger the organization, the more diverse th membership and the more difficult it may be to gain consensus on issue: Douglass (1995) suggests that there may be too many organizations repre senting the interests of older people which are doing too little for too fev The myriad older people's organizations themselves have diverse agenda that may be at odds with one another, and while the organizations coalesc from time to time (as they do under the umbrella of the Leadership Counc on Aging) and work collaboratively to greater effect, disagreements can b profound. Furthermore, the response of older people themselves is neithe always predictable nor assured.

So, for example, with the support of many older people's organization: Congress in 1988 passed the Medicare Catastrophic Coverage Act (MCCA) legislation that would have placed a cap on the out-of-pocket expenditure c Medicare beneficiaries, expanded benefits provided under Medicare, an aided the very poor. While the legislation seemed a 'win-win' situation i the words of former US Assistant Secretary for Aging Fernando Torres-G (1992: 80), victory was short-lived. Not all older people's organizations ha favoured the Act, and, after passage, opponents succeeded in mounting a effective campaign for its repeal. Objection was by no means universal, an many organizations for older people continued to support the MCCA. Non the less, the vocal and organized opponents were apparently the mor persuasive group, and within a year, the MCCA was repealed.[3]

The MCCA was to be financed not through payroll taxes, as are Socia Security and the hospital insurance portion of Medicare, but by highe Medicare premiums and a surtax on the income of older people themselves It was the method of financing that so many elderly found objectionable even though relatively few of them would actually end up paying. Repea caused many Americans to view older people 'as a selfish interest group' according to Torres-Gil (1992), one that wanted benefits without paying fo them. The perception of older people as 'greedy geezers' took hold, at leas in the eyes of members of the media. Repeal also made it clear, if it had no been before, that older people's organizations could not necessarily 'delive their members.

Other instances of disagreement within as well as among old age organi zations could be cited, the Social Security benefit 'notch' issue being a prim one. When in 1972 Congress approved cost-of-living adjustments for Socia Security benefits, it did so incorporating a calculation method that, in effec dually compensated future retirees for the effects of inflation (US Genera Accounting Office 1988: 25). The result was a benefit windfall that place the financial stability of the Social Security system at risk. By 1977, Congres acted to correct this miscalculation, adjusting the benefit calculation formul for persons born after 1916 (that is, people who had not reached the earl retirement age of 62 in 1977) and creating a 'notch' in the process.[4] Conse quently, some Social Security beneficiaries, although receiving what they ar due, collect lower benefits than recipients with comparable work historie

**Table 13.1** Distribution of the US population aged 65+ by race and Hispanic origin: 1997, 2015 and 2030 (per cent)

| Race/Hispanic origin | 1997 | 2015 | 2030 |
|---|---|---|---|
| Non-Hispanic white | 84.9 | 79.4 | 74.6 |
| Non-Hispanic black | 7.9 | 8.4 | 9.2 |
| Hispanic | 4.8 | 8.0 | 11.2 |
| American Indian, Eskimo[*] | 0.4 | 0.5 | 0.5 |
| Asian/Pacific Islander | 2.0 | 3.6 | 4.5 |
| Total | 100.0 | 100.0 | 100.0 |

*Source*: US Department of Commerce, Bureau of the Census (1996b: Table 2)
[*] This category also includes Aleuts

and earnings records born a year or two (or perhaps even only a few days) earlier. This discrepancy has understandably not pleased the affected beneficiaries, who question the fairness of their lower benefits. Elimination of the notch has been the focus of intense lobbying by some older people's organizations, while others, citing the need for fiscal responsibility, have opposed restoration of the higher benefits, despite the fact that some of their members would gain as a result.

If older people fail to speak with one voice today, they are even less likely to do so in the future, a possibility on which policy makers may not have focused. The growing heterogeneity of the US population, both old and young, coupled with the growing activism of special-interest groups, points to greater 'specialization'. Associations for black, Hispanic and Asian older people already exist, and offshoots from some of them seem likely, in view of the rapid growth and diversity of some of those populations. Non-Hispanic whites account for about 85 per cent of the total population of older people today, but that proportion is projected to fall to about 79 per cent in 2015 and to 75 per cent in 2030 (Table 13.1). Little change in the non-Hispanic black older population is anticipated, but particularly sharp increases are expected for Hispanics (who can be of any race). Currently comprising only 4.8 per cent of the older population in the United States, Hispanics may account for 8 per cent in 2015 and over 11 per cent in 2030. As a percentage of the total older population, Asian and Pacific Islanders will also grow almost as rapidly as Hispanics, although from a far smaller base. Both the Hispanic and Asian populations encompass persons from a range of countries and with very different characteristics and needs, all or some of whom might feel that they would be better served by more specialized groups.

The impact of these demographic shifts could be modest at the national level but very pronounced in certain states, such as Texas, California and New York, where the 'minority' older people will be concentrated and where they could eventually come to comprise the majority of older people. There are also signs of a widening gap in health insurance and pension coverage, with the result that 'heterogeneity in retirement will continue to be an important aspect of economic well-being among older people in America, and may even grow' (Smeeding 1997: 5). The needs and concerns of the rapidly growing very old population will be different from and perhaps in conflict with the needs and concerns of the young old. Generalizations about older people are questionable enough at the present time; they may be even less valid in the future.

Vast numbers aside, this growing diversity of the older population may further dilute the 'message' of old age organizations. None the less, these organizations provide an important mechanism for older Americans who do want to try to influence the policymaking process. As interest groups, they may also serve as rich and valuable resources of research, information and well-articulated arguments for the very legislators they seek to persuade. And as Day (1990: 132) notes, 'advocates of old-age benefits in the national and state legislatures use the interest groups' information and endorsements to help advance their own legislative priorities'.

### Older voters

Of course, older people need not be members of organizations to be perceived as influential. Were they to vote as a group, their sheer numbers and propensity to go to the polls could have a significant impact on politics at all levels. As it turns out, however, older people do not function as a monolithic voting bloc any more than they act as a single-interest group. Although older people (65 and older) vote in greater numbers than younger citizens, the middle-aged are not far behind.[5] If older people all voted the same way on a specific issue, they would demonstrate an 'awesome' power (Connor 1992: 158) and might well determine outcome, but even with respect to issues such as Social Security and Medicare, in which virtually all older people have a clear, vested interest, they are not in agreement about benefits improvements or how, for example, to guarantee the long term solvency of the Social Security system. Today's older people are more likely to identify themselves as Democrats than as Republicans and to say they voted for William Clinton over George Bush in 1992 or Robert Dole in 1996. None the less, a large minority of older voters report that they are Republicans (US Department of Commerce, Bureau of the Census 1996c Table 455). Predicting how older people will vote can be a hazardous under taking.

Peterson and Somit (1994) suggest that when it comes to the political influence of older people, 'the emperor really has no clothes' – on most issues they differ little in their opinions from younger persons. However because members of Congress tend to 'share [the] widespread perception of a huge, monolithic, senior citizen army of voters', the practical significance of differences in values, beliefs and expectations is misunderstood, much to the satisfaction of old age interest groups. For members of Congress, then the perception becomes the reality, and so, 'barring some remarkable and improbable demonstration to the contrary, the putative cohesiveness of this huge segment of our voting population can be expected to give older people an increasing political weight in the decades to come' (Peterson and Somit 1994: 178).

Not everyone would agree. McKenzie (1993) speculates that the political influence of older people may actually have peaked and may begin to decline, not only because of the growing diversity of the older population – although that will be a factor – but because of the growing political effectiveness of younger groups and the emergence of new political groups organized around non-age issues. It has often been noted that, in the United States at least, 'all politics is local', meaning that what is important to people occurs in their own backyards. Thus, what concerns older persons at the state and local level may be very different from what captures their attention at the national level; it may well be more pressing, and will vary greatly by state and locale. Flood relief, affirmative action, the minimum wage, welfare reform, age discrimination and environmental matters are just a few of the issues – not all of them 'age'-dependent by any means – that have recently energized some members of one large older people's organization in different regions of the country. These same issues may be of marginal interest to older people elsewhere in the US.

Age may be a more significant determinant of political outcomes at the state and local level than at the national level, especially in states like Florida which have a very high concentration of older residents.[6] Lemov (1996) writes of the impact that ageing communities can have on school budgets, but it is not only schools that are potentially at risk. Sociologist Charles Longino (in Lemov 1996) speculates that future industrial development efforts could be blocked by older people looking for 'quality' places to live. Throughout the country, local communities are engaged in efforts to entice retirees to move to those communities, as young retirees with money to spend are viewed as desirable additions to cities and towns. A concentration of retirees in certain localities could, however, have a far greater impact on local spending and decision making than civic leaders in those locales realize, and in ways that diverge from past patterns. Far more research on the politics of local ageing is called for before definitive conclusions can be drawn.

MacManus (1996) contends that age is often, but not always, a good predictor of political action. In fact, age may mask other more significant differences that influence voting behaviour, even with respect to school finance. For example, although numerous instances of older people voting down school bond issues can be cited, a national survey by Harootyan and Cohen (1995) leads to the conclusion that age may be a less important determinant of who will support or oppose increased school funding than are attitudes about public education and opinions about the adequacy of current funding levels. In the United States, property taxes are a key source of revenues for public education. Older people, according to Harootyan and Cohen, tend to regard their property taxes as too high, but that is the case for younger taxpayers as well, especially those between the ages of 18 and 29. Older people would like to see less reliance on property taxes, and they join the young in expressing a preference for alternatives such as petrol taxes or gambling revenues to finance public education. But, on the whole, 'those who feel that public schools are performing well for the amount of property taxes they pay are more likely' to vote to increase spending (Harootyan and Cohen 1995: 9).

Though issues of particular concern to older people (such as Medicare emerged during the 1996 presidential campaign, Binstock (1997) has observed that older voters were no more influenced by those issues than younger voters, at least at the national level. In fact, contend Binstock and Day (1996: 365), 'age differences in policy attitudes are relatively small' 'Much more striking', they insist, 'are the cleavages that cut across cohorts such as economic, educational, racial and ethnic, gender, and partisan divisions' (p. 364; see also Peterson and Somit 1994).

In sum, there appears to be little empirical evidence to support the contention that age is a powerful predictor of political attitudes and behaviour. Special-interest groups, particularly those with well-financed political action committees, do influence politics in the United States. Age, however does not appear to be a common denominator in the special interest of politics. None the less, this is no guarantee that older people or their representative organizations will docilely accept significant benefit cuts to the programmes that most affect them. In fact, more relevant than age in the future of politics in America may be the sense of entitlement that certain programmes have fostered.

According to Weil (1997), groups that feel entitled to particular benefits do a better job of organizing themselves than groups that receive benefits but that lack a sense of entitlement to them. Though lawmakers may be less receptive to expanding programmes for older people than they were in the past, they cannot help but be aware of the special interests that will confront them when they turn to dealing with the problems of programmes whose beneficiaries believe they have an earned right, or entitlement, to those benefits. No sense of entitlement in the United States is stronger than that associated with Social Security, which just happens (for the most part) to be an age-based programme[7] and which also happens, as will be discussed below, to be unsustainable in its present form over the long run.

Finally, it remains to be seen whether the behaviour of the ageing and eventually old baby boomers will be more age-dependent than that of older people today. This cohort of 76 million people born between 1946 and 1964 has had an enormous impact on virtually every aspect of American society, from the moment the first ones appeared on the scene. They are expected to define and redefine ageing and retirement to suit themselves, and it is possible that with them, age will become a greater predictor of public support for or opposition to issues. The heterogeneity of the baby boom population, however, would suggest that other variables have a stronger influence on voting behaviour, although not all observers are in accord on this point.

Torres-Gil (1992: 136), for one, apparently feels that some sort of generational cohesion that will 'pit [the boomers] against other age groups' is inevitable, if only to enable boomers 'to preserve whatever senior-citizen benefits and programmes they require'. He is correct about the political muscle that those baby boomers could wield, '*assuming they have common objectives*' (emphasis added); what remains to be seen is whether the baby boomers do identify and care about cohort-specific objectives. By the time all 76 million baby boomers have reached old age, many of them – especially those in the 'second wave' – may already have been forced to make do with fewer benefits and programmes than older people 'require' today.

## Barriers to political participation

Political participation encompasses a wide range of activities, from writing letters to elected officials, signing petitions, joining politically active associations and interest groups, speaking out on issues, working on political campaigns, voting, contributing money to candidates, lobbying, and running for and serving in office. Barriers to many of these forms of participation are relatively few and often self-imposed as a result of apathy or lack of interest. Citizenship is required to run for office or vote, which obviously means that the growing number of non-citizen immigrants are unable to express themselves at the polls or as candidates. However, anyone, including illegal immigrants, can engage in most of the other activities, although language barriers and low levels of educational attainment will restrict the activities of many.

Running for state and national office takes money, a great deal of money in the United States, and few older people have the financial resources to mount a successful campaign for office, but that is the case for most younger people. Age alone, however, cannot be said to be an insurmountable barrier to getting nominated or winning elections, as evidenced in the recent candidacies of George Bush and Robert Dole, the election of Ronald Reagan, and the 1996 re-election of one Senator well in his nineties. Age, in fact, provides the experience and access to the well-heeled contacts that are needed to win elections.

A lack of knowledge about the political process as well as a lack of confidence in one's ability to make a difference may keep many older persons, especially immigrants, from taking advantage of the types of political activity open to everyone. Illiteracy or the inability to articulate a convincing argument may limit the ability of people to get their messages across, but age, *per se*, is not the culprit. It is also highly doubtful that many campaigns or candidates would shun the contributions, financial or otherwise, of older persons. Campaigns are heavily dependent on volunteers, and older persons, in general, often have the time to volunteer. It is no coincidence that on election days around the country, older persons are highly visible in their role as poll watchers.

The caregiving responsibilities, health limitations and transportation problems that often increase with age can serve as impediments to engaging in many types of activities, but even the bedridden can write to their members of Congress. While the lone individual has been known to influence City Hall, as it is put in the United States, and while members of Congress cannot afford to ignore their constituents, greater power lies in numbers. Millions of older people will continue, therefore, to rely on special interest groups, including unions and professional associations, to speak for them in the political arena.

**Table 13.2**   Numbers and percentages of the US population aged 65+ and 85+, for 1990, 1996 and projected for 2000 to 2050 (numbers in thousands)

| Date | 65 and over | | 85 and over | |
|------|------|------|------|------|
| 1990 | 31,080 | 12.5% | 3,022 | 1.2% |
| 1996 | 33,872 | 12.8% | 3,747 | 1.4% |
| 2000 | 34,709 | 12.6% | 4,259 | 1.6% |
| 2010 | 39,408 | 13.2% | 5,671 | 1.9% |
| 2020 | 53,220 | 16.5% | 6,460 | 2.0% |
| 2030 | 69,379 | 20.0% | 8,455 | 2.4% |
| 2040 | 75,233 | 20.3% | 13,552 | 3.7% |
| 2050 | 78,859 | 20.0% | 18,223 | 4.6% |

*Source*: Hobbs with Damon (1996: Table 2–1); US Bureau of the Census (1996b: Table 2)

## The future politics of age

Unlike Japan, ageing *per se* has not risen to the top of the political agenda in the United States. Perhaps this is because, on the one hand, by its own standards as well as those of other developed nations, the United States is still relatively young; perhaps, on the other, the projected insolvency of Social Security's old-age and survivors insurance trust fund remains some years in the future.

Only 12.8 per cent of the US population is aged 65 or older; by 2020, older people will still only account for 16.5 per cent (Table 13.2), leaving the country younger than some European nations today. To date, most of the discussion on the implications of an ageing population has taken place in think-tanks, in scholarly and policy journals, and at academic conferences and seminars rather than in the halls of the US Congress or State Capitols, but that will have to change in light of the projected growth in expenditure for programmes documented in the introduction to this chapter.

To a great extent, the future politics of old age in the United States will be dominated by the debate on Social Security and Medicare, which from a budgetary perspective at the national level are really the programmes that matter most.[8] Almost all retirees collect Social Security benefits and have access to health insurance through Medicare, and all but a handful of US workers pay Social Security (FICA) taxes under an implicit intergenerational contract that 'promises' that they, too, will collect benefits in old age. The problem is that neither Social Security nor Medicare can continue on its present spending course. In the case of old age benefits, revenues currently exceed expenditure, and a large trust fund is accumulating. However, as the baby boomers begin to retire, costs will rise rapidly. The number of covered workers per Social Security beneficiary is expected to fall from about 5 in 1960 to 3.3 today to 2 in 2030 and 1.9 in 2060 (see Employee Benefit Research Institute 1997). Beginning about 2010, outgoings will exceed income, necessitating use of interest on the Social Security trust funds to pay benefits. Eventually, timely payment of benefits will require drawing down the large trust fund reserves, and by 2029, under current projections, the reserves will be exhausted (Board of Trustees, Federal Old Age and Survivors Insurance and Disability Insurance Trust Funds 1997).

The system will not be broke, as workers will still be paying Social Security taxes that are expected to cover about 77 per cent of expenditure. None the less, if the system is to be returned to actuarial balance, some adjustment in the form of benefit cuts and/or tax increases will be necessary to maintain the present redistributive, pay-as-you-go system. How deep the cuts and how steep the tax increases will depend on how soon reforms are implemented.

A major problem is the difficulty among the 'experts' in achieving consensus on how best to restructure either Social Security or Medicare. This can be seen in the prolonged effort of the 1994–6 Advisory Council on Social Security, which had been established under Section 706 of the Social Security Act 'to advise the public, the Administration, and Congress on how best to prepare [Social Security and Medicare] for the future' (Advisory Council on Social Security 1997: 6).[9] In contrast to previous councils, no 'best' way or single set of recommendations could be agreed upon by the 13 members of this council, who instead proposed three very different approaches (highlighted below) to restoring solvency to the Old Age and Survivors Insurance Trust Fund.

The Medicare problem is far more pressing. Expenditure for Medicare already exceeds revenues, and Medicare trust fund moneys are being tapped to keep the system afloat. Under current projections, the Hospital Insurance Trust Fund (Part A of Medicare) will be able to pay benefits until about 2001. Immediate action is necessary just to stave off insolvency (Boards of Trustees 1997). In the spring of 1997, President Clinton asserted that he would 'now push for broad changes in Medicare and other federal benefit programmes to prevent them from exploding in cost in the next century' (Peterson and McManus 1997), but as a lame-duck president, his influence may be limited. Legislators, especially those who face re-election every two years, are hardly eager to tackle Social Security and Medicare, and the same can be said, for the most part, of the voting public. The issues are complex and the solutions proposed largely unpalatable or of uncertain success. However, President Clinton has undertaken a national initiative to promote discussion and debate on Social Security, with an eye towards proposing reform legislation in 1999.

The problem might not be so critical if older people were less reliant on Social Security and Medicare than happens to be the case. At present, Social Security is the only or the predominant source of income for more than six in ten older households in the United States,[10] and without it, older people would be more dependent on their families for support. Social Security accounts for over half of the income of all older people's households and a far higher percentage of the incomes of the non-married. For about one in five non-married older people, Social Security is the *only* source of income (Grad 1996: Table VI.B.2). The Economic Report of the President (1997: 99) states that some 15 million people would fall below the poverty level were it not for Social Security. Unpublished computations by AARP's Public Policy Institute indicate that the 1995 older person's poverty rate of 10.5 per cent would have risen to 47.9 per cent if Social Security benefits were excluded.

The proportion of retirees solely or primarily dependent on Social Security will undoubtedly fall in the future, although perhaps not as sharply as might have once been envisaged. A growing proportion of future retirees can expect to receive private pension income, but private pension coverage has stagnated in recent years, with the result that only about half of all full-time workers participate in any type of employment-based pension plan. This stagnation has been coupled with a shift from defined benefit pension plans to defined contribution plans, which means that many workers will reach retirement age without traditional defined pension benefits. Too few pre-retirees are saving adequately for retirement. Hence, while a rosy retirement future is on the cards for many, all signs point to a continuing high dependency on Social Security for millions of older Americans well into the future (Zedlewski *et al.* 1989; Sandell and Iams 1996). In the absence of major health care reform in the United States, Medicare will continue as the primary source of health care for American older people. Ensuring the solvency of these two systems would appear critical to the well-being of many millions of future retirees.

## Younger age groups and the politics of age

*Confidence in and support for programmes for older people*

Policy makers, old age advocates and proponents of America's programmes for older people worry about the extent to which eroding confidence in Social Security, in particular, might weaken support for that, as well as other, programmes, for older people. Young people have more readily admitted to believing in unidentified flying objects (UFOs) than in the likelihood that Social Security will be there when they need it (Dixon 1994). It is hard to know what to make of this observation, but the American press has had a field day with the finding. With somewhat less fanfare, the polling firm DYG, Inc. has reported that confidence in Social Security is on the wane, falling sharply between 1985 and 1995. The proportion of respondents who were confident about its future fell from 45 per cent to 36 per cent over the ten years, and those who were 'not at all confident' rose from 17 to 27 per cent (DYG, Inc. 1995: 55). Retirees express far more confidence in Social Security than non-retirees, perhaps because they have a shorter timeframe to worry about and because reform proposals are likely to have less effect on them than on younger persons. The 1996 Retirement Confidence Survey also reveals that workers are far less confident about Social Security's ability to pay promised benefits than are retirees (Yakoboski 1996), a difference that has widened over time (DYG, Inc. 1995).

So far, though, even in the face of declining confidence, some programmes remain overwhelmingly popular with the public, and Social Security and Medicare are among them. According to national public opinion poll data gathered by DYG, Inc. (1995: 11), 'virtually everyone (96 per cent) views Social Security as essential to retirement income and sees Medicare as the only way older Americans could possibly get adequate health care (92 per cent)'.

In reviewing some 40 years of pubic opinion polls, Reno and Friedland (1997) likewise observe continued strong support for Social Security, despite varying levels of confidence in its future. Not only have Social Security taxes been viewed more favourably than other types of taxes but also, when asked, large majorities of Americans express preference for even higher taxes over reducing benefits. Similarly, Cook (1996) cites opinion research demonstrating widespread public support for maintaining and even increasing benefits to older people, opinions that appear to have remained remarkably stable over time. Whether such enthusiasm would persist in the face of actual tax increases is another question – recent proposals for higher taxes to reform Social Security do not generate much enthusiasm (Yakoboski 1996: 14) – but the American public seems to understand and appreciate what Social Security has accomplished, not the least of which is to free adult children from much of the burden of supporting older parents and in-laws.

Still, observers take reports of declining confidence seriously and do not assume that continued high support for Social Security or Medicare can be taken for granted. At least two of the proposals made by the 1994–6 Advisory Council on Social Security are, according to Smeeding (1997: 4), designed to 'boost confidence in the system for younger workers [as well as] to increase their return on Social Security contributions'.

In the mind of Cook (1996: 343), 'the current political climate for older people is decidedly hostile'. Again, the word 'hostile' seems an overstatement, but it is clearly less promising than in the past. The politics of ageing in the United States, once so giving, is now questioning, a development that cannot help but have bearing on the outcome of the debate about the future of old age programmes in America. Older people may outvote the young,[11] but policy makers must pay attention to the willingness (and, of course, the ability) of younger voters to pay required taxes. Young workers who do not believe that Social Security will be around when they retire cannot be expected to greet rising Social Security taxes with much enthusiasm.

## The money's worth or 'me vs. social insurance principle'

Younger workers have also begun to ask whether they will get their 'money's worth' from Social Security or whether investing their payroll contributions elsewhere would provide them with higher returns. Whatever the limitations of money's worth analyses (Liemer 1995), questions about return have become part of the political landscape, fuelled by the forces that stand to make a tremendous amount of money if Social Security payroll taxes – even a portion of them – become available for investment in the stock market.

Today's Social Security beneficiaries have received a handsome 'return' on their contributions to Social Security, if that is an accurate way to describe getting back all of one's own and one's employer's payroll contributions in a relatively short period of time. Future retirees will have to wait much longer, on average, before that occurs, and for some it may never happen. Cohen and Male (1992) estimate that with the exception of single high earning males, most retirees in the future will continue to recover all of their payroll taxes, but Bajtelsmit, Johnson and Nugent (1997) are not so positive. They report that it will take more than 23 years for average-wage workers retiring in 2025 to recover all their and their employers' contributions plus interest, in contrast to just three years for comparable retirees in 1980; they also note that average life expectancy upon age of receipt will be lower than the 23 years. Moreover, since benefit cuts or tax increases will be necessary to pay benefits to future retirees, the actual payback period will be longer.

The question that privatization proponents ask is whether, especially in booming stock market conditions, it makes sound financial sense to perpetuate a system that requires investment in US government securities returning substantially less than the stock market, which averaged 10.5 per cent annually between 1926 and 1995 (Vanguard Marketing Corporation 1997). Although annual and short term market fluctuations have been considerable, it is undoubtedly the case that many beneficiaries would be better off if they could invest in equities instead of Social Security. Privatizers, however, typically overlook the insurance value of disability and survivors' benefits or the risk to workers of market failure.

What is so significant about the three reform proposals proffered by the 1994–6 Advisory Council on Social Security is that each of the three, to admittedly varying degrees, would open the door to equity investment of some portion of Social Security income. In the most conservative or traditional of the proposals, only a portion of the currently growing trust fund reserves would be invested. In the second, referred to as 'traditional with a twist' (Quinn 1997), workers would be required to contribute an additional 1.6 per cent of their earnings to a new individual account whose moneys could be allocated among a small number of stock and bond funds. The third proposal would radically transform Social Security into a two-tier system paying a flat benefit equal to about 65 per cent of the current poverty threshold for an older individual living alone (the first tier) and a benefit based on the earnings from 5 per cent of wages invested in a mandatory personal savings account (the second tier). The three plans propose other modifications as well, but for the purpose of this discussion, those modifications are less significant than the fact that money's worth and investment return issues are clearly no longer issues of concern merely to the disaffected fringe. They have moved to the mainstream and will feature prominently in forthcoming debate on Social Security reform.

*Intergenerational equity or 'getting my share'*

A growing federal deficit, coupled with the rise in transfer payments to older people, has led to assertions that older people are consuming too many resources at the expense of the young. Moreover, there are fears that when today's young get old, the resources will not be there to provide them with their fair share. No matter that the federal deficit cannot be blamed on Social Security (whose reserves are, in fact, being used to cover other budget expenditure and thus make the deficit appear smaller than it is), the fact that expenditure for Social Security and Medicare is so visible and resources for discretionary spending on programmes for other age groups so low has raised questions about intergenerational equity.

Over the past decade or so, efforts have been made to foster what might be regarded as a 'politics of the young', as witnessed by the creation of several organizations of largely younger persons seeking to draw attention to what they have seen as an excess of resources going to both the baby boomers and older people. During the mid-1980s, for example, Americans for Generational Equity (AGE), founded by a US Senator, attempted to promote generational equity throughout society, which was threatened as a result of excess resources consumed by the baby boomers. Lead or Leave, an organization once reputed to have nearly one million members, and chapters in all states, sought to get politicians to take the lead in dealing with generational issues so that the burden of dealing with older people's support costs would not fall exclusively on the young. Social Security was not its only target, but the group warned of generational warfare if leaders did not act right away. Third Millennium is yet another such organization seeking change that will cut or reduce benefits to older people to lessen the burden of support on future young generations.

Intergenerational equity was not prominently mentioned in many of the articles between 1984 and 1992 that Cook and colleagues (1996) examined, but those that did were 'inflammatory in content', language that might describe some of the rhetoric of the intergenerational equity groups. Inflammatory language notwithstanding, the groups seem to have had little success so far in fanning the flames of intergenerational warfare, (AGE and Lead or Leave have become moribund), perhaps because the bogeyman is not so apparent in the faces of parents and grandparents. Even so, the importance of these groups should not be minimized. AGE, for example, may never have become a potent political force, but it has left a legacy, according to Quadagno (1990: 640) as a result of its 'reshaping . . . the debate . . . all future policy choices will have to take generational equity into account'.

*Greedy geezers*

Related to the intergenerational equity issue is the perception that not only is too much going to the old, but the old do not need all of what they are getting. If this argument is pursued to its logical end, the very success of Social Security and Medicare in improving the fortunes of older people may prove to be their undoing, at least in their present form. Cost considerations, coupled with the fact that older people are no longer disproportionately destitute, have led to recommendations for greater targeting or even means-testing benefits to ensure that publicly funded benefits go only to those who need them. Williamson, Shindul, and Evans (1985: 252) wonder whether 'the basic problem with current public policies benefiting the aged [might be] that they fail to account for the prominent differences that presently exist in the aged population'. Significant differences exist, for example, in the health care needs of the very old and young old, in economic well-being of men and women, and in the support needs of the old married and non-married.

Not only might greater targeting make sense from a resource perspective, but it might also defuse intergenerational tensions if younger persons could be assured that they were supporting persons who really needed help but were not squandering resources on those who could do without. Certainly in the United States, targeting based on need is not a new concept in age-based programmes. Means-tested programmes include, but are not restricted to, Supplemental Income (SSI), which pays monthly benefits to low-income older, blind and disabled people; the Low-Income Home Energy Assistance Programme, which provides energy assistance to the needy; Medicaid; and the Senior Community Service Employment Programme, which provides subsidized work for very low-income elderly. But with the exception of Medicaid, means-tested programmes that benefit older people in the United States are relatively small, low-budget items whose reduction or elimination would have little impact on federal expenditure. Much more could be gained from means-testing Social Security or Medicare, or so means-testing advocates believe. For example, the Concord Coalition has developed a specific proposal that would subject *both* Social Security and Medicare to a sliding-scale means test starting at family incomes of $40,000 per year. (This proposal is sometimes referred to as affluence testing.[12])

What distinguishes means-tested programmes from Social Security and Medicare is that few older people have a stake in them, and those who do are less likely to be active politically. Politicians need not fear the voting booth power of the recipients. Means-tested programmes compete with each other during the annual budget appropriations process and often fall victim to cost cutting they can ill afford. The vulnerability of means-tested programmes for older people was readily apparent in 1996 when Congress eliminated SSI payments for legal immigrants as part of a massive overhaul of the welfare system. While it might be the case that universal programmes end up overserving some older people and underserving others (Harootyan 1981; Williamson *et al.* 1985), it is precisely the universality of Social Security and Medicare that accounts for their widespread public support. Means-testing might undermine that support, as well as result in a weakening of the guarantees provided to the needy. As Wilbur Cohen (1958) once wrote, 'a programme for poor people is a poor programme'.

## Conclusion: no sure bets

The growing numbers of older people in the United States will be a potent influence in American political life for decades to come. They may not vote as a bloc – indeed, as discussed elsewhere in this chapter, age appears to account for few differences in political attitudes – but policy makers do not seem to realize this (Peterson and Somit 1994). Moreover, there is always the possibility that older people *will* coalesce as a group and express themselves forcefully in the voting booth. Politicians, contend Peterson and Somit (1994: 178), are loath to risk the 'possible electoral consequences', including being voted out of office, should older people actually do this. Future cohorts of older persons will be better educated and may as a consequence be more active politically, a prospect that may not be lost on policy makers.

Despite their growing diversity, older people, and perhaps especially those nearing old age with interests and concerns akin to those of their seniors, are not likely to sit idly by as the public benefits and programmes on which they are, or will be, heavily dependent are subjected to slashing or fundamental reform. None the less, while politicians may fear the potential power of older people's vote, the same demographic changes that are producing more older voters are producing the rising support burdens alluded to elsewhere in these pages. On the one hand, older people cannot have what cannot be paid for. On the other hand, many older people now and in the future can count on little other than Social Security and Medicare.

Congress will also be under pressure to respond to accusations on the part of younger Americans that their future is being mortgaged to pay for the old, to demands for a 'better deal' than Social Security, and to waning confidence that Social Security will even be around for them. Both directly through political action and indirectly through their interest groups, America's older people will indeed play a critical role in shaping the debate on entitlement reform. But as workers and taxpayers, in particular, the young will also have their say. In the best tradition of American politics, one assumes that the politics of age in the future will, of necessity, be a politics of compromise.

## Notes

1 This refers to Social Security and Medicare. Medicare provides access to health care to older and disabled people, although the vast majority of the programme's enrollees (88 per cent in 1995) are elderly (US Social Security Administration 1996: Tables 8B3).

2 Medicaid is a federal-state entitlement programme that provides medical assistance to certain poor individuals and families. Medicaid has played an increasingly important role in providing long-term care to impoverished older people (US Social Security Administration 1996: 112), which is why it is frequently included with programmes for senior citizens. Long term care is not available under Medicare.

3 According to Torres-Gil (1992: 81), Assistant Secretary for Aging in the Clinton administration, 'no other major legislation had ever been enacted and repealed within a year due to political pressure'.

4 Because many workers born before 1917 were already receiving the higher benefits and might experience financial hardship if their benefits were cut, Congress opted not to reduce the benefits of persons born before 1917 (Social Security Administration 1991).

5 Indeed, prior to the mid-1980s, middle-aged Americans had higher reported registration and voting rates than the 65+ population (US Bureau of the Census 1996a).

6 Currently, 19 per cent of Florida's population is aged 65 or older, a figure projected to rise to 26 per cent by 2025 (Campbell 1996).

7 Disability and survivors' benefits may, of course, be paid to the young, but most recipients of Social Security are 62 or older.

8 Assuredly, there are other public programmes of importance to many older people in the United States, but none can be compared to Social Security or Medicare. In fact, it is not clear how many Americans could even identify and describe those programmes, but they know and approve of Social Security.

9 Section 706 was repealed in 1994; under the Social Security Independence and Program Act, a permanent Social Security Advisory Board was established.

10 The Social Security Administration actually uses the term aged 'unit', a term, that in the context in which it is used, does not have much meaning to most people. 'Household' has been substituted for 'unit' in this text.

11 In the 1994 November election, for example, 61 per cent of the 65+ population reported having voted, in contrast to only 20 per cent of potential voters between the ages of 18 and 24 and 39 per cent of the 25–44 age group.

12 Social Security and the insurance value of Medicare benefits that caused family income (earned and unearned) to exceed $40,000 would be reduced under the Concord Coalition's plan. The reduction would start at 10 per cent of benefits for persons with annual family incomes of between $40,000 and $50,000 and rise to 85 per cent for those with incomes of $120,000 or more. A key feature of this plan is that retirees with the highest income would be assured some Social Security benefits (15 per cent).

The views expressed in this chapter are the author's and do not necessarily reflect those of the AARP.

# 14

## Conclusion

GERHARD NAEGELE AND ALAN WALKER

The contributions contained in this volume provide information on three dimensions of the general topic of *The Politics of Old Age*:

1 *policies and politics*: policy developments in the countries studied with regard to the older populations;
2 comments on the *political behaviour* of older people, as reflected, for example, in their voting behaviour, their political opinions or their respective patterns of political participation;
3 references to the scope and limits of *political representation*: that is, the representation of the political interests of older people by older people themselves and the different forms of representation these take.

In this chapter we will draw together a few general conclusions, based on these aspects of the politics of old age, and make some proposals for action relating to policies for an ageing population.

### Policies for older people

Policies for older people – and this is a general trend which has also been reflected in the earlier chapters – are primarily understood as being social policies related to income security in old age, as well as covering the social risks of ageing such as home care or nursing care. However, this is a rather unconvincing narrowing-down of the subject of old age to the 'classical' area of social policies for older people, and it ignores the reality that old age has now become a topic covering a whole cross-section of politics. In addition to the socio-political dimensions, policies for older people increasingly clearly refer to other political spheres such as the economy, health, the labour market, family life, housing, transport, education and even aspects of national security. The ageing of society no longer only affects the social security system, and has now reached almost all social sectors which are under political influence or control.

Such a comprehensive, cross-departmental view of old age as an object of national politics, however, is not very widespread. In the Netherlands, the debate on this appears to be just beginning. In the Federal Republic of Germany, too, the study commission 'Demographic Change', set up by the German federal parliament, is a remarkable exception to the rule. In Germany, study commissions are usually set up for the preparation of decisions on wide-ranging and significant issues. The aim of this commission, which is to present its final report in the summer of 1998, is to examine the consequences of demographic change for the individual and for society and make appropriate suggestions for policies. At the same time, it is concerned with the demographic consequences in such varying areas as the economy, family issues, social networks, housing, social and political integration or migration, and of course with the classical topics related to social security (Deutscher Bundestag 1994).

If policies concerning old age are limited mainly to the area of social security, it is no wonder – as discussed in nearly every chapter – that demographic changes and thus policies for older people are primarily examined nowadays from the point of view of costs – if they are not already seen as being a financial threat. In this context, there is already talk in Germany of the 'burden of older people'. Policies relating to older people are coming under increasing economic pressure becasue of both a growing shortage of public funds and the supposed crisis in the welfare state. Two aspects of this should be emphasized.

First, to focus solely on the 'costs of old age' is to completely ignore the benefits which the ageing of society brings for the overall development of the national economy. The fact that older people can and indeed must be seen as a productive force for the overall economy is not given any attention, and the balancing of the costs and benefits of the consequences of demographic processes does not take place. For example, the ageing of society in many respects promotes the development of new, or the expansion of existing, markets and thus secures or creates jobs and incomes for those who are not old – this is most clearly shown in the field of personal social services and/or in the area of health. Thus, the German Council of Experts for Concerted Action on Health – a body which advises on health-related issues – explicitly mentions in a special report published recently that health in Germany is both a 'cost factor and future market', and expressly refers to the increasing number of older people as consumers of health services (Sachverständigen-rat 1996). Similarly the 1998 European Commission Report on Ageing and Technology emphasizes the market opportunities for assistive and other technologies created by an ageing society (European Commission 1998). Certain segments of private consumer goods markets are booming solely as a result of the increase in the older population; as the income of successive cohorts of older people increases, so too does their purchasing power. Even if, as for example in Germany, a considerable proportion of the income of older people is saved, this still has beneficial effects on the national economy, as money markets also profit from it.

Second, it cannot be accepted that financing problems observed in social security systems in Western Europe are attributable exclusively or even mainly to demographic shifts or the ageing of society. Thus for example in the Federal Republic of Germany, the financial difficulties faced by the pension insurance system can be put down primarily to a drop in the contributions received as a result of mass unemployment and the increasing exclusion by employers of groups of employed people from social security protection, as well as the enormous number of those going into early retirement in recent years and the resulting shifting of costs to the pension insurance scheme. These difficulties, in other words, are also attributable to a large extent to the situation in the labour market (Walker 1997; Naegele and Schmidt 1998). Moreover, as far as the rising costs of health in Germany are concerned, it can be said that demographic effects can be singled out as a causal factor for only a very small proportion of people. Rather, there is a severe lack of efficiency in the health service as well as a variety of mechanisms which stimulate the increase in costs; these *appear* to be connected to the demographic trend (for example the trend towards the overspecialization of doctors, excessive medical treatment for older patients, the use of new and very expensive treatments [Naegele 1998]), but in fact are not.

Nevertheless, policies for older people – and this has been underlined by almost all of the chapters from Europe and especially the one from the US – are increasingly required to justify proposed spending in terms of demographic shifts. In Europe, too – albeit not (yet) as distinctly as in the United States – the serious question of intergenerational justice is being brought up, especially in Italy, the Netherlands and Germany. The internal cohesion of a society stands or falls by the balance of give-and-take between the large groups in that society. The generational contract as defined in the social security system is based on this key principle, and is incorporated into the idea of intergenerational reciprocity and the general belief in the necessity of solidarity between the strong and the weak. If these principles are now at risk, we must take heed and react.

However, we need to make a more precise analysis of the causes first of all. To see demography as the *only* starting point for adjustments to the social security system would be, to take a very narrow view of things. It would be inappropriate as a 'new' policy for older people because it ignores other causal factors (such as the situation in the labour market or the lack of efficiency in the healthcare system). This error can currently be observed in many Western European countries. On the other hand, we should not deny that intergenerational imbalances exist. The growing poverty of families with children or of those who are unemployed affects general policies concerning older people; raising the income of older people may no longer be justified, given the fact that in some countries such as Italy and Germany they are increasingly better-off anyway. Older people, though – even in Europe – still belong to those social groups where there is an above-average risk of impoverishment, as in the United Kingdom, and especially in Central/Eastern Europe. There is no justification here for a reduction in the level of material provision for old age.

Any necessary adjustment of the social budget to suit changed economic conditions would (according to the principle of solidarity) have to take into consideration the respective economic capacity of the groups affected. However, we should disregard any supposed differences in productivity between different groups of the population: on closer examination, they may not even exist. In the end, there are – and this was brought out again and again in various chapters – as many striking disparities in lifestyles and living conditions in the social group known as 'older people' as there are, incidentally, in the younger and middle generations. Consequently, 'broad brush' policies can all too easily overlook and possibly even reinforce these disparities, as is usually the case with gender differences, for example.

However, this should not be justified solely on demographic terms, because demographics alone do not warrant the change being made (Walker 1990). On the other hand, if status quo policies for older people aim to distribute the burden unselectively on to the shoulders of the younger and middle generations in a manner which does take account of the needs of the younger generations, this too is intolerable. Whatever the case, comprehensible and socially balanced criteria must be taken as a basis when cutting social benefits. Likewise, the financial situation of older people as a whole must be taken into consideration. Where there is a high degree of poverty among older people, a further reduction in the level of income should be ruled out automatically. Furthermore, just as with other population groups, different countries have very different economic bases for the provision of services to all the various subgroups of older people.

In several countries – especially conservative ones – 'new' policies for older people are being called for and, to some extent, are already being practised. These are seen as an 'appropriate' reaction to the demographic challenges facing the social security system; this was typically the case in the United Kingdom under the Conservative governments of Thatcher and Major and, more recently, Germany and Sweden. The aim of these 'new' policies for older people is the (partial) privatization of the coverage for social risks related to old age, in accordance with the individualism principle. Often, the reasons given are that the new policies are fairer for young *and* old – frequently an excuse for the introduction of private old age pension insurance schemes.

As soon as things go this far, any doubts one may have had are entirely justified. A policy of privatization of the coverage of the social risks of old age necessarily leads (at other levels of social life) to (new) conflicts and thus to subsequent risks for relations between the generations. There is undoubtedly an unbreakable link between everyday intergenerational solidarity and the principles of both the generational contract and solidarity as enshrined in social welfare legislation in many countries. These cornerstones of previous policies for older people are prerequisites for solidarity between the generations. To deliberately sacrifice them would necessarily reinforce the tendency of *bellum omnium contra omnes*; for those who do not expect solidarity will not themselves show solidarity. In other words, making private insurance schemes the basis of policies for older people would mean weakening the willingness to practise solidarity, which undoubtedly exists within the various generations, has been confirmed by many studies, and is particularly pronounced in the provision of care by family members.

Various chapters have drawn attention to one very specific aspect of the solidarity between generations which ought to be acknowledged and accordingly expanded as a future focal point of policies for older people. The starting point for this can be found in catchphrases now frequently used in the field of gerontology such as 'the potential of older people' or 'the productivity of old age'. It is claimed that there is as yet no suitable means by which these terms can be put into practice and tested. On the contrary! Forced early retirement for older people – mentioned in almost every contribution in this book and brought about by the state of the job market, company strategies of 'hiving-off' labour and the overall economic crisis – can be observed in Western and Eastern Europe as well as the US, and points to a continuation of the practical devaluation of the productivity of older people (Walker 1997).

Against this background, the belief in the 'productivity of older people', as vociferously declared by scientists and politicians alike, would necessarily degenerate into empty rhetoric, if, in the future, paid employment remained closed to the older generation. The conditions for this must be improved or created so that older people can prove themselves in their professional lives if they wish and if they are allowed. What is more, this would also be in line with the supposedly threatened generational contract. However, a precondition of this is a change in employment policies relating to older people and the development and use of measures for promoting the integration of older people into employment (Walker 1997). Such a change is currently not in sight. To put it another way: the generational contract in the social security system is not threatened because more people are growing old, but because they are being prevented from making a productive contribution to society.

If the current system of retirement is maintained – and there are no indications that there will be any fundamental changes in the medium term – then it is all the more important that we provide for a socially 'productive' utilization of the potential of older people after they have retired. From the point of view of intra- and intergenerational solidarity, this could mean the promotion of solidarity as it is practised among older people. The aim of this would be for older people to use their potential for productivity for the benefit of others – both young and older people who are in need of help and assistance (Naegele 1994); preferably along the lines of the motto 'I for myself together with others for myself and for others' (Tews 1994: 60). The fact that, at least among the younger groups of older people, there is a certain willingness and quite a considerable degree of potential for commitment to public causes, self-help, cooperation within associations for older people, voluntary work, civic work and so on has been mentioned in different ways in earlier contributions and is already the focal point of discussions which are starting up in many countries, for example France, concerning the redefinition of the role of older people.

Admittedly, there are in individual countries' models such as old age expert services, projects using empirical knowledge and such like. However,

in none of the countries mentioned could we speak of a sufficiently developed overall concept. The theory of 'structural discrepancy' (Riley and Riley
1994), according to which the potential of older individuals is increasingly
drifting away from the opportunities offered by society to use this potential,
is especially applicable to the retirement phase, especially with the continued
trend towards early retirement and the lengthening of the advanced old age
phase. To eliminate this discrepancy would be a development-related task
and the focus of modern and future-oriented policies for older people, at
least for as long as the concept of productivity remains applied solely to paid
employment. To overcome this would be a permanent task of policies for
older people in the future.

## Political behaviour of older people

Those chapters which go into explicit detail about the political behaviour of
older people reveal consistent tendencies: the level of electoral participation
of older people – as compared with younger age groups – is above average,
at least with people aged up to 75 or 80. They are more strongly affiliated to
the established parties, whereas younger voters are more likely to switch
allegiances than older voters. In many countries, party members are made
up of an above-average number of older people, yet the latter have below-
average representation at management level or among elected representatives. Political parties comprising only older people – it remains to be seen
what will happen with the trend in the Netherlands – have hardly a chance,
as is the case in Germany, the UK, Sweden and the US. Conventional as
opposed to spectacular forms of political activity are preferred here.

The considerably higher level of electoral participation, like the affiliation
to the established parties, seems to indicate greater trust among older people
in the existing forms of political participation within the scope of parliamentary democracy. This, in turn, supports the assumption that older people find
sufficient representation for themselves and their specific interests and needs
through the established and ruling institutions of the (welfare) state, including the social groups and political parties which support them.

The fact that parties encompassing only older people find so little support
among the older population – even in the Netherlands they are in the minority – is as little of a surprise as the empirically numerous pieces of evidence
which show that being old is no authoritative means of predicting political
opinions and behaviour. The reasons for this are obvious: in addition to the
apparent trust in the efficacy of parliamentary democracy, there are no
genuinely old age-related topics or interests which could be bundled up and
channelled into one political party for older people. Voting behaviour is
influenced by more than the typical subjects related to old age: for example
housing policies in the US or national security in Germany. Even massive
cuts in the social security systems which affect older people to an above-
average degree, such as in the United Kingdom or – less markedly – in
Germany, have not led to the political mobilization of the older population
into organizing a group for themselves. On the contrary, those who are most
affected (that is, older women) are quite apparently the most loyal voters of

hose parties which carry the political responsibility for these cuts, at least in Germany and the UK.

Added to this is the failure among older people, as reported in almost all of the preceding chapters, to affiliate themselves to one homogeneous group known as 'older people', which consequently prevents any group consciousness being developed in the political sense. The very chronological self-definition as 'old' is being pushed further and further into the background. Older people do not desire the label of a 'party for older people' and possibly the related idea of being identifiable as a member of a 'special' social group. Rather, as the case of Germany shows and, indeed, those of most EU countries (Walker and Maltby 1997), older people see themselves as being an integral (albeit older) part of society as a whole – and consequently also vote for the large national parties.

The heterogeneity of older people as a group itself fits this concept. It is clear from all the contributions to this volume that older people differ in a variety of ways, particularly according to affiliation to groups, economic resources, gender, age ('younger old people', 'very old people'), region (for example, older Northern Italians and Southern Italians, East Germans and West Germans) or ethnic background. Within the subgroups of older people there are significant internal differences to be observed, if one looks at the internal structure of 'older immigrants' in the US, for instance. Here, even older Asian immigrants differentiate themselves according to numerous ethnic subgroups without obvious common interests or needs.

Nevertheless, tendencies towards political mobilization can indeed be observed among older people, as many contributions have clearly shown. However, this does not take place outside the established supporting bodies and structures for developing political opinion, but within them or under their auspices. On the one hand, the existing large political parties are of prime importance here, for example, in Austria, Germany and Sweden, where parties have their own 'sections for older people'. Furthermore, there is a strong connection between the incipient political mobilization of older people and trade unions, at the initiative of older people themselves, especially in Italy and the UK. However, it should be said that these are not always grassroots movements within the established structures but rather – and perhaps primarily – incentives 'from above' as well, that is initiatives controlled from above, with the interests of the parent organization in the foreground. Thus, for example, those organizations for older people founded in Germany by the two largest parties, the CDU and the SPD, are also a reaction from the heads of the parties to the demographic changes in the electorate itself and should therefore be seen as an attempt to present themselves in an attractive light to the older voting public.

It is sometimes assumed that age cohort effects (more education, more professional experience among women, higher incomes in old age, generally higher levels of activity, more practised mobility) would contribute to a change in the political behaviour of future cohorts of older people. Whether this is true or whether greater political activity outside the established supporting bodies and structures for developing political opinion will result from this, is an open question about which we can only speculate at present.

The little reported experience regarding this issue points in two directions On the one hand, there could be a kind of 'depoliticization' of old age, with a great many more personal and individual interests than those which concern the common good or political life being pursued in the retirement phase. Even most of the above-mentioned projects for 'productive old age' and many of the regional and local forms of representation for older people which will be discussed in the next section are by no means considered to be 'political'.

On the other hand, the large political organizations such as the parties and trade unions will be forced to offer their older members more scope and opportunities for cooperation, as older members make far stronger demands for such things. In other words: against the background of demographic changes in the established structures themselves, the situation may result in older people – who are excluded, to a great extent, from attaining leading positions or holding office and thus from having any influence and power – becoming more involved at the membership level. This trend will not necessarily lead – as experience in Germany has shown, where this process has just got under way – to a 'surge' in topics related to old age within organizations or parties. Rather, we can expect that the general tasks and goals of the respective parent organization will be increasingly dealt with and examined from the older person's point of view. It is precisely this which would correspond with the cross-sectional character of the subject of old age within politics which we mentioned at the beginning.

## Patterns of political participation

A conceptualization of political participation and the representation of the interests of older people which is confined solely to the conventional political system seems to be too limited. This would emphasize only the traditional forms of involvement and participation in politics – political parties, parliaments, committees, and so on – that is, the established political forums. Of course, this sector is significant for older people too: in some Western European countries there is inadequate representation of this group on official committees and other bodies. This has led to criticism, both by older people themselves and by other relevant societal groups mainly representing the intellectual and political elites in the countries concerned. Nevertheless, a much broader concept of political significance is favoured here, one which includes the whole area of social participation, and thus goes beyond the narrow definition of the political system. This view understands the active role of older people in helping to build the social and economic fabric of all areas of society, by comprehensive political and social participation and representation. This concept, therefore, goes far beyond the representation of the local interests of older people – for example in their role as tenants, road users, or as users of numerous social services, institutions and facilities available to them – and proposes using the skills and potential of this group to contribute to areas which have overall social relevance beyond the specific interests of older people. This includes the various sectors of the economy, education, culture and so on.

The chapters in this volume provide examples of quite different forms of the political and social representation of older people. These intermediate forms between self-representation and external representation (even by those who are not old) cannot always be clearly defined such as:

- professional lobbying without the active participation of older members;
- state-organized forms of representation with a mainly advisory function for state forums, usually in relation to socio-political topics of national importance;
- organizations for older people sponsored by the respective large parties, again with the focus on national and/or socio-political themes;
- forms of representation arising from the trade union movement or supported by the trade unions, with a strong focus on trade union and/or socio-political matters at a national level;
- representative bodies of older people at a regional and local level and, if necessary, their merging at a national level with differing degrees of authority, having primarily an advisory function in relation to various, though extensively old age-related issues with a regional or local character;
- interest groups in old people's homes and related facilities, usually with advisory and supervisory functions.

In view of the widely differing political structures of the states represented in this book – for example, predominant centralization in France, which accords greater significance to the national level, and the strongly decentralized structures in Germany and in the Netherlands, which theoretically means greater influence at local authority level – the political involvement of older people varies widely from country to country. The institutional framework for the political involvement of older people also varies widely, as do cultural background, willingness to get involved and interest.

Although there are elements of political participation of older people and a tendency for the speedy growth in the number of committees, representative organizations and so on to varying degrees on all levels, the legal and institutional base is inadequate in many cases. Statutory provisions for co-determination by older people in institutions are common. The Netherlands has taken the lead in this respect. Moreover there are currently very intensive statutory provisions and institutional measures at local level. This is particularly the case in countries in which this level has extensive powers. The legal basis of senior citizens' committees with relatively wide-ranging powers is also particularly developed in the Netherlands. In principle, it is necessary either to expand existing statutory frameworks for the political involvement of older people in the countries concerned, or to create new ones.

There is an increasing appreciation at all levels across Europe of the necessity for (better) representation of the interests of older people in the public and political sectors. There are not just demographic reasons for this – the increasing proportion of older people making up the total population in all European countries. Reference must also be made to the attempts in almost all Western European countries to reorganize or even cut down on social welfare provision. The era of fiscal austerity and the convergence criteria of the Maastricht Treaty in the EU Member States have greatly constrained the financial resources available to the public sector and have reduced the scope for redistribution, which affects older people in particular because they are the largest group of welfare state beneficiaries (Beck *et al.* 1997).

In this respect, it must also be recorded critically that there is a growing discrepancy, common to almost all countries, documented in this book, between the quantitative and qualitative increase in the significance of age in public life and the representation of self-interests by those directly concerned. For example, in most Western European countries, older people are underrepresented in the established political bodies and institutional structure. There is a special pensioners' lobby in only the UK and the Netherlands – disregarding any question whether it has any actual power. Even at a regional level, special senior citizens' committees do not exist in all Western European countries, as in Germany, the Netherlands, the UK and in Sweden as well as in the other Scandinavian countries for example. However, co-determination and decision-making powers vary widely, and are institutionally based. For example, senior citizens' committees in the Scandinavian countries already have extensive responsibilities which go far beyond a purely advisory capacity and include decision-making powers and consultation rights in budgetary and personnel matters. Overall, however, many more decisions are made *about* older people than *with* them, and in particular older people make few decisions in those matters which directly affect them.

In the future, old age policy must increasingly try to reach a just balance of interests between all sectors of the population in a country, region and town. In this process of negotiation too, the interests of some older people – as a group of current consumers of welfare rather than contributors – must be taken more into account. This could certainly then lead to discussions about the relative position of older people and their apparently justified interests compared to the interests for example, of (even) more disadvantaged social groups, such as immigrants, single parents, the long term unemployed and their families. For many reasons, older people must be involved more than before in these discussions and plans affecting their quality of life, and they must have equal say as one of the affected parties.

The question of an appropriate form of representation thus arises. It will be necessary to maintain various forms of representation at different levels. These should strongly reflect each individual state's cultural and national previous experiences. This particularly applies to Central Eastern European countries in which the political participation of older people – at least outside of the former parties – is just beginning to take shape. No standard European-wide solution is possible. However, a constant exchange of information between countries is required, perhaps on the model provided by a book like this, in order to benefit from the experiences of others.

Although there can be no 'standard' form of representation for each country, particular requirements relating to national- or regional-specific solutions can be drawn up. The main assessment criterion should be authority: what must be examined is the extent to which the existing or proposed forms of representation of interests are authorized to speak on behalf of those affected. From this point of view, 'grassroots projects' and democratically developed (elected) forms of representation doubtless have the highest degree of authority. This cannot be assumed *per se* for delegatory forms of representation which have been used by a number of regional or national political bodies in Western European countries. Do these forms of representation simply act as an 'extended arm' of the interests of third parties, such as the main political parties, while officially claiming to speak 'on behalf of everyone'?

What topics are to be taken up, and whose interests represented? Distinguishing between groups of senior citizens who are less old and very old, female and male, healthy and infirm/requiring care, well-off and poor, native and foreign, shows that there is no such thing as a 'standard' set of needs of older people. The danger of the representation of particular interests thus becomes acute. Simply being an 'older person' is thus no guarantee of always representing the interests of older people as a whole.

The interests of the weaker groups of the older population must primarily be taken into account, because experience shows that these groups in particular are least able to represent their own interests or organize themselves politically, on account of their usually restricted living conditions (see Chapter 2). There is thus a great danger of the interests of both groups of people being lumped together and represented in the political and public spheres, without necessarily reflecting the interests of weaker groups of older people. However, this would not be justifiable in terms of policy affecting older people, and would *de facto* mean a further privileging of those categories among older people who are already socially privileged. There is no 'intergenerational solidarity' on the sole basis of belonging to the group defined as 'older people'. On the contrary, many objective contrasts of interest exist between the individual social categories of older people, based on their belonging to different social or ethnic groups, for example. In view of the increasingly tight financial constraints on social redistribution, perhaps these contrasts will be more obvious in the future. This makes it all the more important to consider the interests of 'powerless' older people in future negotiation processes.

This also places significant restrictions on self-organization and political self-representation. The interests of the underprivileged, the 'powerless' and/or the 'voiceless' (such as the poor, infirm or migrant older people) must also be expressed in the existing and planned representative bodies which claim to speak 'for everyone'. Such representative bodies must also be examined to see if this is actually the case, or whether their internal composition contradicts their claim. It also follows that the future path of political 'self-organization of older people' certainly cannot be summarized as 'older people speak for themselves'. In the future, it will be necessary for third parties, who need not be older people or one of those affected, to assume representation of the interests of this group too. Ideally, they should consult bodies representing the interests of older people, but this is not essential.

## Solidarity between the generations

Although (improved) representation of the interests of older people is an important social and socio-political objective, unanswered questions – including the risks associated with a grouping justified exclusively or primarily on the basis of the age calendar and concerning the representation of interests – must not be ignored. On the one hand, there are many interests and matters which are certainly not 'age-specific', but exist across all age groups and are primarily justified in content. For example, the desire for a qualitatively superior social infrastructure, a comfortable and cost-effective public transport system, urban regeneration, traffic calming and so on are proof of a more pronounced identity of interests on a local level between various social and age groups. On the other hand, the desire for a clean environment or internal and external security applies across all groups on a national and European level. It is therefore also important to interpret and pursue these interests as the common concerns of various social groups, including all age groups, which simultaneously raises the question of appropriate partners for cooperation.

Yet steady pressure for one's own interests must give rise to the question of whether forcing these interests through wherever possible will disadvantage another social group. 'Solidarity between generations' is demanded, and rightly so. This also means placing the interests of one's own age group in relation to those of other age groups, and making sure there is equal appreciation and consideration of interests. It is certainly not wrong to fear that the so far (still) largely unknown 'generation conflict' in the Western European countries might be fuelled by a stronger and more self-assured representation of the interests of older people. This addresses a serious problem, resulting both from demographic shifts and also from the massive disparities in some Western European countries in the material and financial situations of the different subgroups of older and younger people. In some Western European countries, some older people are nowadays materially better off than many young families with children and most single parents.

In this respect, it is also true that demanding rights always entails the question of obligations. Although this statement applies equally to all social groups, it must also include older people. If they articulate their justified interests to everyone in general and demand their relevant rights, it may be anticipated that at the same time they will also disclose what they wish to do for society, in return for and as an expression of 'solidarity between the generations'. A living contract between generations will have little time for any harping back to what they had achieved earlier, particularly not in any negotiation resulting from a tightening of financial constraints, though of course past financial contributions to social security systems must be recognized.

If the interests affecting countless age groups are in no way age-specific, who are the appropriate cooperation partners for the existing bodies which represent the interests of older people? If supposedly 'independent', any proximity to governments and major political parties will give rise to scepticism. The question of alliances and cooperation would arise repeatedly to compromise objectives currently pursued, and there would be no natural 'coalition partners' for the bodies representing the interests of older people. Depending on the topic, target group and circumstances, these could be the trade unions or other political parties, charities and welfare organizations, other non-governmental organizations, consumer protection groups, citizens' initiatives and so on. How the respective representative bodies find and assert their independence from the ruling political elites will be crucial to the authority of their claim to speak 'on behalf of older people'.

This certainly does not preclude the possibility of representation of older people which is close to the government or parties, as has already been the case for some years in some Western European countries (such as Germany). On the contrary, it is at least as important to represent the affairs of older people within established forms of politics as well as through other channels of political influence. This is necessary to counter the exclusion of older people from established decision-making bodies, as in some other European countries. However, in these cases, political independence can no longer be claimed: in practice, frequently persons and functions are the same in each respective organization.

An important question for the future will be how to ensure that the interests of older people as consumers ('customers') and users of social services are guaranteed. The more social services and related provisions are available on the market, and the more older people become dependent on these, the more important this becomes. Even now, for example, the demand for quality assurance in care is highly topical in some Western European countries, and one of the questions which emerges is that of the representation of consumer interests of those requiring care. However, in many EU countries there have not yet been any role models or experience. Positive examples can be found particularly in Sweden, the UK and the Netherlands.

We conclude where we began: the politics of old age have entered a critical new phase in the EU. This is also true in Hungary and, to a lesser extent (in terms of timing), the US. Whether or not older people are able to enjoy full citizenship (both national and European) depends on a combination of bottom–up mobilization by older people and top–down actions by national and European policy elites. Much hinges on the outcome of these political developments, which contain both conflictual and consensual possibilities: the meaning of old age in contemporary Europe, the representativeness of democratic institutions and the maintenance of intergenerational solidarity.

# References

Abrams, M. and O'Brien, J. (1981) *Political Attitudes and Ageing in Britain*. Mitcham: Age Concern England.

Actes du Colloque de la Roche-sur-Yon (1992) *Faire de la démocratie autrement*, Premières rencontres nationales des Conseils de sages et d'anciens, Journée du 13 février. Paris: L'Harmattan.

Advisory Council on Social Security (1997) *Report of the 1994–1996 Advisory Council on Social Security, Volume I, Findings and Recommendations*. Washington, DC: US Social Security Administration.

Age Concern England (1994) *Pensioner Organisations in England*. London: Age Concern Briefings.

Age Concern England (1995) *Core Information*. Volume I. London: Age Concern.

Age Concern England (1996) *Pensioner Organisations in England*. London: Age Concern England.

Alber, J. (1994) Soziale Integration und politische Repräsentation von Senioren, in G. Verheugen (ed.) *60plus. Die wachsende Macht der Alten*. Köln: Bund-Verlag: 145–68.

Alber, J. (1995) The social integration of older people in Germany, in A. Walker (ed.) *Older People in Europe: Social Integration*. Brussels: Commission of the European Communities, DGV: 111–62.

Allsop, J. (1984) *Health Policy and the National Health Service*. London: Longman.

Almond, G.A. and Verba, S. (1963) *The Civic Culture*. Princeton, NJ: Princeton University Press.

Amt der Tiroler Landesregierung (ed.) (1993) *Leitbild Seniorenreferat*. Innsbruck: unpublished manuscript.

Andersson, B. (1983) Pensionärsrörelsen: utnyttjade och outnyttjade maktresurser. Exemplet Göteborg 1938–79, in B. Oden, A. Svanborg and L. Tornstam (eds) *Äldre I Samhället: Förr, Nu och Framtiden, del 2: Probleminventeringar*. Stockholm: LiberFörslag.

Archambault, E. (1993) *Defining the Nonprofit Sector: France*. The Johns Hopkins University Institute for Policy Studies, Working Paper No. 7. Baltimore, MD: Johns Hopkins University Press.

Argoud, D. (1991) *Participation sociale: agir avec les retraités. Le Conseil des sages de la Roche-sur-Yon*, Rapport préparatoire au colloque de Versailles. Paris: Fédération CRI.

Argoud, D. (1997) Die Vertretung der Interessen der Senioren in Frankreich – Zu einer Neudefinition des Stellenwertes des Rentners in der Stadt? in A. Carrell, V. Gerling, C. Marking, G. Naegele and A. Walker (eds) *Politische Beteiligung älterer Menschen in Europa*. Bonn: Bundesministerium für Familie, Senioren, Frauen und Jugend.

Artner, M., Klein, I., Riedel, B. and Strümpel, C. (eds) (1996) *Ehrenamt zwischen Anspruch und Wirklichkeit* (Eurosocial Report No. 59). Wien: Europäisches Zentrum.

Askham, J., Henshaw, L. and Tarpey, R. (1993) Policies and perceptions of identity. Service needs of elderly people from black and minority ethnic backgrounds, Chapter 11 in S. Arber and M. Evandrou (eds) *Ageing, Independence and the Life Course*. London: Jessica Kingsley.

Association of Metropolitan Authorities and Association of County Councils (1995) *Who Gets Community Care: A Survey of Community Care Eligibility Criteria*. London: AMA/ACC.

Audit Commission (1986) *Making a Reality of Community Care*. London: HMSO.

Baars, J., Knipscheer, K. and Breebaart, E. (1992) *The Impact of Social and Economic Policies on Older People in the Netherlands*. Amsterdam: Vrije Universiteit.

BAGSO (ed.) (1996) *Portraits '96. Mitgliederverzeichnis*. Bonn.

Bahr, C., Leichsenring, K. and Strümpel, C. (1996) *Mitsprache. Bedarfsfelder für politische Mitsprache älterer Menschen in Österreich*. Vienna: European Centre for Social Welfare.

Bajtelsmit, V.L., Johnson, R.D. and Nugent, M.M. (1997) *The Impact of Social Security Reform Proposals on Individual Taxpayers*. Fort Collins, CO: Colorado State University, Department of Finance and Real Estate.

Baldwin, P. (1990) *Class Bases of the European Welfare State, 1875–1975*. New York: Cambridge University Press.

Barber, B. (1984) *Strong Democracy. Participatory Politics for a New Age*. Berkeley/Los Angeles/London: University of California Press.

Barnes, M. and Walker, A. (1996) Consumerism versus empowerment, *Policy and Politics*, 24(4): 375–93.

Beauvoir, S. de (1977) *Old Age*. Harmondsworth: Penguin Books (first published as *La Viellesse*, 1970).

Beck, W., van der Maesen, L. and Walker, A. (eds) (1997) *The Social Quality of Europe*. The Hague: Kluwer International.

Beresford, P. and Green, F. (1996) Income and wealth, *Critical Social Policy*, 16(1): 95–109.

Berg, H. van den (1991) Ouderen in de samenleving. Van 'do to' naar 'do, Tijdschrift voor' Agologie.

Bernadotte af Wisborg, G., Claesson, C.B., Lundberg, O. and Thorslund, M. (1996) Drug usage and self-reported health among a cross-sectional population aged over 75 years, *Clinical Drug Investigation*, 12: 156–69.

Binstock, R. (1983) The aged as a scapegoat, *The Gerontologist*, 23: 136–43.

Binstock, R.H. (1991) From the great society to the aging society – 25 years of the Older Americans Act, *Generations*, 15(3): 11–18.

Binstock, R. (1992) Older voters and the 1993 presidential election, *The Gerontologist*, 32(5): 601–6.

Binstock, R.H. (1997) The 1996 election: older voters and implications for policies on aging, *The Gerontologist*, 37(1): 15–19.

Binstock, R.H. and Day, C.L. (1996) Aging and politics, in R.H. Binstock and L.K. George (eds) *Handbook of Aging and the Social Sciences*, 4th edition. San Diego, CA: Academic Press.

Birnbaum, J.H. (1997) Washington's second most powerful man, *Fortune*, 12 May: 122–6.

Blake, M. (1997) 'Grey power? Political mobilization among pensioners in Sweden', IGP masters thesis, Stockholm: Stockholm University.

Bloch-Lainé, F. and Garrigou-Lagrange, J.M. (1988) *Associations et développement local*, Paris: L.DJ.

Board of Trustees, Federal Old-Age and Survivors Insurance and Disability Insurance Trust Funds (1997) *The 1997 Annual Report of the Board of Trustees of the Federal Old-Age and*

*Survivors Insurance and Disability Insurance Trust Funds*. Washington, DC: US Government Printing Office.

Boards of Trustees, Social Security and Medicare (1997) *Status of the Social Security and Medicare Programs: A Summary of the 1997 Annual Reports*. Washington, DC: Boards of Trustees.

Boccella, N. (1982) *Il Mezzogiorno sussidiato*. Milano: Angeli.

Bone, M., Gregory, J., Gill, B. and Lader, D. (1992) *Retirement and Retirement Plans*. London: HMSO.

Boulard, J.C. (1991) *Vivre ensemble*, Report on the frail elderly submitted to the National Assembly on June 20. Paris: National Assembly.

Brunner, M. (1996) *Âge et politique. Le comportement politique des personnes âgées en Suisse* (Études et Recherches, No. 34). Genève: Université de Genève/Département de Science Politique.

Bundesministerium für Arbeit und Soziales (ed.) (1994) *Seniorenbericht*. Wien: BMAS.

Bürklin, W. (1987) Alte Wähler morgen: Graue Panther oder konservative Stammwähler der CDU? in Deutsches Zentrum für Altersfragen (ed.) *Die ergraute Gesellschaft*. Berlin: DZA: 116–40.

Campbell, P.R. (1996) *Population Projections for States by Age, Sex, Race, and Hispanic Origin: 1995–2025*, PPL-47. Washington, DC: US Bureau of the Census, Population Division.

Carell, A., Gerling, V., Marking, C., Naegele, G. and Walker, A. (1997) (eds) *Politische Beteiligung älterer Menschen in Europa*. Bonn: Bundesministerium für Familie, Senioren, Frauen und Jugend.

Carter, T. and Nash, C. (1992) *Pensioners Forums – An Active Voice*. Guildford: Pre-Retirement Association.

CEC (1993) *Social Protection in Europe*. Luxembourg: OOCEP.

Centraal Bureau voor de Statistiek (1994) Statistiek der verkiezingen 1994, *Tweede Kamer*, 3 mei. Voorburg/Heerlen: CBS.

Centraal Bureau voor de Statistiek (1996) *De Leefsituatie van de Nederlandse Bevolking, 1995*. Kerncijfers. Voorburg/Heerlen: CBS.

CER (1997) *Gli anziani in Italia*. VI Rapporto, Roma: Ediesse.

CLEIRPPA Infos (1993) *Activités d'utilité sociale des retraités et des personnes âgées*, Hors série, Bulletin d'informations du CLEIRPPA. Paris: CLEIRPPA.

CNRPA (1995) *Retraités et représentativité*, Rapport du CNRPA, avril. Paris: CNRPA.

Cohen, J. and Rogers, J. (1995) Secondary associations and democratic governance, in E.O. Wright (ed.) *Associations and Democracy*. London: Verso.

Cohen, L. and Male, A. (1992) *Old Age Insurance: Who Gets What for Their Money*. Issue Brief No. 15. Washington, DC: American Association of Retired Persons.

Cohen, W. (1958) *Retirement Policies Under Social Security*. Berkeley and Los Angeles: University of California Press.

Commission against Poverty and Marginalization (1996) *Le politiche locali contro l'esclusione sociale*. Rome: Presidenza del Consiglio dei Ministri.

Commission on Social Justice (1994) *Social Justice: Strategies for National Renewal*. London: Vintage.

Connor, K.A. (1992) *Aging America: Issues Facing an Aging Society*. Englewood Cliffs, NJ: Prentice Hall.

Cook, F.L. (1996) Public support for programs for older Americans: continuities amidst threat of discontinuities, in V.L. Bengtson (ed.) *Adulthood and Aging*. New York: Springer.

Council for Social Affairs (1993) Basic declaration of the European Union and the Ministers assembled in the Council of Social Affairs on 6 December 1993 on the occasion of the official end of the European Year for Older People and Solidarity Between the Generations, *Official Journal of the European Community*, No. C343/1.

Cumming, E. and Henry, W.E. (1961) *Growing Old, The Process of Disengagement*. New York: Basic Books.

Daatland, S.O. and Szebehely, M. (1997) Tjenstene og Utviklingen in Sammenheng', in S.O. Daatland (ed.) *De Siste årene*. Oslo: NOVA.

Dane Age (1990) *New Horizons – New Elderly*. Copenhagen: Senior Forlaget.

Davies, B. and Ward, S. (1992) *Women and Personal Pensions*. London: HMSO.

Day, C.L. (1990) *What Older Americans Think: Interest Groups and Aging Policies*. Princeton, NJ: Princeton University Press.

Dekker, P. and Ester, P. (1993) *Social and Political Attitudes in Dutch Society. Theoretical Perspectives and Survey Evidence*. Rijswijk: Social and Cultural Planning Office.

Department of Health (1989) *Caring for People: Community Care in the Next Decade and Beyond*, Cm 849. London: HMSO.

Department of Health and Social Security (1981) *Growing Older*, Cm 8173. London: HMSO.

Department of Social Security (1991) *Options for Equality in State Pension Age*, Cm 1723. London: HMSO.

Department of Social Security (1993) *The Growth of Social Security*. London: HMSO.

Deutscher Bundestag (ed.) (1994) Zwischenbericht der Enquete-Kommission Demographischer Wandel – Herausforderungen unserer älter werdenden Gesellschaft an den einzelnen und die Politik. Zur Sache, Themen parlamentarischer Beratung, 4. Bonn: Bundestagsdruckerei.

Dieck, M. (1993) Entwicklungslinien der Altenpolitik in der Bundesrepublik Deutschland, in H.-U. Klose (ed.) *Altern der Gesellschaft. Antwort auf den demographischen Wandel*. Köln: Bund-Verlag: 187–212.

Dieck, M. (1996) Demographische Entwicklung – Konsequenzen für die Gesellschaft, in B. Hoppe and C. Wulf (eds) *Altern braucht Zukunft*. Hamburg: EVA-Wissenschaft: 273–85.

Di Francia, C. (1992) Anziani, istituzione e società: gli organi di rappresentanza degli anziani, *Tutela*, 2.

Dixon, J. (1994) Poll finds young Americans doubt social security future, *Washington Post*, 24 September.

Dochweiler, H. (1993) Erfahrungen mit der politischen und verbandlichen Organisation von Alten-Interessen, in Fritz-Erler-Akademie der Friedrich-Ebert-Stiftung (ed.) *Solidarität der Generationen. Perspektiven des Älterwerdens der Gesellschaft in Deutschland und Europa*. Freudenstadt: FEA-Manuskripte: 35–41.

Douglass, E.B. (1995) Professional organizations in aging: too many doing too little for too few, *Generations*, 19(2): 35–6.

DYG, Inc. (1995) *Social Security and Medicare Anniversary Research: A Study of Public Values and Attitudes*. Washington, DC: DYG, Inc.

Economic Report of the President (1997) Washington, DC: US Government Printing Office.

Employee Benefit Research Institute (1997) *The Basics of Social Security*. Washington, DC: EBRI.

Endl, M. and Leichsenring, K. (1994) *Mitbestimmungsmöglichkeiten für ältere Menschen in Österreich. Zwischenbericht zum Projekt 'Mitsprache'*. Wien: Europäisches Zentrum.

Eriksen, T.E. (1988) The adjustment of old age benefits and its impact on the financing of the schemes providing the benefits – the Swedish experience, *Current Problems of Pensions Schemes*. Geneva: International Social Security Association.

Esping-Andersen, G. (1985) *Politics Against Markets*. Princeton, NJ: Princeton University Press.

Esping-Andersen, G. (1990) *The Three Worlds of Welfare Capitalism*. Oxford: Polity Press.

Estes, C. (1979) *The Ageing Enterprise*. San Francisco, CA: Jossey-Bass.

Estes, C.L. (1982) Austerity and aging in the US, *International Journal of Health Services*, 12(4): 573–84.

Estes, C. (1986) The politics of ageing in America, *Ageing and Society*, 6: 121–34.

Estes, C.L. (1991) The new political economy of aging: introduction and critique, in M. Minkler and C. Estes (eds) *Critical Perspectives on Aging*. New York: Baywood: 3–18.

Europa Research Group (1993) *Senior Citizens in Europe*. Mainz: Johannes-Gutenberg University (mimeo).

European Commission (1998) *The Ageing Population and Technology: Challenges and Opportunities*, ETAN working paper. Brussels: European Commission.

Eurostat (1996) *Social Protection Expenditure and Receipts, 1980–94*. Luxembourg: Eurostat.

Evers, A. (1997) Consumers, citizens and coproducers. A pluralistic perspective on democracy in social services, in G. Flösser and H.U. Otto (eds) *Towards More Democracy in Social Services*. Berlin and New York: de Gruyter.

Evers, A. and Pruckner, B. (1995) *Pflege in der Familie? Politik, die hilft. Tagungsbericht.* Wien: Bundesministerium für Jugend und Familie.

Evers, A., Leichsenring, K. and Pruckner, B. (1993) *Alt genug, um selbst zu entscheiden – Internationale Modelle für mehr Demokratie in Altenhilfe und Altenpolitik.* Freiburg: Lambertus-Verlag.

Evers, A., Leichsenring, K. and Pruckner, B. (1994) Payments for care: the case of Austria, in A. Evers, M. Pijl and C. Ungerson (eds) *Payments for Care: A Comparative Overview.* Aldershot: Avebury.

Falkingham, J. (1989) Dependency and ageing in Britain: a re-examination of the evidence, *Journal of Social Policy*, 18(1): 55–68.

Falkingham, J. and Victor, C. (1991) *The Myth of the Woopie? Incomes, the Elderly and Targeting Welfare*, WSP 55. London: Suntory Toyota International Centre for Economics and Related Disciplines.

Ferge, A. (1997) *Nyugdíjreform kérdőjelei* (Questions of Pension Reform), mimeo.

Ferrera, M. (1993) *Modelli di solidarietà.* Bologna: Il Mulino.

Fessel and GfK/IFES (1989) *Politische Kultur in Österreich.* Studie 1989/47.005. Wien.

FKF (Swedish Confederation of Insurance Offices) (1997) *Nytt Pensionsystem*, internet website, http://www.fk.se/pension/nyttpen.htm.

Flora, P. (1981) Solution or source of crisis? The welfare state in historical perspective, in W. Mommsen (ed.) *The Emergence of the Welfare State in Britain and Germany.* London: Croom Helm.

Florea, A., Costanzo, A. and Cuneo, A. (1995) The social integration of older people in Italy, in A. Walker (ed.) *Older People in Europe: Social Integration.* Brussels: Commission of the European Communities, DGV: 229–61.

Fogt, H. (1992) *Politische Generationen.* Opladen: Westdeutscher Verlag.

Gallard, L. and Argoud, D. (1995) L'engagement associatif des retraités français, *Retraite et société*, 10: 41–61.

Gaullier, X. (1995) Le 'quinqua' est l'avenir de la société, *Libération*, 19 October.

Gehmacher, E. (1990) SPÖ: Wähler und Mitglieder 1945 bis 1990, in E. Fröschl, M. Mesner and H. Zoitl (eds) *Die Bewegung. Hundert Jahre Sozialdemokratie in Österreich.* Wien: Westview: 520–30.

Gerlich, P. (1991) Politische Kultur der Subsysteme, in Dachs *et al.* (eds) *Handbuch des politischen Systems Österreichs.* Wien: Manz-Verlag.

Gilbert, N. (1993) From 'welfare' to 'enabling' state, in A. Evers and I. Svetlik (eds) *Balancing Pluralism. New Welfare Mixes in Care for Older People.* Aldershot: Avebury.

Ginn, J. (1993) Grey power: age-based organisations' response to structured inequalities, *Critical Social Policy*, 13(2): 23–47.

Ginn, J. and Arber, S. (1991) Gender, class and income inequalities in later life, *British Journal of Sociology*, 42(3): 369–96.

Ginn, J. and Arber, S. (1993) Pension penalties: the gendered division of occupational welfare, *Work, Employment and Society*, 7(1): 47–70.

Ginn, J. and Arber, S. (1994) Heading for hardship: how the British pension system has failed women, Chapter 13 in S. Baldwin and J. Falkingham (eds) *Social Security and Social Change: New Challenges to the Beveridge Model.* Hemel Hempstead: Harvester Wheatsheaf.

Ginn, J. and Arber, S. (1996) Patterns of employment, pensions and gender: the effect of work history on older women's non-state pensions, *Work Employment and Society*, 10(3): 469–90.

Ginsburg, N. (1992) *Divisions of Welfare*. London: Sage.

Glennerster, H. and Hills, J. (1998) *The State of Welfare: The Economics of Social Spending*. Oxford: Oxford University Press.

Gottschlich, M., Panagl, O. and Welan, M. (eds) (1989) *Was die Kanzler sagten. Regierungserk-lärungen der Zweiten Republik 1945–1987*. Wien: Braumüller.

Grad, S. (1996) *Income of the Population 55 or Older, 1994*. Washington, DC: US Government Printing Office.

Green, F., Hadjimatheou, A. and Smail, R. (1984) *Unequal Fringes: Fringe Benefits in the United Kingdom*. London: Bedford Square Press.

Guillemard, A.M. (1986) *Le Déclin du social. Formation et crise des politiques de la vieillesse*. Paris: PUF.

Guillemard, A.M. (1990) Les paradoxes de la politique vieillesse, *Revue Française des Affaires Sociales*, 3: 127–52.

Guillemard, A.M. (1991) *La Retraite en mutation*. Paris: Recherche FEN.

Guillemard, A.M. *et al.* (1994) *Solidarité intergénérations et citoyenneté: quels nouveaux rôles pour les retraités*. Université Paris 1-Panthéon Sorbonne, Université de Liège, Rapport Fédéra-tion CRI.

Gustafsson, H. (1988) *Local Government in Sweden*. Uddevala: Svenska Institutet.

Haller, B. and König, I. (1997) *Graue Panther. Zur Wahrscheinlichkeit und Intensität der politis-chen Mobilisierung der älteren Generation in Österreich*. Wien: Institut für Konfliktforschung (unv. Endbericht einer Studie im Auftrag des Bundesministeriums für Wissenschaft, Verkehr und Kunst).

Hamnett, C. and Mullings, B. (1992) A new consumption cleavage? The case of residential care for the elderly, *Environment and Planning*, 24: 807–20.

Hancock, R. and Weir, P. (1994) *More Ways than Means. A Guide to Pensioners' Incomes in Britain During the 1980s*. London: Age Concern Institute of Gerontology.

Hancock, R., Jarvis, C. and Mueller, G. (1995) *The Outlook for Incomes in Retirement*. London: Age Concern Institute of Gerontology.

Hannah, L. (1986) *Inventing Retirement. The Development of Occupational Pensions in Britain*. Cambridge: Cambridge University Press.

Harding, T., Wistow, G. and Meredith, B. (1996) *Options for Long Term Care: Economic, Social and Ethical Choices*. London: HMSO.

Harootyan, R.A. (1981) Interest groups and aging policy, in R.B. Hudson (ed.) *The Aging in Politics: Process and Policy*. Springfield, IL: Charles C. Thomas: 74–85.

Harootyan, R.A. and Cohen, L.M. (1995) *Public Education Financing: Support for Increased Funding and Tax Preferences*. Washington, DC: American Association of Retired Persons.

Harris, J. (1981) Some aspects of social policy in Britain during the Second World War, in W. Mommsen (ed.) *The Emergence of the Welfare State in Britain and Germany*. London: Croom Helm.

Harvey, D. (1989) *The Condition of Postmodernity*. Oxford: Blackwell.

Henwood, M. (1990) *Community Care and Elderly People: Policy, Practice and Research Review*. London: Family Policy Study Centre.

Héran, F. (1988) Au coeur du réseau associatif: les multi-adhérents, *Economie et Statistique*, 208, mars.

Hills, J. (1993) *The Future of Welfare. A Guide to the Debate*. York: Joseph Rowntree Founda-tion.

Hills, J. (1996) Does Britain have a welfare generation? in A. Walker (ed.) *The New Gener-ational Contract*. London: UCL Press.

Hills, J. (1997) *The Future of Welfare*, revised edition. York: Joseph Rowntree Foundation.

Hobbs, F.B. with Damon, B.L. (1996) *65+ in the United States*, US Bureau of the Census, Current Population Reports, Special Studies, 23–190. Washington, DC: US Government Printing Office.

Hoggett, B. (1989) The elderly mentally ill and infirm: procedures for civil commitment and guardianship, in J. Eerkelaar and D. Pearl (eds) *An Ageing World. Dilemmas and Challenges for Law and Social Policy*. Oxford: Oxford University Press: 517.

Hojnic-Zupanc, I. (1996), Elderly and technology, in Z. Széman and V. Gáthy (eds) *Aging and Technology. Exploring European Old Age in East and West*. Saarijarvi: STAKES: 6–13.

Holm-Christensen, E. (1997) Denmark, in Report of the Dutch-Danish-German Expert Meeting: Senior Citizens, Elderly Consumers, held in Maastricht 1996. Utrecht: Realiseer.

Holsteijn, J.J.M. van and Niemöller, B. (eds) (1995) *De Nederlandse kiezer 1994*. Rijksuniversiteit Leiden: DSWO Press.

Holz, G. (1993) Altern und Politik. Zur gegenwärtigen und zukünftigen Macht der Alten, in B. Hoppe and C. Wulf (eds) *Altern braucht Zukunft*. Hamburg: EVA-Wissenschaft: 248–72.

Hudson, R. (ed.) (1981) *The Ageing in Politics*. Springfield, IL: Charles C. Thomas.

Hudson, R.B. (1978) The 'graying' of the federal budget and its consequences for old age policy, *The Gerontologist*, 18(5): 428–40.

Hudson, R.B. (1980) Old-age politics in a period of change, in N.G. McCluskey and E.F. Borgatta (eds) *Aging and Society*. London: Sage: 147–89.

Hutton, S., Kennedy, S. and Whiteford, P. (1995) *Equalisation of State Pension Ages: The Gender Impact*. Manchester: Equal Opportunities Commission.

IRP [Istituto di Ricerche sulla Popolazione] (1997) If there is an old person at home, *Demotrends*, 1 (October).

ISFOL (1996) *Rapporto*. Milano: Angeli.

Jenkins, J.C. and Klandermans, B. (eds) (1995) *The Politics of Social Protest*. London: UCL Press.

Johnson, P. (1994) *The Pensions Dilemma*. London: IPPR.

Johnson, P. and Falkingham, J. (1992) *Ageing and Economic Welfare*. London: Sage.

Johnson, P., Conrad, C. and Thomson, D. (eds) (1989) *Workers Versus Pensioners: Intergenerational Conflict in an Ageing World*. Manchester: Manchester University Press.

Jowell, R., Brook, L., Prior, G. and Taylor, B. (1992) *British Social Attitudes Survey. The Ninth Report*. Aldershot: Gower.

Jowell, R., Witherspoon, S. and Brook, L. (1990) *British Social Attitudes Survey. The 7th Report*. Aldershot: Gower.

Kaelble, H. (1987) *Auf dem Weg zu einer europäischen Gesellschäft. Eine Sozialgeschichte Westeuropas 1880–1980*. München.

Kaufman, O. (1996) Landesbericht Frankreich, in B. Shulte (ed.) *Altenhilfe in Europa. Rechtliche, Institutionelle und Infrastrukturelle Bedingungen – Vergleichender Gesamtbericht*. Bonn: Kohlhammer.

Kersbergen, K. von (1995) *Social Capitalism. A Study of Christian Democracy and the Welfare State*. London.

KF [Association of Municipalities] (1994) *Support and Development of Local Authorities*. Stockholm: KF.

Knipscheer, C.P.M. (1995) Een samenleving voor ouderen of met ouderen? in J. Munnichs, C. Knipscheer, N. Stevens and T. van Knippenberg, (eds) *Ouderen en Zingeving*. Baarn: Ambo: 32–47.

Köbben, A.J.F. and Nelissen, C. (1989) Oud en machteloos? Over het aandeel van ouderen in politiek en bestuur. Utrecht: Nederlands Instituut voor Zorg en Welzijn.

Köhler, P. (1997) Landesbericht Dänemark, in B. Schulte, (ed.) *Altenhilfe in Europa*. Bonn: Kohlhammer.

Kohli, M., Rein, M., Guillemard, A.M. and van Gunsteren, H. (eds) (1991) *Time for Retirement*. Cambridge: CUP.

Kohli, M., Künemund, H. and Wolf, J. (1994) Von Solidarität zu Konflikt? Der Generationenvertrag und die Interessenorganisation der Älteren, in G. Verheugen (ed.) *60plus. Die wachsende Macht der Alten*. Köln: Bund-Verlag: 61–74.

Kohli, M., Neckel, S. and Wolf, J. (1997) Krieg der Generationen? Die politische Macht der Älteren. Funkkolleg Altern, Studieneinheit 20, Studienbrief 7. Deutsches Institut für Fernstudien (DIFF) (eds). Tübingen: DIFF-Eigenverlag.

KSH [Central Statistical Office] (1996) *Magyar statisztikai zsebkönyv '95* (Hungarian Statistical Yearbook '95). Budapest: KSH.

Kühnert, S. and Gloddeck, P. (1996) Participation of seniors in the Federal Republic of Germany, paper prepared for the Expert-Meeting 'Senior Citizens, Elderly Consumers', Maastricht, November. Dortmund.

Künemund, H. (1994) Senioren im Deutschen Gewerkschaftsbund, in J. Wolf, M. Kohli and H. Künemund (eds) *Alter und gewerkschaftliche Politik. Auf dem Weg zur Rentnergewerkschaft?* Köln: Bund-Verlag: 32–49.

Laczko, F. and Phillipson, C. (1991) Great Britain: the contradictions of early exit, in M. Kohli, M. Rein, A.M. Guillemard and H. van Gunsteren (eds) *Time for Retirement*. Cambridge: Cambridge University Press: 222–51.

Lamison-White, L. (1997) *Poverty in the United States: 1996*. Bureau of the Census, Current Population Reports, Series P60-198. Washington, DC: US Government Printing Office.

Leibfried, S. (1992) Towards a European welfare state? in S. Ferge and J. Kolberg (eds) *Social Policy in a Changing Europe*. Frankfurt: Campus/Westview: 227–59.

Leichsenring, K. (1996) Payments for care in selected European countries, in Fondazione Finney (ed.) (1996) *What Kind of Legal and Social Protection for Frail Older Persons? The Ageing Society and Personal Rights*. Rome/Brussels: Fondazione Finney/ Commission of the European Union: 274–9.

Leichsenring, K., Bahr, C. and Strümpel, C. (1997) Politische Mitbestimmungsmöglichkeiten älterer Menschen in Österreich, in A. Carell, V. Gerling, C. Marking, G. Naegele and A. Walker (eds) *Politische Beteiligung älterer Menschen in Europa*. Bonn: Bundesministerium für Familie, Senioren, Frauen und Jugend.

Lemov, P. (1996) Welcome to Eldertown, *Governing*, 10(1): 18–21.

Lenoir, R. (1979) L'invention du troisième âge, *Actes de la Recherche en Sciences Sociales*, 26–7, mars-avril.

LF [Association of County Councils] (1995) *The County Councils in Sweden*. Stockholm: LF.

Liemer, D.R. (1995) A guide to social security money's worth issues, *Social Security Bulletin*, 58(2): 3–20.

Lilley, P. (1992) Speech to the International Conference on Social Security 50 Years After Beveridge, 27 September, York, published as a press release.

Lloyd-Sherlock, P. and Johnson, P. (1996) *Ageing and Social Policy. Global Comparisons*. London: Suntory Toyota International Centre for Economics and Related Disciplines.

Lundberg, O. and Kåreholt, I. (1996) The social patterning of mortality in a cohort of elderly Swedes, *Yearbook of Population Research in Finland*, 33. Helsinki: Population Research Institute.

Lundsgaard, M. and Raahauge, C. (1997) A summary of patterns of cooperation between local authorities and senior citizens councils in Denmark, in *Report of the Dutch-Danish-German Expert Meeting*. Utrecht: Realiseer.

Mabbett, D. (1997) *Pension Funding: Economic Imperative or Political Strategy*, Discussion paper No. 97/1. Uxbridge: Brunel University Department of Government.

MacManus, S.A. (1996) *Young versus Old: Generational Combat in the 21st Century*. Boulder, CO: Westview.

Magyarország, Szegénység és Szociális támogatások [Hungary, Poverty and Social Supports] (1996) World Bank Country Study. Washington, DC: World Bank.

Majce, G. (1992) *Altersbild und Generationenverhältnis in Österreich*. Wien: Institut für Soziologie.

Manton, K., Stallard, E. and Corder, L. (1995) Changes in morbidity and chronic disability in the US elderly population: evidence from the 1982, 1984 and 1989 National Long Term Care Survey, *Journal of Gerontology*, 50B: S104–S204.

Marsh, A. (1975) The dynamics of dissatisfaction and protest in British politics, conference paper, Iowa City.

Mathiesen, C.J. (1997) Dänische Seniorenorganisationen und ihre Bemühungen, Einfluss auf die Seniorenpolitik und die praktische Fürsorge für ältere Menschen zu nehmen, in A. Carell, V. Gerling, C. Marking, G. Naegele and A. Walker (eds) *Politische Beteiligung älterer Menschen in Europa*. Bonn: Bundesministerium fur Familie, Senioren, Frauen und Jugend.

Mayer, K.-H. (1994) Bildung und Förderung von Seniorenvertretungen. Ein Gebot der politischen Vernunft, in G. Verheugen (ed.) *60plus. Die wachsende Macht der Alten*. Köln: Bund-Verlag: 33–42.

McKenzie, R.B. (1993) Senior status: has the power of the elderly peaked? *American Enterprise*, 4(3): 74–80.

Medical Research Council (1994) *The Health of the UK's Elderly People*. London: MRC.

Meijer, R. (1996) *Recht en Zzorg*. Dongen: Wetgering rondoms de Zorg.

Merton, R. (1968) *Social Theory and Social Structure*. New York: Free Press: 106.

Michel, R. (1990) Les retraités dans la commune, *Notre Temps*, 251, novembre: 42–8.

Michelletti, M. (1991) Swedish corporatism at a crossroads: the impact of new politics and new social movements, in J.-E. Lane (ed.) *Understanding the Swedish Model*. London: Frank Cass.

Michelletti, M. (1993) Interest groups in transition and crisis, in C.S. Thomas (ed.) *First World Interest Groups: A Comparative Perspective*. Westport, CT: Greenwood Press.

Michelletti, M. (1995) *Civil Society and State Relations in Sweden*. Aldershot: Avebury.

Midwinter, E. (1992) *Citizenship: From Ageism to Participation*. Dunfermline: Carnegie United Kingdom Trust.

Mills, C.W. (1956) *The Power Elite*. New York: Oxford University Press.

Ministère de la Solidarité, de la Santé et de la Protection Sociale (ed.) (1994) *Informationsschrift CNRPA*. Paris: MSSPS.

Minkler, M. (1986) 'Generational equity' and the new victim blaming: an emerging public policy issue, *International Journal of Health Services*, 16(4): 539–51.

Minkler, M. (1991) Generational equity and the new victim blaming, Chapter 5 in M. Minkler and C. Estes (eds) *Critical Perspectives on Aging. The Political and Moral Economy of Growing Old*. New York: Baywood.

Minkler, M. and Estes, C. (eds) (1991) *Critical Perspectives on Aging. The Political and Moral Economy of Growing Old*. New York: Baywood.

Mirabile, M.L. (ed.) (1996) Il lavoro e l'invecchiamento: la tutela della salute futura come compatibilità del welfare. Rapporto di ricerca, dattiloscritto, novembre.

Mishra, R. (1981) *Society and Social Policy. Theories and Practice of Welfare*. London: Macmillan.

Mishra, R. (1986) Social analysis and the welfare state: retrospect and prospect, in E. Oyen (ed.) *Comparing Welfare States and their Futures*. Aldershot/Vermont: Gower: 20–32.

Myles, J. and Quadagno, J. (eds) (1991) *States, Labor Markets and the Future of Old Age Policy*. Philadelphia, PA: Temple University Press.

Naegele, G. (1994) Zur Forderung nach mehr Beteiligung älterer Menschen am öffentlichen und politischen Leben – zwischen Fiktion und Realität, *Sozialer Fortschritt*, 10: 232–9.

Naegele, G. (1999) Demographie und Sozialepidemiologie, in G. Igl and G. Naegele (eds) *Perspektiven einer sozialstaatlichen Umverteilung im Gesundheitswesen*. München/Wien: Oldenbourg.

Naegele, G. and Schmidt, W. (1998) Anmerkungen zur Zukunft der Generationenbeziehungen, in L. Velken *et al.* (eds) *Jung und Alt. Beiträge und Perspektiven zum Wandel der Generationenbeziehungen*. Dortmunder Beiträge zur angewandten Gerontologie, 6. Hannover: Vincentz-Verlag: 89–122.

National Audit Office (1990) *The Elderly: Information Requirements for Supporting the Elderly and Implications of Personal Pensions for the National Insurance Fund*. London: HMSO.

National Pensioners' Convention (1998) *Pensions not Poor Relief. The National Pensioners' Convention's Submissions to the Government Pension Review*. London: NPC.

Neckel, S. (1993) Altenpolitischer Aktivismus. Entstehung und Variation eines Politikmusters, *Leviathan 21*, 4: 540–63.

Negri, N. and Saraceno, C. (1996) *Le politiche contro la povertà' in Italia*. Bologna: Il Mulino.

Neubauer, E. (1994) Politik mit und für Senioren. Das Beispiel der Bundesarbeitsgemeinschaft der Seniorenorganisationen (BAGSO) in G. Verheugen (ed.) *60plus. Die wachsende Macht der Alten*. Köln: Bund-Verlag: 23–32.

Neugarten, B.L. (1974) Age groups in American society and the rise of the young-old, *Annals of the American Academy of Political and Social Science*, 415: 189–98.

O'Connor, J. (1977) *The Fiscal Crisis of the State*. London: St Martin's Press.

OECD (1988a) *Reforming Public Pensions*. Paris: OECD.

OECD (1988b) *Ageing Populations – The Social Policy Implications*. Paris: OECD.

OECD (1994) *New Orientations for Social Policy*. Paris: OECD.

Office for National Statistics (1997) *Living in Britain. Results from the 1995 General Household Survey*. London: The Stationery Office.

Olk, T. (1997) *Motive, Kompetenzen und Interessen zur politischen Partizipation bei älteren Menschen. Expertise*. Halle.

Olsson, S.E. (1993) *Social Policy and Welfare State in Sweden*. Lund: Arkiv.

Olsson Hort, S.E. and Sparks, S. (1993) Privatization of old age care in Sweden: a study of three municipalities in Stockholm, paper presented at a research conference at the University of Lund.

Országos Nyugdíjbiztosítási Főigazgatóság [National Pension Insurance Administration] (1996) *Statisztikai Évkönyv 1995* (Statistical Yearbook 1995). Budapest: NPIA.

Paci, M. (1984) Il sistema welfare italiano fra tradizione clientelare e prospettive di riforma, *Welfare State all'Italiana*. Bari: Laterza.

Paci, M. (1996) *Storia dell'Italia repubblicana*, vol. 3, book 1. Torino: Einaudi.

Paillat, P. (1995) Chiffres: les maires en métropoles, *Gérontologie et Société*, 74, octobre: 73–4.

Palme, J. (1990) *Pension Rights in Welfare Capitalism*. Stockholm: Swedish Institute for Social Research.

Palme, J. and Wennemo, I. (1996) Social security under reform: the Swedish case, unpublished paper, Institute for Social Research, Stockholm.

Pampel, F.C. and Williamson, J.B. (1989) *Age, Class, Politics and the Welfare State*. Cambridge: CUP.

Pampel, F., Williamson, J. and Stryker, R. (1990) Class context and pension response to demographic structure in advanced industrial democracies, *Social Problems*, 37(4): 535–50.

Parsons, T. (1963) Old age as a consummatory phase, *The Gerontologist*, 3: 53–4.

Pensionistenverband Österreichs (ed.) (1996) *Zahlen – Daten – Fakten*. Wien: Pensionistenverband.

Perista, H. (1995) The social integration of older people in Portugal, in A. Walker (ed.) *Older People in Europe: Social Integration*. Brussels: Commission of the European Communities DGV: 340–59.

Peterson, J. and McManus, D. (1997) Clinton to push for reform of Medicare, Social Security, *Los Angeles Times*, 24 May.

Peterson, S.A. and Somit, A. (1994). *Political Behavior of Older Americans*. New York: Garland.

Plasser, F. and Ulram, P.A. (1987) Das Jahr der Wechselwähler. Wahlen und Neustrukturierung des österreichischen Parteiensystems 1986, in A. Khol, G. Ofner and A. Stirnemann (eds) *Österreichisches Jahrbuch für Politik 1986*. München/Wien: Oldenbourg: 51–123.

Plasser, F., Ulram, P.A. and Seeber, G. (1996) (Dis-)Kontinuitäten und neue Spannungslinien im Wählerverhalten: Trendanalyen 1986–1995, in F. Plasser, P.A. Ulram and G. Ogris (eds) *Wahlkampf und Wählerentscheidung. Analysen zur Nationalratswahl 1995*. Wien: Manz: 155–209.

Platz, M. and Petersen, N.F. (1995) The social integration of older people in Denmark, in A. Walker (ed.) *Older People in Europe: Social Integration*. Brussels: Commission of the European Communities, DGV: 46–74.

Presidenza del Consiglio dei Ministri/Fondazione Finney/Labos (1996) *Guida ai servizi per gli anziani*. Roma: Fondazione Finney.

Prinz, C., Rolf-Engel, G. and Thenner, M. (1996) *Neue Wege der eigenständigen Alterssicherung von Frauen. Ausgangslage und Reformmodelle*. Wien: Europäisches Zentrum (Forschungsbericht im Auftrag der Bundesministerin für Frauenangelegenheiten).

PRO (1990) *The National Organization of Pensioners: Sweden*, information booklet, Stockholm: PRO.

Quadagno, J. (1988) *The Transformation of Old Age Security, Class and Politics in the American Welfare State*. Chicago: University of Chicago Press.

Quadagno, J. (1990) Generational equity and the politics of the welfare state, *International Journal of Health Services*, 20(4): 631–49.

Quadagno, J. (1991) Interest group politics and the future of old age security, in J. Myles and J. Quadagno (eds) *States, Labour Markets and Old Age Policy*. Philadelphia, PA: Temple University Press: 36–58.

Quinn, J.F. (1997 revised) *Social Security Reform: Marginal or Fundamental Change?* 1996 Boettner Lecture at the Boettner Center of Financial Gerontology, Philadelphia, PA.

Reggentin, H. and Dettbarn-Reggentin, J. (1990) *Wir wollen Unruhe in die Ratsparteien bringen*. Seniorenbeiräte und -Vertretungen in der Bundesrepublik. Forschungsbericht. Bonn: Stiftung Mitarbeit.

Reinhard, H.J. (1996) Assistance for the old in Europe in B. Schulte (ed.) *Altenhilfe in Europa. Rechtliche, institutionelle und infrastrukturelle Bedingungen – Vergleichender Gesamtbericht*. Bonn, München

Reno, V.P. and Friedland, R.B. (1997) Strong support but low confidence: what explains the contradiction? in E.R. Kingson and J.H. Schulz (eds) *Social Security in the 21st Century*. New York: Oxford University Press.

Rijsselt, R. van (1995) The social integration of older people in the Netherlands, in A. Walker (ed.) *Older People in Europe: Social Integration*. Brussels: Commission of the European Communities, DGV: 306–39.

Rijsselt, R. van, Schuyt, T. and Graveland, I. (1994) Burgerschap van ouderen; theoretische implicaties van een praktische opgave, in J. Baars, C.P.M. Knipscheer and T.N.M. Schuyt (eds) *Zelfstandigheid en ouder worden, een inleiding*. Utrecht: Lemma.

Riley, M.W. and Riley, J.W. jr. (1994) Individuelles und Gesellschaftliches Potential des Alterns, in P.B. Baltes, J. Mittelstraß and U. Staudinger (eds) *Alter und Altern: Ein interdisziplinärer Studientext zur Gerontologie*. Berlin: Verlag de Gruyter: 437–60.

Ristau, M. and Mackroth, P. (1993) Latente und aktive Altenmacht. Seniorenorganisationen, Gewerkschaften und Parteien, *Forum Demographie und Politik*, 3(Mai): 110–36.

Rödel, U., Frankenberg, G. and Dubiel, H. (1989) *Die Demokratische Frage*. Frankfurt a.M.: Suhrkamp.

Rosanelli, M. and Wolf, J. (1994) Die Italienischen Rentnergewerkschaften, in J. Wolf, M. Kohli and H. Künemund (eds) *Alter und Gewerkschaftliche Politik*. Köln: Bund-Verlag: 97–121.

Roth, D. and Emmert, T. (1994) Wahlverhalten der Senioren, in G. Verheugen (ed.) *60plus. Die Wachsende Macht der Alten*. Köln: Bund-Verlag: 169–88.

Sachverständigenrat (1996) *Sachverständigenrat für die Konzentierte Aktion im Gesundheitswesen. Gesundheitswesen in Deutschland – Kostenfaktor und Zukunftsbranche*. Bonn.

Salon, C. (1993) *Conseil des anciens, conseil des sages. Les personnes âgées au coeur de la cité. L'exemple de la ville de Mulhouse*. IEP de Grenoble, DEA Études politiques.

Sandell, S.H. and Iams, H.M. (1996) Women's future social security benefits: why widows will still be poor, paper prepared for the annual meeting of the Population Association of America, New Orleans.

SCB [Swedish Central Bureau of Statistics] (1994) *Sveriges Framtida Befolkning*. Stockholm: SCB.

SCB (1997) *Statistical Yearbook*. Stockholm: SCB.

Scharf, T. (1993) Erfahrungen mit der politischen und verbandlichen Organisation von Alten-Interessen, in Fritz-Erler-Akademie der Friedrich-Ebert-Stiftung (ed.) *Solidarität der Generationen. Perspektiven des Älterwerdens der Gesellschaft in Deutschland und Europa*. Freudenstadt: FEA-Manuskripte: 7–13.

Schmidt, J. (1995) *Wohlfahrtsverbände in Westeuropa. Zur Bedeutung nationaler Entwicklungspfade in der Sozialpolitik*, in T. Rauschenbach, Ch. Sachße and T. Olk (eds) *Von der Wertgemeinschaft zum Dienstleistungsunternehmen. Jugend – und Wohlfahrtsverbände im Umbruch*. Frankfurt a.M.: Suhrkamp: 428–55.

Schopflin, P. (1991) *Dépendance et solidarités. Mieux aider les personnes agées*. Paris: Documentation Française.

Schüller, H. (1995) *Die Alterslüge. Für einen neuen Generationevertrag*. Berlin: Rowohlt-Verlag.

Schüller, H. (1997) Wir Zukunftsdiebe. Wie wir die Chancen unserer Kinder verspielen. Berlin: Rowohlt-Verlag.

Schulte, B. (1993) Die Entwicklung der europäischen Sozialpolitik, in H. Winkler and H. Kaelble (eds) *Nationalismus – Nationalitäten – Supranationalität. Europa nach 1945*. Stuttgart.

Schulte, B. (1995) Sozialstaat und Europäische Union, in P. Clever and B. Schulte (eds) *Bürger Europas*. Bonn: Kohlhammer-Verlag.

Schulte, B. (ed)(1996) *Altenhilfe in Europa. Rechtliche, institutionelle und infrastrukturelle Bedingungen. Schriftenreihe Bd. 132.1 des Bundesministeriums für Familie, Senioren, Frauen und Jugend*. Bonn: Kohlhammer-Verlag.

Schuyt, T.N.M. (1990) Van Verzorgingsstaat naar Verzorgingskapitalisme; nieuwe modellen voor verzorgingsbeleid, *Beleidswetenschap*, 4(2): 99–111.

Schuyt, T.N.M. and Zanden, G.H. van der (1994) Netherlands, in J.I. Kosberg (ed.) *International Handbook on Services for the Elderly*. Westport, CT/London: Greenwood Press: 88–304.

Schweitzer, H. (1996) Politische Teilhabe und gesellschaftliches Engagement, in Kuratorium Deutsche Altershilfe (ed.) *Rund ums Alter. Alles Wissenswerte von A bis Z*. München: Beck-Verlag: 248–56.

Seniorenbüro des Landes Salzburg (ed.) (1993) *Gern älter werden im Land Salzburg*. Salzburg: Amt der Salzburger Landesregierung.

Sgritta, G.B. (1993) Il mutamento demografico rivoluzione inavvertita, *Il Mulino*, 1: 15–29.

Shragge, E. (1984) *Pensions Policy in Britain: A Socialist Analysis*. London: Routledge and Kegan Paul.

Smeeding, T.M. (1997) *Reshuffling Responsibilities in Old Age. The United States in a Comparative Perspective*. Syracuse, NY: Syracuse University, Center for Policy Research (mimeo).

Sociaal en Cultureel Planbureau (1994) *Sociaal en Cultureel Rapport 1994*. Rijswijk/Den Haag: SCP/VUGA.

Sociaal en Cultureel Planbureau (1996a) *Sociaal en Cultureel Rapport 1996*. Rijswijk/Den Haag: SCP/VUGA.

Sociaal en Cultureel Planbureau (1996b) *Sociale en Culturele Verkenningen 1996*. Rijswijk: SCP.

Social Security Administration (1991) The facts on social security 'notch' babies, *Social Security Courier*, October.

SOU (1988) *Pensionärerna – inflytande och medbestämmande: Betänkande av utredningen om pensionärsinflytande*, 1988 (65). Stockholm: Allmänna Förlaget AB.

Sparks, S. (1994) 'Privatization of social services: home-help in three Swedish municipalities', IGS masters thesis, Stockholm University, Stockholm.

SPF (1997) *Välkommen till Sveriges Pensionärsförbund.* Stockholm: SPF.

Spicker, P. (1991) The principal of subsidiarity and the social policy of the European community, *Journal of European Social Policy*, 1(1): 3–14.

Ståhlberg, A.C. (1990) Life-cycle income distribution of the public sector: inter- and intra-generational effects, in I. Persson (ed.) *Generating Equality in the Welfare State: The Swedish Experience.* Oslo: Norwegian University Press.

Ståhlberg, A.C. (1991) Lessons from the Swedish pension system, in T. Wilson and D. Wilson (eds) *The State and Social Welfare: The Objectives of Policy.* London and New York: Longman.

Stolle, D. and Rochon, T.R. (1996) Social capital, but how? Associations and the creation of social capital, paper presented at the 10th International Conference of Europeanists, Chicago.

Streck, W. and Schmitter, P.C. (1991) From national corporatism to transnational pluralism: organized interests in the single European market, *Politics and Society*, 19: 133–64.

Street, D. (1993) Maintaining the status quo: the impact of old-age interest groups on the Medicare Catastrophic Coverage Act of 1988, *Social Problems*, 40(4): 431–44.

Street, D. (1997) Special interests or citizens' rights? Senior power, social security and Medicare, in M. Minkler and C. Estes (eds) *Critical Gerontology: Perspectives from Political and Moral Economy.* New York: Baywood.

Subileau, F. (1995) La participation électorale des personnes âgées, *Gérontologie et Société*, 74: 8–19, octobre.

SWS-Bildstatistiken (1996) Die Nationalratswahl im Rückblick, *SWS-Rundschau*, 36(1): 113–20.

Szebehely, M. (1994) Care for the elderly in Sweden and the United Kingdom: practice, policy and debate, unpublished paper, Stockholm University, Stockholm.

Szebehely, M., Lingsom, S. and Platz, M. (1997) Hemhjälpsutvecklingen: Samma Problem, Skilda Lösningar? in S.O. Daatland (ed.) *De Siste årene.* Oslo: NOVA.

Tews, H.P. (1987) Die Alten und die Politik, in Deutsches Zentrum für Altersfragen (ed.) *Die ergraute Gesellschaft.* DZA Schriftenreihe, 21. Berlin: DZA: 141–88.

Tews, H.P. (1994) Alter zwischen Entpflichtung, Belastung und Verpflichtung, in G. Verheugen (ed.) *60plus. Die wachsende Macht der Alten.* Köln: Bund-Verlag.

Tews, H.P. (1996) *Für und wider die Seniorenvertretungen Expertise.* Heidelberg.

Thane, P. (1978) The muddled history of retiring at 60 and 65, *New Society*, 3 August: 234–6.

Théry, H. (1993) *Les activités d'utilité sociale des retraités et des personnes âgées*, Séances des 9 et 10 février 1993, Collection avis et rapports du Conseil économique et social. Paris: Direction des Journaux Officiels, 3, 22 mars.

Thomas, H. (1996) *Vieillesse dépendante et désinsertion politique.* Paris: L'Harmattan, Logiques politiques.

Thornton, P. and Tozer, R. (1994) *Involving Older People in Planning and Evaluating Community Care: A Review of Initiatives.* York: Social Policy Research Unit.

Thorslund, M., Norström, T. and Wernberg, K. (1991) The utilization of home help in Sweden: a multivariate analysis, *The Gerontologist*, 31(1): 116–19.

Timmermans, J.M. (1996) 25 Jaar Ouderenbeleid: Het verhaal achter de zes nota's, *Een Ouderendebat.* Utrecht: NIZW: 5–17.

Timmermans, J.M. (1997) *Rapportage ouderen 1996.* Rijswijk: VUGA; Den Haag: Sociaal en Cultureel Planbureau.

Torres-Gil, F. (1992) *The New Aging: Politics and Change in America.* Westport, CT: Auburn House.

Torres-Gil, F. (1993) Interest group politics: generational changes in the politics of aging, in V. Bengtson and A. Achenbaum (eds) *The Changing Contract Across Generations.* New York: Aldine: 239–58.

Townsend, P. (1962) *The Last Refuge: A Survey of Residential Institutions and Homes for the Aged in England and Wales.* London: Routledge and Kegan Paul.

Townsend, P. and Walker, A. (1995) *Revitalising State Pensions*. London: Fabian Society.

Ulram, P.A. (1991) Politische Kultur der Bevölkerung, in H. Dachs *et al.* (eds) *Handbuch des Politischen Systems Österreichs*. Wien: Manz: 466–74.

US Congress Congressional Budget Office (1997) *The Economic and Budget Outlook: Fiscal Years 1998–2007*. Washington, DC: US Government Printing Office.

US Department of Commerce, Bureau of the Census (1996a) *Percent Reported Voting and Registering by Age and Region in November Elections: 1964–1994*. Washington, DC: Bureau of the Census Web Page, www.census.gov.

US Department of Commerce, Bureau of the Census (1996b) *Population Projections of the United States by Age, Sex, Race, and Hispanic Origin: 1995 to 2050*. Washington, DC: US Government Printing Office.

US Department of Commerce, Bureau of the Census (1996c) *Statistical Abstract of the United States 1995*. Washington, DC: US Government Printing Office.

US General Accounting Office [GAO] (1988) *Social Security: The Notch Issue*. Washington, DC: GAO.

US Social Security Administration (1996*) Social Security Bulletin Annual Statistical Supplement*. Washington, DC: US Government Printing Office.

Vanguard Marketing Corporation (1997) Vanguard plain talk about realistic expectations for stock market returns, *Investor Education*. (www.vanguard.com).

Véron. J. (1995) L'âge du pouvoir, *Gérontologie et Société*, 74: 9–19, octobre.

Verté, D., Ponjaert-Kristoffersen, I. and Geerts, C. (1996) Political participation of elderly in local policy, in A. Carrell, V. Gerling, C. Marking, G. Naegele and A. Walker (eds) *Politische Beteiligung älterer Menschen in Europa*. Bonn: Bundesministerium fur Familie, Senioren, Frauen und Jugend.

Vicarelli, G. (1988) Problematiche territoriali dello sviluppo del servizio sanitario nazionale, in 'Il bene-salute tra politica e società' supplement, *Democrazia e diritto*, 6: 117–26.

Ville des Rennes (ed.) (1995) *Citoyens agés dans la ville. Analyses, réflexions et propositions pour 2010*. Rennes: Les Cahiers de Rennes. Centre Communal d'Action Sociale.

Vincent, J. (1996) Who's afraid of an ageing population? *Critical Social Policy*, 16(2): 33–44.

Viriot-Durandal, J.P. (1996) Les retraités manifestent! Analyse d'un mouvement social, *Années Documents Cleirppa*, 241: 1–10, novembre.

Walker, A. (1982) The meaning and social division of community care, in A. Walker (ed.) *Community Care: The Family, The State and Social Policy*. Oxford: Blackwell/Robertson: 13–39.

Walker, A. (1986) The politics of ageing in Britain, in C. Phillipson, M. Bernard and P. Strong (eds) *Dependency and Interdependency in Old Age – Theoretical Perspectives and Policy Alternatives*. London: Croom Helm: 30–45.

Walker, A. (1990) The economic 'burden' of ageing and the prospect of intergenerational conflict, *Ageing and Society*, 10: 377–96.

Walker, A. (1991) Thatcherism and the new politics of old age, in J. Myles and J. Quadagno (eds) *States, Labor Markets and the Future of Old Age Policy*. Philadelphia, PA: Temple University Press: 19–36.

Walker, A. (1993) Whither the social contract? Intergenerational solidarity in income and employment, Chapter 2 in D. Hobman (ed.) *Uniting Generations. Studies in Conflict and Cooperation*. London: Age Concern England.

Walker, A. (ed.) (1996) *The New Generational Contract. Intergenerational relations, Old Age and Welfare*. London: UCL Press.

Walker, A. (1997) *Combating Age Barriers in Employment*. Luxembourg: Official Publications of the European Communities.

Walker, A. and Maltby, T. (1997) *Ageing Europe*. Buckingham: Open University Press.

Walker, A., Guillemard, A.M. and Alber, J. (1993) *Older People in Europe: Social and Economic Policies*. Brussels: Commission of the European Communities.

Walker, A., Maltby, T. and Walker, C. (1996a) Landesbericht Vereinigtes Königreich, in B.

Schulte (ed.) *Altenhilfe in Europa. Rechtliche, institutionelle und infrastrukturelle Bedingungen – Vergleichender Gesamtbericht.* Bonn: Kohlhammer.

Walker, A., Walker, C. and Ryan, T. (1996b) Older people with learning difficulties: a case of double jeopardy, *Ageing and Society*, 16(1): 125–50.

Ward, R.A. (1977) Aging group consciousness: implication in an older sample, *Sociology and Social Research*, 61: 496–519.

Weil, D. (1997) The genesis and evolution of social security, conference presentation 30 May. Washington, DC: American Enterprise Institute.

Westergaard, J., Noble, I. and Walker, A. (1989) *After Redundancy*. Oxford: Polity Press.

Wetenschappelijke Raad voor het Regeringsbeleid [WRR] (1996) *Tweedeling in perspectief*. Den Haag: SDU Uitgevers.

Wilkinson, M. (1993) British tax policy 1979–90? Equity and efficiency, *Policy and Politics*, 21(3): 207–17.

Williamson, J., Evans, L. and Powell, L. (1982) *The Politics of Aging: Power and Policy*. Springfield, IL: Charles C. Thomas.

Williamson, J.B., Shindul, J.A. and Evans, L. (1985) *Aging and Public Policy: Social Control or Social Justice?* Springfield, IL: Charles C. Thomas.

Wilson, G. (1993) The challenge of an ageing electorate: changes in the formation of social policy in Europe? *Journal of European Social Policy*, 3(2): 91–105.

Wolf, J. (1990) Krieg der Generationen? Sozialstaatliche Verteilung und politische Handlungspotentiale Älterer in der 'alternden' Gesellschaft, *Prokla*, 20(80): 99–117.

Wolf, J., Kohli, M. and Künemund, H. (eds) (1994) *Alter und gewerkschaftliche Politik. Auf dem Weg zur Rentnergewerkschaft?* Köln: Bund-Verlag.

World Bank (1994) *Averting the Old Age Crisis*. New York: Oxford University Press.

Yakoboski, P. (1996) *Daring to Touch the Third Rail?* Washington, DC: Employee Benefit Research Institute.

Young, K. (1984) Political attitudes, in R. Jowell and C. Avery (eds) *British Social Attitudes*. Aldershot: Gower: 11–46.

Zedlewski, S.R., Barnes, R.O., Burt, M.K., McBride, T.D. and Meyer, J.A. (1989) *Needs of the Elderly in the 21st Century*. Washington, DC: Urban Institute.

# Index

# THE POLITICS OF OLD AGE IN EUROPE

The politics of old age in Europe have entered a critical new phase. This timely collection of essays by leading authorities examines the new politics of old age from the perspectives of individual countries and the European Union as a whole. Case studies of Austria, France, Germany, Italy, the Netherlands, Sweden and the UK provide a broad representation of EU countries. In addition there are case studies of Hungary and the USA to provide comparative reference points in Central/Eastern Europe and North America. Each country study provides an overview of the politics of old age (main developments, organizations and actors), an account of recent developments and measures taken by national or local government to increase the participation of older people, analysis of the barriers to participation and a forward look at the likely direction of policies, forms of representation and generational relations. The country examples are preceded by European overviews of political participation and representation, the machinery of representation and recent innovations. The authors provide an introduction to the key issues and review the main lessons in a concluding chapter.

*The Politics of Old Age in Europe* will be of interest to policy makers and practitioners working with older people, as well as students of social policy, political science and gerontology.

## The editors
Alan Walker is Professor of Social Policy at the University of Sheffield and specializes in social gerontology and European social policy. He chaired the European Commission's Observatory on Ageing and Older People and currently chairs the European Foundation on Social Quality.

Gerhard Naegele is Professor of Social Gerontology and Director of the Institute of Gerontology at the University of Dortmund. He specializes in social gerontology, social policy and poverty research.

## The contributors
Sang-Hoon Ahn, Sara Arber, Dominique Argoud, Christiane Bahr, Adalbert Evers, Lucia Lameiro García, Jay Ginn, Anne-Marie Guillemard, Sven E. Olsson Hort, Kees Knipscheer, Kai Leichsenring, Maria Luisa Mirabile, Gerhard Naegele, Sara E. Rix, Bernd Schulte, Theo Schuyt, Charlotte Strümpel, Zsuzsa Széman, Alan Walker and Jürgen Wolf.

ISBN 0-335-200